D0583360

7 5c

WASHINGTON AT WAR: 1941-1945

WASHINGTON
AT
WAR:
1941-1945

by Scott Hart

PRENTICE-HALL, INC.
Englewood Cliffs
New Jersey

For Jonathan Hart

Winston Churchill's speech, "The White House Christmas Tree," is reprinted from *War Speeches, Volume II,* by Winston S. Churchill, by permission of Cassell and Company Limited, London; Houghton Mifflin Company, Boston; and McClelland and Stewart Limited, Toronto.

Material originally printed in the following newspapers is used by permission of the respective publishers: *The Washington Daily News, The Washington Star, The Washington Post,* and *The Times-Herald.*

Library of Congress Catalog Card Number: 76-99967
Printed in the United States of America · T
13-945550-7
Prentice-Hall International, Inc., London
Prentice-Hall of Australia, Pty. Ltd., Sydney
Prentice-Hall of Canada, Ltd., Toronto
Prentice-Hall of India Private Ltd., New Delhi
Prentice-Hall of Japan, Inc., Tokyo

Acknowledgments

The preparation of this book would have scarcely been possible without the help of my friends. They gave freely of their time to dig into their memories of the war years for anecdotes to brighten the narrative, and in many instances devoted valuable hours in a search for facts in the libraries. Now, a simple expression of thanks seems woefully inadequate—but I may pay the compliment of saying that I had expected nothing less of them.

Some of these friends seemed ever at my side from the start. Among them were Val Trimble, who lived the war times in Washington and is possessed of wonderful powers of recall. In the Washingtoniana Division of the Central Library here, Miss Sue Shivers, the chief, and Miss Francine J. Inman, assistant, followed the progress of my research closely, and with skill and enthusiasm gave me valuable guidance. Also, I am deeply indebted to Hope Chamberlin, a World War II chronicler, whose research helped delineate some of the human-interest facets contained in the narrative.

Valuable assistance was given by Thomas G. Corcoran, a renowned personality of the Roosevelt New Deal era and now a prominent Washington attorney; Christine (Sadler) Coe, former Washington newspaperwoman now associated with *McCall's* magazine; Martin E. Dietz and William Clark Daffron, former newsmen in the capital; Herman Allen, a member of the Associated Press Bureau in Washington during the war; Mrs. Florian H. Thayn, head of the art and reference library, Office of the Architect of the Capitol; E. M. Eller, distinguished historian; Foster Hunter, a specialist in Washington history and collector of rare books and manuscripts; George E. Schroebel of the staff of the Union Station Corporation; William W. Morrison, assistant to the director of the National Gallery of Art, and Diosdado M. Yap, veteran Washington correspondent and authority on the Far East.

The names of others who helped so importantly are strewn through the narrative, and may be easily detected. But I should like to underline the names of Marshall Andrews and Walton Onslow as two who went widely out of their way to help bring to the story any merit it may have.

I owe an especial debt of gratitude to Miss Diane Giddis, my editor at Prentice-Hall, who guided me throughout the preparation of the narrative. It was a joy to work with someone with so fine a talent, combined with patience.

Finally, about myself: I lived the war years in Washington, first as a reporter on the *Post* and later as a staff correspondent in the Washington bureau of *Time* magazine. Consequently, I had a front-row seat and emerged from the experience with many memories and impressions. Memory is tricky, of course, after a quarter of a century, and I did not trust my memory. In writing the story, I checked out everything insofar as was possible. The obvious difficulty was in selecting from huge piles of available material what was most interesting and, perhaps, most significant. My aim was fixed solely on the city of Washington during the war, and the life that its inhabitants led. To have diffused this focus with official intrigues, the wide backdrop of the war, and other military activities was beyond my scholarship and, moreover, would have resulted in a literary stew or a narrative of several volumes. In any event, if I have kindled nostalgia among those who lived the times in Washington—or have satisfied the interest of others who want to know what it was like—I have succeeded in what I set out to do.

I have done my best to avoid factual error; but in a narrative of such breadth, error is almost bound to occur. None of the persons who helped me with the story is responsible for these inaccuracies.

Scott Hart
Washington, D.C.

CONTENTS

Contents (*continued*)

CHAPTER ONE

MORNING MEANS ANOTHER DAY

ON THE MORNING of December 7, 1941, Washington inhabitants awakened thanking God it was Sunday. For all but the Defense Program people who responded to their immediate supervisors' mandate that for six or seven days shalt thou labor, Sunday was a break in an ever-expanding chain of work days. The more fortunate people might turn over in bed and go back to sleep, or yawn and stare at the wall, engaging in various important introspections crushed out in the grind of weekdays.

There was much to consider seeing or ignoring in the course of a Sunday morning's drowsy deliberations. The Don Cossacks Chorus, with basses thundering from depths of ancient sorrows, would appear at Constitution Hall, home of the Daughters of the American Revolution. The Washington Redskins were sharpened for a game with the Philadelphia Eagles, the final game of the season in age-worn Griffith Stadium. Sammy Baugh would take to the air and the ball would speed like a bullet, in a display of a marksmanship brilliant enough to bring thousands to their feet. Later, Rosita Royce, the "Dove Girl," would flaunt herself at the Gayety Theatre on 9th Street, a hurly-burly thoroughfare of penny arcades and pawn shops, peopled with all manner of pitchmen and con men—a place, indeed, with everything that people of circumspection might secretly desire.

It was a Sunday like so many had been and should be, always. For Washington, compared to other cities, was not only a beautiful but a good town, or at least had been until 1933

1

when the New Deal brought in swarms of people, to be followed by those who had arrived eighteen months ago to handle the National Defense Program. This alone was enough to ponder while staring at the wall. And there was another matter to wonder on. Everybody knew that Hitler, a success at wallpapering, a failure at painting, now triumphantly bludgeoning Europe with lightning strokes, would eventually involve the United States.

There were many little indications of this, because a war, however distant, sensitizes men's minds. For instance, marriage licenses had about doubled since Europe began rumbling—had climbed from 5,680 in 1939 to 10,554 in 1941. The men viewed their brides in a wistful way: these would be the girls they would leave behind them. And that was a disturbing thought while staring at the wall on a Sunday morning. Was it as dangerous to leave the girls behind as to face bullets? Meanwhile, the single women were pursuing a primary goal—marriage, and the chances had widened. A girl in an elevator had said to another, "I'm going to get me an admiral and I don't care whether he's vice or rear." The other girl was silent; her thoughts were her own. Maybe she would settle for a sergeant.

Thousands of these defense workers had come into Washington through the immensity of Union Station, and there was no single reason why they had come. Some may have been brought by the words chiseled high upon the southeast front of the Vermont granite building:

> LET ALL THE ENDS THOU AIMEST AT BE
> THY COUNTRY'S—THY GOD'S—AND TRUTH'S
> BE NOBLE AND THE NOBLENESS THAT
> LIES IN OTHER MEN—SLEEPING BUT
> NEVER DEAD—WILL RISE IN MAJESTY
> TO MEET THINE OWN.

In any case, Washington had spoken to them. A fool would know that much. But nobody knew just when the United States would be at war.

President Roosevelt knew it even while his personal bodyguard was taking the little scottie named Fala for his daily walk.

Judge Samuel I. Rosenman, the President's stubby aide and speech writer, knew it as he entered the White House with scarcely more than a nod to the Secret Servicemen. Bernard Baruch, with the never-failing courtliness of his South Carolina aristocratic heritage, knew it while sitting on a bench in Lafayette Park across Pennsylvania Avenue from the White House, raising his eyes in a sad and unobtrusive way at young servicemen striding past without any knowledge that this lonely-looking man who wore age so well could influence whether they lived or died.

Thousands had known of approaching war for eighteen months as the most powerful preparations for war in the nation's history were begun. But those of the innermost circles had not wanted to alarm the people, so they had not confided in them completely. The United States was arming itself for defense, went the official statement, but the words were ominous. From Warm Springs, Georgia, the "second White House," the President had remarked on November 29, 1941, "It is always possible that our boys in the Military and Naval Academies may be fighting for the defense of American institutions by next Thanksgiving." On November 30, 1941, a story in the *Washington Post* had reported, "Japan threatens to purge Asia of U.S. and Britain." Even in the relaxing Georgia environment Roosevelt was not deaf to Japanese Premier Hideki Tojo's bluster that Japan would have to do everything possible to "wipe out with a vengeance British and U.S. exploitation in the Far East."

Obligingly (whenever officially and humanly possible) White House Press Secretary Steve Early had called a news conference. But deep within the government lay a perhaps irrational fear of telling the American people that some frightful bloodletting impended. And there seemed a deeper dread of letting the people know why the blood would flow—much less what might be expected when the fighting was finished. It was enough to say that the fighting, if it came, would be in self-defense.

Historians have since pondered why the people weren't told bluntly what they would be fighting for. When the young men

25 years before marched away to World War I they were making the world safe for democracy. So they fought in that innocent frame of mind with willingness and bravery, later to discover that they had made America safe for Prohibition and a decade of young ladies in short skirts with hosiery caught up by garters just above the knees; for "Yes, We Have No Bananas"; for high-placed laziness and saxophones that moaned syncopatedly; for stocks and bonds which a bottomless pit devoured in 1929; for Silent Cal boyishly raiding the White House refrigerator by night; and, before him, for the cronies of Harding, some of whom carried off nearly everything except the Treasury, which defied their efforts to lift it. Perhaps the simplest explanation is that the government feared that the people would remember the old song, "Never Let the Same Bee Sting You Twice." And it is generally best to let good enough alone. The balances were delicate enough.

The men and women who lay abed or went to defense offices that Sunday morning didn't know about a high-level function held on Thursday evening, December 4, at the very proper Carlton Hotel, a mere two blocks and a park from the White House. The originator and headman of the function was Donald M. Nelson, whom the Administration had brought to Washington from Sears Roebuck's upper echelon to be the executive director of the Supply Priorities and Allocations Board—an excursion into the thickets and quagmires of bureaucracy which it is safe to say Nelson would never have consented to except from the pull of patriotic duty. Now a member of the newly imported defense-production hierarchy, he was a man who could equally well administer a huge business or mend a fractured human relationship. He had watched production trouble develop and seen the need for the New Deal Administration and the conservative dollar-a-year industrialists to find at least a paper-thin flooring to move upon together. To the big names brought in for production leadership under the aegis of defense, the Administration had come to mean the old New Deal and the New Deal meant ruination. So Nelson had arranged a dinner of conciliation with the head Dealer, Vice President Henry Wallace.

The 24 carefully chosen persons acted precisely as people should in the soft lights and hush of the hotel. Politeness abounded, and the only startling sounds came from the pop of champagne corks. Wallace, image of the New Deal and outwardly as humble as the wrapping on a stick of dynamite, made a brief self-conscious talk and drew token applause. The only grim face was that of Secretary of the Navy Frank Knox. This man who could remember being a Rough Rider with Teddy Roosevelt knew the signs and could sense the rhythms of oncoming war. He was asked for a few words. After cautioning that what he had to say should be kept within the four walls, he said that the situation was dangerous. He foresaw war in the Pacific at any moment and ventured that it might be starting at the very hour of Nelson's party. But he wanted no alarm. The Navy, he assured his intent listeners, was ready. Historian Bruce Catton, privy to the Secretary's prediction, would remember Knox's assertion that the Navy would not be caught napping.

Proposals had flown for days between the United States and Japan, in anything but harmony. The President the day before had read an intercepted message between the Japanese architects of war and exclaimed, "This means war."

Indeed, if the late sleepers on December 7 had got to their newspapers they would have been informed by veteran reporter Mark Sullivan that "at the moment this is written we are extremely close to war with Japan." Sullivan believed that if it came, it would be "wholly a war for our naval and air forces, not for our soldiers."

And yet, somehow, most people hoped someone would find a way out of war with Japan. Roosevelt, unlike the British before the war, was not a man to muddle through; he was a clever manipulator. And he had said that he hated war. Moreover, there was another hope in the public mind: Japan was war-crazed but it wasn't crazy enough to fight the United States, whose clang of martial industry could be heard across the yet untroubled Pacific. And despite Japan's recent stomping of frailer nations, the Japanese remained genial theatrical characters suitable to a comic-opera stage lilting with music and strung with colored lanterns. The war would come from the Atlantic side sometime in the future—more likely than from Japan.

On the morning of December 7, the subdebutantes of the capital compiled the names of Christmas party guests which they had scribbled furtively in their notebooks when the teachers weren't looking. They were planning a big Christmas.

Downtown, far from the girls' Spring Valley and Chevy Chase homes, Secretary of State Cordell Hull, a tall gaunt man with misty eyes and a quiet deliberateness that he had brought with him to Washington from the Tennessee hills, a calm man but not one to be tampered with, met with Secretary of War Henry Stimson and Secretary Knox at the State Department. The two soon left, Stimson for his wood-crested residence, Woodley, and Knox for his Department. After their departure, Hull conferred with his Far Eastern experts. The telephone rang. The Japanese Embassy requested an appointment for Ambassador Admiral Kichisaburo Nomura and Special Envoy Saburo Kurusu with the Secretary at 2 P.M. He agreed to see them at 1:45 P.M.

Early that morning Chief of Staff General George C. Marshall looked at the day and readied himself for a recreational horseback ride. He was aware of the imminent danger of war but could not know exactly when it would explode upon the country. Perhaps he realized that the word "defense" was a politically adroit euphemism for war and that amid all the talk of "defense" he should think in terms of war and its demands on the treasure, the young manhood, and the spirit and capacity for endurance of the nation. He was all soldier. It had been stamped on his bulldog face during his youthful years at the Virginia Military Institute where he had engaged in athletics with a fury and endured painful hazing like a man. Everyone liked the young Pennsylvanian who had come down to be a cadet in "the West Point of the South." Marshall had distinguished himself in World War I, and thereafter when ordinary soldiers looked at him they saw a soldier, and when Roosevelt talked with him he found not only a soldier but a realist endowed with a brain. He did pose one problem: where could he best be used when the war began—as commander at the front or in Washington where it was evident, even with no war in progress, that a strong man must sit astride the War Department and oversee the continual building of fighting forces?

Marshall knew where he would want to be. But on this morning, with its indeterminate sky, he was interested in recreation. For years he had indulged a bent toward recreation at its proper time and place. He approved of the Department's policy of allowing officers to rejuvenate themselves periodically. For the General, an occasional morning horseback ride was recreation and also work, because the quietude of the bridle paths gave him a chance to think. He had once observed that nobody could think after 2 P.M.

Outside General Marshall's quarters, a sergeant stood holding a bay horse. The General mounted and trotted away from the red brick buildings of Fort Myer spread widely along a crest across the Potomac from Washington. When he returned he could see in the rising day the Washington Monument piercing the sky and on the east the bronze statue called the Goddess of Freedom rising from her perch on the top of the Capitol dome. The symbolic goddess had been placed there in December 1863, while crowds below howled acclaim and the iron guns of 68 forts guarding the seat of government roared in salute. Now on this December morning the city lay sprawled in a Sunday calm.

Marshall strode into his quarters, and after a few minutes the telephone rang. He was wanted at the War Department, but the caller did not tell him to hurry. The General showered and dressed, and reached his office around 11:10 A.M. The messages on his desk convinced him that a crisis impended. Uppermost was information that the Japanese envoys had requested an audience with Secretary Hull, carrying the look of a cover for something about to happen. Marshall sent an alert to all Pacific commands.

The people of Washington went about their usual affairs. On Meridian Place, N.W., between important 14th and 16th streets, a young married woman serving as a defense worker looked from her fourth-floor apartment to the fourth-floor windows across the courtyard and murmured, "It simply can't be true." Neighborhood gossips had related that during a recent party there the hostess had either fallen or been thrown from the opposite window and struck the grass without completely spilling a drink clutched in her hand.

The morning wore on. The people read the headlines *FDR Sends Note to Hirohito. . . . Jap Convoys Near Thailand.* This was not good, but it was at least far away. And the weather was promising. From a December low of 31 degrees, the temperature had grown comfortable by midmorning, though the sky was intermittently overcast, and the mere ten-mile-an-hour wind didn't bite. Simply a good day to lounge at home and listen to one of the four radio networks. Or maybe to prepare for that promised brunch, a social ritual requiring the hostess to provide juice, ham and eggs, jam, and a brisk swig sometime around noon.

Otherwise, the places of public worship enjoyed a heyday for reasons having nothing to do with soul-searchings about defense. Prior to the New Deal upsurge, Washington had been a Southern town in character, and the church a dominant interest, though not necessarily an influence. Joining in now as defense workers were thousands of small-town people from all about the country whose lives had revolved around the activities of their churches. The eyes of Julia Ward Howe in the war year of 1861 had "seen the glory of the coming of the Lord" despite all the hell-raising in Willard's Hotel where she stopped, and the Lord, indeed, had arrived in December 1941. The ministers, quite naturally, delighted in surveying the packed pews. But unlike the ministers of 1861, who had joined with the newspaper editors and politicians to foment strife, little if anything sounded from the pulpits on December 7 related to Germany or Japan. The worshipers listened, went outside, stood around a few minutes to enjoy an ordinary Sunday morning and went home. Some hastened to brunches: some, mindful of flesh, made off to other rendezvous.

Places of rendezvous were frustratingly scarce December 7, 1941, mainly because the capital's population had risen from approximately 200,000 to over 700,000 in two decades, creating an apartment and room crisis. Frequently, three or four girls slept in one room, causing one to complain that "I must step across desks all day in the office and across beds and baggage in the night." But the girls, being human and understanding, accommodatingly left the premises when a compatriot in defense came in with a boy friend. Morale was a word whose meaning they appreciated. Averaging in age between eighteen and twenty five, they were sufficiently mature to know that the home fires were important.

The morning gave way to noon. On the 13th floor of the National Press Building, just north of Pennsylvania Avenue at 14th Street, scarcely anyone was about the Press Club bar or lounges. It was just as well, because the highballs that sold for 35 cents were prohibited on Sunday, and few would have wanted the available wine and beer. Club assistant manager Ernie Ball, whose entire metabolism was calibrated to the weekday crushes, reflected that "this is just another Sunday." From the windows of this tallest building in Washington the streets looked normal. There were a few strollers with no apparent destination. Ball looked at the switchboard beside the cigar counter and the bulbs were dark.

Outside, once more, the sky was unsure. The gray stone of the Washington Post Building, visible on E Street from one of the windows, seemed even darker than usual. Sunday required only a skeleton news staff, and most of those were at lunch.

A lanky reporter walked out of the newsroom into the sports department, throwing only a glance at the small marble bust of John Philip Sousa, placed there in honor of his "Washington Post March." The reporter began wondering what he could write; the city editor had made off, leaving no assignment. There was news, of course, on so-called city-side Sunday events, but it was unexciting. On the national side, Secretary Knox had issued a formal statement describing our Navy as second to none. And, earlier that week, the Third Supplemental National

Defense Appropriation Bill, totaling some $38.5 billion, had passed the House by an overwhelming 309 to 5. Moreover, the nation was doing well in the air. National Aeronautics Association President John J. Jouett forecast that within twelve months annual airplane production would exceed 50,000.

It was a dull day, probably even dull for little Steve Vasilakos, the peanut vendor on Pennsylvania Avenue beside the White House, who was sometimes good for a story.

The lanky reporter sat at his desk, and after a while noticed that others had come in and they, too, appeared aimless. The Associated Press machines clattered behind a glass enclosure. Then the sound stopped for longer than usual, and resumed. A young reporter went to take a look and after a few moments called, "Somebody come back here. What's going on?"

The AP machines rang twelve bells, at that time the signal for a flash:

FLASH   WHITE HOUSE SAYS JAPS ATTACK PEARL HARBOR.

This was followed immediately by the customary bulletin:

BULLETIN

Washington, Dec. 7 (AP)—*President Roosevelt said in a statement today that the Japanese had attacked Pearl Harbor, Hawaii, from the air.*

BULLETIN MATTER

The attack of the Japanese also was made on all Naval and Military "activities" on the Island of Oahu.

The President's brief statement was read to reporters by Steven Early, Presidential Press Secretary. Sometime shortly after the first Flash (exactly when is not known) came a second Flash. It may have interrupted the Bulletin matter or have come after it. It was:

FLASH   SECOND AIR ATTACK REPORTED BY ARMY AND NAVY BASES IN MANILA.

The young man's face grew concerned, but then he relaxed and said that it was probably a war game in motion out there. The clock on the city room wall was somewhere around 2:35 P.M. Steve Early had originated the message on orders from the President, and had told an aide to connect the three press associations on one line.

"All on?" he asked, and was told they were.

"This is Steve Early at the White House. At 7:35 A.M., Hawaiian time, the Japanese bombed Pearl Harbor. The attacks are continuing and . . . No, I don't know how many are dead."

In thousands of Washington homes radios choked off programs to announce the attack. Many people did not believe it, and newspaper switchboards became jammed with inquiring, frantic calls.

The Japanese envoys had failed to appear until 2:05 P.M., twenty minutes after the agreed-upon time. Secretary Hull chose to make them wait for fifteen minutes.

At about the same time, President Roosevelt, relaxed in a turtleneck sweater, was eating from a tray. He looked up occasionally for a word from his alter ego, Harry Hopkins, whose frail body never slowed his energies. The Navy Department had received a coded message, and it moved fast up the echelons to Knox, who telephoned the President. Pearl Harbor had been attacked. Roosevelt said one long-remembered word: "No." Then he recovered fast. He turned calm and telephoned Hull. He wanted, Roosevelt told him, the emissaries treated coolly.

But that was beyond the mountain code of the Tennessean. When he confronted the Japanese they received a burst of "mule-skinner" language. (There is a wide discrepancy in accounts of what he said.) The Secretary then hastened to the White House and was joined by Knox and General Marshall. A message was brought to the President: Vice President Wallace was hurrying in from New York.

Outside, a December wind was stiffening, and the sun fought a battle for the sky.

The President telephoned Lord Halifax, the British Ambassador. Halifax was experienced in crises, too, at Munich and in his days as Viceroy of India. He listened while seated in his office, which resembled more a gentleman's study or library than a place of business. Halifax was a slender six-feet-two and his face was long and gray and generally he wore somber clothing which deepened the gray of his face. But behind the gray he loved the flaming colors of life. He was social-minded, which, of course, an ambassador must be, and the hostess who snared him penciled a score. But spiritually he was inflexible. When people had begun staring at him in his church, he had changed to a lesser-known place of worship near Capitol Hill, far from his aloof Embassy on fashionable Massachusetts Avenue. A profoundly religious man, he loved quiet thoughts and the manifestations of God in nature. He often walked in Rock Creek Park, apparently conscious of the tree-scraped skies and the fragrance of damp grass. But now, on this Sunday, he communicated by radio-telephone with London, and what he said was the first London knew of Pearl Harbor.

Elsewhere in the White House that morning, thirty-nine men and women had entered the east entrance for luncheon with Mrs. Roosevelt in the upstairs Blue Parlor. These were government and service personalities to whom the First Lady owed a social obligation. At 2:45 P.M. Mrs. Roosevelt shook hands with them in parting, and the guests, stunned by the news, left quietly.

Donald Nelson had been lunching at the Headwaters Farm of Secretary of the Interior Harold Ickes, in nearby Maryland, with Senator Tom Connally of Texas, and Supreme Court Justice Hugo Black, who not long before had ridden out a blasting Senate storm to get on the court over a charge that he had once belonged to the Ku Klux Klan. Connally, chairman of the Senate Foreign Relations Committee, had oriented the talk to the Japanese, while Ickes poked at his eyeglasses which continually slid down the bridge of his nose. Beyond the pillared house, his chickens enjoyed the fairly pleasant day, and more distantly the pigs grunted for fun or food. Ickes, Nelson,

Black, and Connally had agreed that immediate war with Japan
was unlikely.

At 3 P.M., as he was riding back to Washington, Nelson was
set bolt upright by the message from the radio in his car.

At Pearl Harbor, the roar of Japanese planes diving and
ascending could be heard over the explosions while Honolulu
FBI Special Agent-in-Charge Robert L. Shivers phoned headquarters in Washington 5,000 miles away. Director J. Edgar
Hoover was in New York and Shivers' voice reached him
through the FBI's private line.

"The Japanese are bombing Pearl Harbor," Shivers said.
"There is no doubt about it—those planes are Japanese. It's war.
You may be able to hear the explosions yourself. Listen." The
receiver was placed near a window, and Hoover heard the roar.
He ordered war plans long in preparation to be put into effect.
Then he went to LaGuardia Airport and boarded a plane for
Washington.

At 3 P.M. that Sunday, 2,500 America Firsters awaited the
arrival in Pittsburgh of the U.S. Senate's spellbinding
isolationist, Senator Gerald P. Nye of North Dakota. Nye
arrived at Soldiers' Hall as heated as a man coming from a steam
bath. Backstage at the Hall, a Pittsburgh newsman showed him
an Associated Press bulletin. Pearl Harbor had been attacked.
Nye pushed the bulletin aside, saying, "It sounds terribly fishy
to me. Is it sabotage, or is it pen attack?" He took the stage and
cascaded his opinion of the "warmongers" in Washington.
Somewhere along in his speech he told the audience of the
report but cautioned, "I can't somehow believe this . . . there've
been many funny things before." (Unvanquished, he spoke
again that night in a church, but then with a mild concession to
fact. "We've been maneuvered into this by the President," he
said. Then he made for Washington to see what he could do
about the situation.)

Many people, like those at Mrs. Roosevelt's luncheon, didn't
learn until later on of the Japanese attack. Exactly 27,102
football fans—13,000 of them season-ticket holders—sat in

Griffith Stadium while the Redskins engaged the Eagles. Supreme attraction of the day was "Slingin'" Sammy Baugh. More people knew more about what Baugh did daily than of anything going on behind the walls of the capital's buildings. (Indeed, someone had scribbled on a government toilet wall, "You're the only man in Washington who knows what he's doing.") The people knew Sam's life story. From earliest days a baseball, basketball, or football had been his obedient servant. As a youngster in Sweetwater, Texas, he practiced throwing a football through a dangling automobile tire: he put the tire into gyrating motion and found its center like a person poking a finger through a doughnut hole. He raced around as if avoiding tacklers and threw unerringly. Laundry magnate and team owner George Preston Marshall, a man with a showman's flair for half-time extravaganzas, had signed Baugh on. And now the fans screamed his praise—all manner of fans, Army and Navy brass, diplomats, defense workers, and filling station attendants. Washington had it made, and this was a Sunday to remember.

But soon the public address system crackled, and the top Army and Navy men were told to report to their offices. The necks of many onlookers stiffened at the sounds. A call came for popular Philippines Commissioner Joaquin "Mike" Elizalde.

The game ended and the crowds pushed their way from the stadium, elated that the 'Skins had won 20 to 14. Before they had traveled very far they learned that an attack had been made upon Pearl Harbor.

At the White House there was little time for reflection—such as how the surprise had been so successfully sprung. There was much wondering how the nation's 132,000,000 people would react, inasmuch as there had been wide chasms of view concerning the conflict in Europe and the spread of violence in the East. If what the people said, and ever so quietly, could be compressed into a sentence it was, "Why, the little yellow bastards." The vehement reaction contained a core of amazement, for all along the people had been double-talked, and the talk had varied according to expediency. Politicians are frightened men; ever fearful for themselves, they distrust the people. So what would the people do now? If the politicians had read history they would have known that the people would pull together overwhelmingly. They had always come together. And the people now were the sons of the past.

By now, the switchboard lights at the National Press Club were twinkling, and Ernie Ball repeated monotonously, "Yes, it's true." The elevators climbed to the 13th floor and members spilled into the lobby, asking of no one in particular, "What is it now?" and the answer generally was, "It's bad." The members swarmed into the bar and hunched over glasses of beer and wine and then went on to the main lounge, asking questions almost totally unanswerable. They looked from windows upon the streets and at the automobiles moving more swiftly and at small groups of people standing about talking, but with little show of animation.

Behind the gray stone hulk of the *Washington Post*, Alexander F. "Casey" Jones, the superb and irascible managing editor, had arrived and lowered his tall figure into his chair at a desk behind a rail separating him from the newsroom. He looked at some copy piled on his desk and called for his news editors to budget an extra. Now more detailed information about the disaster at Pearl Harbor came in. It was clear that the sitting-duck fleet, the nation's Pacific first-line defense, was ruined. That there had been an appalling toll in deaths was obvious. Jones, World War I veteran, read the accounts and his eyes, ordinarily deep gray pits, reddened in anger and sorrow. (A night city editor had once said of Jones, "He comes storming out here raising hell, but dammit, it always brings out a better paper next morning.") Actually, he needed no one to budget the paper. He could put a paper together or a man in his place with his eyes alone. Pearl Harbor was the paper now, and his eyes settled on the calamity.

Jones looked up at a commotion beside his desk. Robert Tate Allan, the ebullient church editor, had leaped in to announce that he had a scoop: A Georgetown minister, he blurted, had, after long soul-searching, decided to leave town for a pastorate in another city. (There are conflicting accounts of what Jones screamed. Allan recalls that "Mr. Jones's face turned a deep purple.")

It was known by now that Hull had "cursed out" the Japanese envoys. But so many other things were vague. The request for the conference by its very timing was suspicious, its seeming purpose to obtain a few moments for lulling the United States while Japanese warplanes attacked the huddled fleet. The envoys in Washington appeared stunned. They went to the Japanese Embassy, a yellow and elongated building surrounded by gardens, a few blocks away from the British Embassy. The place had appeared quiet, befitting a Washington Sabbath. Then William Beal, a telegraph messenger, knocked on the door and a butler took the telegram. About this time of early afternoon, fifteen taxicabs stopped in fairly rapid succession at the high gate. In all, dozens of Japanese leaped out, some without hats, coats, or ties. Reporters, also, had arrived in taxicabs or in cars driven by photographers. They called to the Japanese, but the few replies came in the Japanese tongue. Two or three could speak enough English to say that they knew no English. The door of the Embassy opened narrowly, and when individuals or groups had slid in, the door closed and the lock snapped. The reporters speculated upon this sudden appearance of so many Japanese. Perhaps they had kept closely in touch with their Embassy, maybe by radio—a faster device than telephone.

A few Japanese reappeared from the Embassy. Within moments flashes brightened the gardens: the Japanese were burning their official documents. They brought these out to an iron grate in boxes with lighted fuses attached to each box. The boxes were metal and about twice the size of a workman's lunchbox. What appeared to be chunks of cement lay on the side of the containers, and inside the metal boxes were smaller wooden ones filled with papers. Vacant space was packed with excelsior. The Japanese talked shrilly in their language, as though to each other or to the orange flames.

One Japanese yelled to reporters who had entered through

the carelessly unlocked gate, "Go away, go away. You must not come." The reporters didn't move. A photographer raised his camera, snapping three Japanese.

The Japanese seemed to be tiny men in the expanse of lawn. One appeared as from nowhere, carrying a wrapped object about the size of three telephone directories. He set the object afire. The glow brought an unearthly life to the backdrop of December's dying leaves on the trees.

A Japanese in a pin-striped suit told the reporters with a broad smile, "No, there is nothing for you here, gentlemen. Please go." The confidential documents were reduced to smoke, but during the process one accumulation shaped into a mushroom (a shape Hiroshima would die under almost four years later).

A reporter asked the man in the pin-striped suit, "What were you burning?"

"Dear sir, those, of course, were my love letters. I hope you will not jump to the hasty conclusion that those were diplomatic documents." He paused, and in an even voice said, "Goodbye. I hope that we may meet under more pleasant circumstances the next time."

An aide was asked if the Embassy had taken extraordinary safety precautions. The reply came fast: "We do not expect to be molested. We have faith in the fairness of the American people."

That afternoon, reporter John D. Morris of the *Post* came to the Embassy and looked around. A large black automobile was parked in the driveway. Several F B I agents talked intently in low voices with the occupants. Morris was a fine reporter, with more than a touch of audacity. He strode to the Embassy door and knocked. A Japanese opened the door and asked what he wanted. Morris said he wanted to talk to the envoys who had met with Secretary Hull. He was told they could not be seen. All right then, would he deliver them a message: why were they conferring when the attack came? The aide returned after a while, saying that the emissaries had not been informed of an impending attack. That was news of the first order. But the

F B I grabbed Morris on his way out and took him to a room in a nearby house. He was questioned: who was he? what was he doing there? Morris showed his press credentials, but those were not enough. The agents phoned the *Post* asking if it had a reporter named John D. Morris on its staff. The reply was Yes. Where was he now? He should be at the Japanese Embassy. The agents wanted a physical description and got it.

Morris hurried to the office to write his story about the denial made by the two envoys—the very guts of the news. The burning of the papers was merely human interest stuff. But the story was spiked (and the newsmen would later try their best to figure out why). The paper, however, found space to disclose that Police Chief Edward J. Kelly had appeared in person at the Embassy and assigned a special detail to the site—an unexpected excursion into foreign affairs from his accustomed routine of pouncing upon brothels or raising hell about traffic snarls.

Downtown and in the residential sections the city lay like a coiled spring, and many wondered when it would snap open. There was some action: recruiting stations prepared for an onrush on a 24-hour basis, seven days a week. And the lines began forming. Meanwhile, the extent of the destruction at Pearl Harbor remained vague. The President, of course, had ordered the Army and Navy to fight back. They had already fought back at Pearl Harbor, but the instances of personal heroism were almost totally unknown.

The Delegate from Hawaii, Samuel Wilder King, had received the news from Radford Mobley, Washington correspondent of the *Honolulu Star-Bulletin*. "My God," King muttered. "Don't they know that Honolulu is not in the Philippines?" (It was widely thought that if an attack came it would be in the Far East.) They went to the Navy Department to see Admiral Chester Nimitz. Mobley saw the face only fleetingly through a doorway, and the face was pale and angry.

Reaction from members of Congress began to come in. Senate Minority Leader McNary asked the nation to "now unite in giving Japan a beating for her aggressive stupidity." Senator

Wheeler of Montana, bullhorn of the isolationist viewpoint, believed that the Japanese "must have been crazy" (which echoed an opinion already expressed by the people). "It means war and we will have to see it through." Representative Hamilton Fish, Jr., of New York, grand panjandrum of the opponents of Roosevelt's foreign policy, said he would urge the House to close ranks behind the President. Senator Vandenberg of Michigan was all for "licking the − − out of them in twenty minutes." In meditative understatement, House Majority Leader McCormack, his Boston Irish up, said that "no matter what have been the views of any American in the past, we cannot tolerate this attack." In the view of bustling, popular Chairman Sol Bloom of the House Foreign Affairs Committee, the President and Secretary Hull had consistently done everything humanly possible to keep the peace. "But now the Army and Navy will take over the situation with a united people behind them, under their Commander-in-Chief."

Senator Thomas of Utah prophesied, "If this attack is approved by the Japanese government, it will result in the destruction of those who started it. Hawaii is an incorporated part of the United States. I am very happy that we have prepared for this." The Congress, said Senator George of Georgia, "will be prepared tomorrow to receive a recommendation from the President declaring war immediately." This did not mean "our entrance into the European war, but we would move nearer to war on that front by cooperating closely with Britain and Russia in the Far East." Cautious Senator Taft of Ohio wanted to grab fast at Japan's throat. "The outrageous attack of the Japanese navy on Hawaii and the Philippines can only lead to a declaration of war by Congress," Taft said. "Undivided and unlimited prosecution of that war must show that no one can safely attack the American people." Now recovered from astonishment, and angry, Delegate King of Hawaii demanded that Japan be destroyed as a military power. Chairman Walsh of the Senate Naval Affairs Committee, frequent opponent of the national foreign policy, now looked to God for help, and would not look back. "We must promptly meet the challenge with all of our resources and courage, and place our faith in God to protect us in this hour of national peril. It is too late now to ponder whether a different international policy would have averted war."

Into the White House came expressions from the Republican top-side. Said Herbert Hoover: "American soil has been treacherously attacked. We must fight with everything we have." Alfred Landon, Roosevelt's second-term opponent and a man not disliked anywhere, said: "Please command me in any way I can be of service."

John L. Lewis, bushy-browed leader of unionized miners, spoke: "When the nation is attacked, every American must rally to its support. All other considerations become insignificant." Charles A. Lindbergh, in the Executive Mansion's doghouse because of his controversial views on Nazi Germany's air force might and future, said: "We have been stepping closer to war every month. Now it has come, and we must meet it as United Americans regardless of our attitude in the past toward the policy our government has followed. . . . Our country has been attacked by force of arms and by force of arms we must retaliate."

A late afternoon in mid-December brings a haunting melancholy as winter nears. In Lafayette Park, the five bronze statues of remembered soldiers fade into the night and the deeper hold of history. The street lights shine inadequately in the darkness of the spaced trees. Yet in the light, the young face of Lafayette glows like a cameo of an aristocratic youth. In the center of the park stands a statue memorializing Andrew Jackson, seventh President, cast from cannon captured at Pensacola during the War of 1812. In the late afternoon of December 7, around the once deadly metal, were fading flowers.

The crowd of men and women increased in the vicinity of the White House with approaching night. Some grabbed at the iron fence and pulled themselves up for a better view. White House police commanded by Secret Service Chief Edmund W. Starling, who walked with the studied jerk of a football player on a muddy field, kept repeating in monotone, "Move on, move on."

And the crowd obeyed. But it moved only a little, shifting and weaving until the wide sidewalk seemed in sway. Mostly the crowd was silent, but occasionally a stranger spoke to a stranger in the way people do in crisis.

Automobiles moved slowly along Pennsylvania Avenue, and faces stared from the car windows at the crowd and at the lights of the White House, where Roosevelt was completing a first draft of the war declaration message. A larger crowd stood and swayed in West Executive Avenue, the narrow thoroughfare between the State Department and the White House. They jammed the double stairway of the Winder Building on 17th Street, a structure which had been the headquarters of Generals Winfield Scott and Ulysses S. Grant, but was more memorable for the visits Abraham Lincoln had paid to learn the turns of war. Along the curbs, a few people held children on their shoulders. Most of the faces were stunned, but a few were angry. Edward R. Andrews, a government employee, spoke quietly. "I was just standing here thinking that there's only one thing to do—get in there and beat the living hell out of them now. They've got it coming." Miss Dorothy Quine, of Boulder, Colorado, a visitor to Washington, appeared puzzled by the inscrutability of the White House lights. "I can't understand it, when Kurusu is here talking about peace," she exclaimed.

At his desk, General Marshall was equally puzzled. (He would later say, " . . . It is inconceivable to me how the attack could have been such a complete, such a total surprise. Previous alerts had been sent. They did not follow orders. They were careless and overconfident—a fatal mistake.")

About the White House, police began searching photographers' carrying-cases. The sound of "Move on, move on," was incessant. A mood of utter mistrust had taken hold of Washington. It affected the Chinese and Filipinos in the capital. They feared they might be mistaken for Japanese, and said so to the press. One of them, a reporter, wore a sign on his coat: *Chinese Reporter—not Japanese.*

During the early night, the sidewalk in front of the White House was blocked off with red lanterns and heavier police details. The Japanese Embassy, despite protection from thirty FBI agents and Chief Kelly's constabulary, additionally safe-guarded itself by employing the Burns Detective Agency. The Munitions Building on Constitution Avenue, a "temporary" structure dating from World War I and now accommodating civilian and military forces, was guarded by Marines. Guards stood at all public utility installations, with 38 allotted to the Washington Aqueduct.

Capital Commissioner Guy Mason made a lengthy inspection, and ventured an opinion: "I don't think the crowds are in a violent mood, but it is our duty to see that the Japanese in this country are given the protection to which they are entitled. There is always the possibility that some fanatic will attempt to bomb the Embassy."

Meanwhile, others saw to the protection of the rest of the population. An easy-going former newsman, District of Columbia Commissioner John Russell Young, now doubling as United States Coordinator of Defense, issued a few words to Civilian Defense Committee chairmen:

> In the present situation it is imperative that the Civilian Defense Committee take caution to complete all defense organization already requested. The order of importance is: complete the Air Raid Warden Service by delivering to deputy, zone and service wardens, the names of men and women to complete all air-raid warden sectors in the city; select a well-qualified woman to organize emergency feeding units; select a well-qualified man or woman to organize emergency housing service.

From Colonel Lemuel Boles, executive director of the District Defense Council, came a reassuring statement. "Washington has nothing to worry about at the present time," he told the people. "Our organization is ready for whatever may come. Even our Air Raid Wardens Division is functioning properly, and in some places we already have thirty to fifty percent of our needed personnel."

Several residents in the Seventh Police Precinct, which

embraced fashionable Georgetown, would deny that Washington had nothing to worry about. Precinct desk officers were told that air-raid wardens were yelling unnecessarily loudly when ordering people to turn off their house lights. One man complained that a night light had been burning in his ailing wife's bedroom, and the wardens had made so much noise that he had had to summon a doctor to quiet his wife.

The dark of December 7 was bright with lights. Behind the lighted windows of the White House, Roosevelt met with his Cabinet at 8:30 P.M. and with Congressional leaders at 9:00 P.M. in the second-floor Red Room Study. Senator Hiram Johnson of California, prominent isolationist, visited the White House for the first time in as long as he chose to remember. This was an inappropriate night for explanations, justifications, or the venturing of opinions. But, of course, someone, and even Johnson, might have something helpful to say to the President. Roosevelt finished with his callers and went back to work. He slept for five hours that night, possibly carrying into slumber the angry challenging words of Senator Connally of Texas: "To hell with what they did to us. What did we do to them?"

Embassy Row was illuminated. Late in the night, light shone in the windows of the cloister-office of Lord Halifax, and in the red-carpeted office of Soviet Ambassador Maxim Litvinoff. He had arrived in Washington only that morning after flying three-quarters of the way around the earth from Moscow. He had received the news by telephone during a luncheon at the residence of Joseph Davies, Presidential advisor on Far Eastern Affairs, a former Ambassador to Russia, and a top Washington socialite. The embassies and legations were cautious, saying, in essence, to reporters' inquiries, "We only know what we hear on the radio."

Lights glowed all night at the National Press Club, where everything is known in advance of the event. But now no one admitted to knowing everything. They did know one thing: this story was too vast, even locally, for the tremendous news-man-power of a city that, with the possible exception of New York, was the news center of the nation. Masses of detail already were overwhelming. These details—what might ordinarily be called trivia—helped make up a larger picture, and that picture promised to be a horrifying one.

No one entirely escaped the night. Mrs. Susan S. Long, part-time maid at the Japanese Embassy, finished her work at midnight. She was tired and there was a long way to go to her home at 1505 West Virginia Avenue, N.W., where her six children were asleep. When she passed through the servants' exit she was stopped by federal agents. They were polite to the extent of tipping their hats, but they were firm.

"You cannot leave, Madam," an agent said. Mrs. Long replied in a lilting Irish voice, "My husband must be at work at 5 A.M. He must heat the school for those children. What of my six little ones? They must go to church, and to school."

"We are only carrying out orders," she was told.

Mrs. Long stood quietly in the half-warmth of the doorway. She was noticeably weighing old indoctrinations. After a few moments she said, "May God bless these wicked people."

Inside the silent Embassy, the Japanese were unaware of her compassion.

CHAPTER TWO

CRY HAVOC–AND INFAMY

DECEMBER 8, 1941, WAS COLD. Few places in Washington feel the whip of wind more uncomfortably than Capitol Hill. It is scarcely a hill but more of a sudden rise commanding a view of the westerly expanses of the city. It had been considered by Washington, Jefferson, Carroll and the other founders as the best site for housing in architectural majesty the young nation's lawmakers and their young American dream.

The Capitol always had affected people according to their individual points of view. From its splendor flowed good or evil. But it was theirs, and though it stood so near to the Atlantic the awesome building was the throbbing heart, the dead center of America. Here, since its construction, was the rallying place of American devotion. In February 1865, Federal and confederate commissioners had met on a ship in Hampton Roads to try to end the Civil War. A Virginian had turned to a Union man and asked, rather wistfully, "How is the Capitol? Is it finished?"

The immensity of the Rotunda often startled visitors. A Midwestern farmer and his wife once gazed up 183 feet to the domed copper ceiling. They tried to equate it with a barn back home on the farm, and wondered how long it might take to fill it with hay.

It was a building that inspired legends. One day a girl had come in, believing that a likeness of Jesus was inlaid on the floor. And a superstition persisted that a black cat unfailingly appeared to wander among the statuary whenever the nation was threatened. No one (of record) thought of the cat that December day, but more than two thousand Washingtonians thought of the Capitol. They would go there in duty or curiosity to see the President arrive to ask for a declaration of war against Japan.

How they managed to escape work is impossible to know; but they selected heavy clothing to keep from suffering on the open spaces of The Hill. The earliest arrivals discovered that Chief Kelly had deployed three hundred of his finest in strategic places among the trees, fences, and bushes. More ominous was the silence of Marines holding bayoneted rifles at every doorway of the building.

The men and women appeared by midmorning; and, precisely as they or their kind had done the previous evening at the White House, they now stood in groups or mass staring at the Capitol. But this crowd was in a different mood: the shock, visibly, had been absorbed. Reporter Charles Mercer of the *Post* viewed the crowd as "American," and in the mood of people who go to baseball games or to revival meetings.

One group of boys began whistling "Maryland, My Maryland," and another group sang, "You're In the Army Now." Soon the Plaza to the east of the Capitol became jammed. Men raised their overcoat collars against the cold. Some people gathered beside portable radios. Outspread morning newspapers fluttered in the wind. The people knew only what they read.

Downtown, a red-haired boy walked into the Marine Corps recruiting station, and soon left, sorrowful. "I'm sorry," the sergeant said twice. The recruiting age could not be shrunk down to thirteen. He was but one volunteer, with lines of potentially eligible men lengthening at the recruiting station. An enchanting recruiting poster portraying the pleasures at Waikiki Beach had within less than 24 hours become meaningless.

Elsewhere downtown, there was trouble for Jesse S. Shima, a slightly-built Japanese and former major-domo for capital socialite and real estate entrepreneur Mrs. Mary F. Henderson. Shima listened uneasily as a court jury returned a verdict compelling him to pay (if he could) $35,000 owed in debts to one Hideyoshi Nagayama. Standing beside both litigants were F.B.I. agents and immigration officials.

Out at the Japanese Embassy it became evident that the human belly wouldn't stay quiet awaiting international settlements. An estimated 49 to 60 diplomats and other personnel (a wide guess in press accounts) had emptied the larders. A functionary telephoned a grocer for about $200 worth of food, including 500 pounds of rice, 75 loaves of white and rye bread, 36 dozen eggs, a case of orange juice, two cases of grapefruit juice, stewed lamb, jams and jellies. When the groceries arrived, the deliveryman refused a check, reminding a Japanese wearing a gray herringbone suit that "your funds are tied up in the bank."

"But we need food badly," the Japanese replied. "All I have had today is a cup of coffee." The deliveryman—probably rehearsed—answered, "I'm sorry, but we cannot wait two or three months for our money." He walked away and the door closed. No doubt, the Japanese had read almost daily that "Christmas is just around the corner," and how loaded the city was with good things to eat. Wine was under heavy sales pressure; spareribs were offered for 22 cents a pound and two pounds of ground beef cost 29 cents. Butter went begging for 39 cents a pound, while the same sum would buy a pound of sliced bacon. Fresh ham cost 29 cents a pound; cigarettes sold for $1.29 a carton.

Members of the elite newspaper Gridiron Club had decided to cancel its dinner scheduled for the following Saturday night at the Willard Hotel. The decision was superfluous. The President was to appear with Wendell Willkie, and Roosevelt was not in the mood for fun.

Little things began making the whole of the day. Something that looked like a radio or a toaster was delivered to the somber brick German Embassy on the downtown stretch of Massachusetts Avenue. The windows upstairs were curtained. But as the object was brought in, the curtains parted and faces in proper Teutonic freeze appeared, the eyes lookd downward and the curtains again closed the view. Hans Thomsen, Hitler's chief representative in the United States, left the Embassy and after a little while returned. Seemingly absorbed in thought, he refused to answer reporters' questions.

Shortly before noon, John De Narco, staff sergeant, 33rd Infantry, stood in the crowd at the Capitol Plaza. His face was almost expressionless. He turned to a bystander, saying, "I guess we all expected it to come. We're just surprised it came so fast. It won't take long to get them." A short while later, Patrolman Jewell Carroll of the Eighth Precinct fell accidentally down the Capitol's marble steps and was carried to a hospital. This caused a flurry. But the President would be along soon and the crowd became tense again. The people looked toward the House wing of the Capitol where the joint session would convene. High up, the goddess stood upon the dome with a face too proud to see from the distance—the distance goddesses should keep. But it was easy to see that her sword was sheathed. Within a few hours the sword figuratively would flare upward.

Far beyond, thousands had tuned in radios; everyone knew what the President would ask, but did not know how much—if any—emotion he would express; and certainly it was not known that one sentence would long live because of one word— "infamy."

The crowd became edgy. Important-looking automobiles arrived from the west. Chauffeurs stepped out and opened the rear doors, and men and women emerged wearing expressions as cold as the day. The people who watched appeared to be more sure of themselves. By now everything was sufficiently clear to them, and simple. The nation had been attacked and they would fight back.

Representative Jeannette Rankin, Montana Republican, arrived, her eyes troubled behind heavy-rimmed glasses. She had voted against war in 1917, and the intervening years had not changed her views. She still had a "deep horror of war and killing," and she would cast the only vote that day against them.

One of the most important arrivals, Mrs. Woodrow Wilson, emerged from her limousine. The President knew that no occurrence within nations or between them erupts spontaneously like a barroom brawl, that occurrences flow from exact cause and effect down the inexorably flowing river of history. Historians who knew him personally believe this thought motivated his decision to have Mrs. Wilson at the Declaration of War session. Symbols are always useful in tying era to era, great cause to great involvement. And Mrs. Wilson, sixty-nine and active, was the reincarnation of the man who had envisioned a better world in which evil men would be eliminated and from their unhallowed graves would arise a federation and everlasting peace. Mrs. Wilson, who had accepted with no show of displeasure the acclaim of her husband in France and who, indeed, had purportedly been the President during her husband's failing months, had dressed for this symbolic appearance in elegant black attire, illuminated by white gloves.

The winds blew harder on Capitol Hill, and across town the winds of fear were rising. Among the possibilities was that the Washington Monument might be sabotaged, and the havoc that would create could only be demonstrated by an Einstein equation. If a bomb with sufficient force were exploded, the 555-foot obelisk would hurl stone all the way from Jimmy Lake's Gayety Theatre on 9th Street (where female performers had no modesty whatever) to ten-mile-distant Alexandria, where the Old Families in Old Town were aghast at the carryings-on and skirt-slinging ways of those newcomers from Washington. The threat was eased by a decision to close the monument at 4 P.M. instead of 6 P.M. It was further decided to take a hard look at the issuance of weather reports. There was no advantage in telling the enemy when good flying conditions lay ahead.

Shortly before noon, a black automobile came to the gravel-topped driveway of the White House south lawn to carry the President to the Capitol. The car was watched every moment by Secret Servicemen, trained to trust nobody, especially on this worst of all days. The F.B.I. with a mere 2,602 agents had, thanks to advance planning, already rounded up nearly 3,000 enemy aliens. But what of potentially dangerous Americans secreted anywhere within the lunatic fringe?

The fear of assassination had never seemed to bother the President. (This assertion can be disputed; some have said—without producing any documentation—that Roosevelt was mindful of the possibility.) He had spent a fitful night, and perhaps missed the two things that relaxed him most—an hour or so with his stamp albums and small talk with Harry Hopkins, a strange man who sometimes looked off and smiled with the wistful uncertainty of a virtuous girl following her first kiss. (Years later, one of Roosevelt's closest, but earlier, associates would say privately, "The President really was a very lonely man." Asked why Roosevelt so persistently sought the company of Harry Hopkins, the reply came, "That's easy. Hopkins always flattered him. He told me once, 'Never, never, say No to him. Always agree. But then do what you choose.' ")

Roosevelt, wearing his blue Navy cape, entered the car. He must have felt the importance of symbols deeply on this day. He was acting not only as President of the people but as commander-in-chief of the nation's armed forces. It was necessary to emphasize his commander-in-chief role because commander he intended to be. Americans never liked the notion of their President wearing a uniform, suggesting as it did the dangerous possibilities of The Man on a Horse. But the cape—reputedly thrown about him once by a Navy officer when he became chilled aboard ship—symbolized the commander's role, and, secretly, subtly, his fondness for the Navy.

The car moved between the bleak trees onto Pennsylvania Avenue. From the sidewalks people stared and said the obvious words: "There he goes," or "We're in it now."

Ahead, the Capitol dome rose like a silver shell above the dark trees, above the dark day, and the worried waiting world. For the onlookers the dome was constant; but the streaming sight on the Avenue carried the eyes along. A Secret Serviceman clung upon each runningboard of the President's car; and on each side were open Secret Service automobiles. Three Secret Servicemen, each armed with a .38-caliber revolver, rode the runningboards and in each open car the agents held riot guns. The automobiles sped to the foot of The Hill, turned right and then left, and climbed.

The crowd upon the Plaza, now feeling the cold intensely, swung about. In its components, it was American from coast to coast, from deepest south to farthest north. It seemed that day a tough old breed that, when frightened, disliked to show it, and when too frightened became angry—anger being the quick killer of fear. The people didn't cry or carry on as, say, French people do in severe crisis or great joy. The crowd knew despite all the huddle that the President had arrived or was nearing, and merely clapped, but in a low and respectful way. After a few moments a spotty cheering rose, which seemed to freeze in the cold air and then be whirled away by the winds.

Inside the Capitol, the joint session sat adorned by Justices of the Supreme Court, the Cabinet, and Mrs. Wilson. Vice President Wallace, his hair less unruly than usual, stood with Sam Rayburn, Speaker of the House, beside an American flag. An ear-pounding yell broke the silence when the President entered, and there was continuous applause. Rayburn's round face was hard when he raised the gavel nearly to his shoulder and banged it down. The President faced the Congress, and his hand went out meticulously and opened a black notebook which looked like those that children use in school. His other hand tightened upon the Reading Clerk's stand. His eyes for a moment roamed the upturned faces, and then he looked down.

"Yesterday, December 7, 1941, a day which will live in infamy, the United States of America was suddenly and deliberately attacked by naval and air forces of the Empire of Japan." The voice known to millions spoke on.

In the Plaza, people listened to portable radios. They heard that severe damage had been done to American naval and military forces, and a reaction showed in their faces. The voice, which could lull, mesmerize, or enrage—according to the listener—was taking its extraordinary effect.

The voice came to what seemed to be the ending: ". . . I ask that the Congress declare that since the unprovoked and dastardly attack by Japan on Sunday, December 7, 1941, a state of war has existed between the United States and the Japanese Empire."

The President had arrived at 12:12 P.M., and at 1:00 P.M. the

Senate acted 82 to 0 upon his request. The House listened to a flurry of speeches, and all were in a fighting mood except Representative Rankin. Then the House voted 388 to 1. At 1:32 P.M. Congress declared war, and at 4:10 P.M. the weary President signed the Resolution in his office.

Roosevelt talked for a while with Soviet Ambassador Litvinoff and then slept on his office sofa for an hour. What he thought as he closed his eyes no one will ever know. Perhaps he gave a thought to the ending of an era—known by the name of the New Deal—and the beginning of another; or perhaps he thought of the people whose destinies he guided.

Representative Rankin, whom no one disliked, had fled for refuge into a telephone booth to avoid questions from reporters who, devilishly, only wanted something to lighten their somber stories. When Roosevelt awakened, he began dictating a speech to the nation for the following night. He could now talk in hard terms about the Japanese.

Before the day ended, Senator Albert B. "Happy" Chandler, Democrat of Kentucky, wanted personal action. Telephoning the White House, he offered to "put on a uniform and go out and fight." He telephoned the same proposal to General Marshall, whose disgust at the Pearl Harbor fiasco-tragedy was at its height. (Later on, Chandler would say, "I haven't had any reply yet, but I'm ready to go whenever they want me.")

Representative Lyndon B. Johnson, Democrat of Texas, restrained what emotion he felt. He simply stated to the White House that he was a member of the Naval Reserve and wanted active duty. In another communication to Secretary Knox he asked for prompt action, and got it.

Within a few days a great many things happened to Washington. The word "war" was substituted for "defense" in the titles of government programs. The pace quickened within all government buildings, down to a faster shuffling of papers. Young men and women groaned at being kept at work beyond dating hours. Many individuals throughout the capital remembered or had heard of the rationing imposed in World War I and began the dirty work of hoarding. They knew what would go off the markets—sugar, coffee, good clothing, good meat, shoes, and gasoline.

But something suddenly happened that troubled the spirit. The light went from the Capitol dome. The people at nighttime looking up Pennsylvania Avenue could scarcely see the dome and the goddess, and some may have wondered why they had for so long taken so much grandeur for granted. Sometimes when the moon was up or the stars grew bright the faint traces of the goddess' robes were limned, and then the lovely bronze woman (whom some believed was an Indian) lived again.

CHAPTER THREE

OF THINGS PAST AND
TURMOIL PRESENT

MOST WASHINGTONIANS HAD not recovered from the first
blow before word of others came through the radios or in the
shouts of "Extra" from the streets. They did know that the
Japanese planes had severely crippled the fleet at Pearl Harbor.
Time passed before the men who should know such things
learned that the hundred-plus aircraft ornamented with the
Rising Sun had destroyed the Battleship Arizona and badly
damaged the Oklahoma, Nevada, California, and West Virginia.
Three destroyers, a minelayer, and a target ship lay damaged.

The Navy, it was learned as information trickled to the
officials, had lost 80 planes, and the Army 97. Of human
casualties, information came with painful slowness. But it
would be learned that 2,117 officers and enlisted men of the
Navy were killed, 876 were wounded, and 960 were missing.
The Army death toll reached 226 officers and enlisted men,
with 396 wounded. Lacking knowledge, men and women in
offices and stores and homes listened to rumors of what might
have happened out there. But they remained calm even when it
became known that the Japanese had enlarged the war with
attacks on Wake Island and its small force of Marines, on Guam
and Midway Islands, and had virtually destroyed the United
States air base in the Philippines.

The calm prevailed on December 11, 1941, when Germany
and Italy declared war on the United States. Congress, vocally
angry that day, responded by declaring war as existing

34

"between the United States and Germany and the United States and Italy."

Eight-column banner headlines became the newspaper norm, and the news in the aggregate was bad. It is beyond dispute that the people were depressed, but it is equally true that they didn't show it too much. There may have been a reason: the United States had never been defeated in war. It had been badly shaken by the Civil War, but it never had lost. This war was a calamity, and a hard job lay ahead, but it could be accomplished. And, meanwhile, Washington was an exciting place to be in, and a place of usefulness.

For thousands, the war brought no radical changes in their way of life, a way of life dating back to June 22, 1940, when occupied (Vichy) France had capitulated to Hitler and the call for defense workers had rung across the land. Civil Service recruiters had fanned out to find young women who could type forty words a minute, and who would agree to a six-month probationary period. There were 53,038 government women workers in Washington in June 1940, and a year later the number had climbed to 77,774—more than 8,000 entering the War Department during the first year of defense emergency. Hundreds found work in the British and other missions in the capital.

The women had come from everywhere in the United States, and what they were like was in the eye of the beholder. A Washington newspaperwoman, with claws extended, typed them as "on the whole, a pretty unsophisticated lot." She calculated their ages as ranging from eighteen to twenty-five, "younger than the typical New York stenographer." She tried to understand why they had come to Washington, and believed it was because of jobs, which averaged between $105 and $120 a month. (The newspaperwoman's judgment is questionable. Viewpoints even at this late date are in conflict. Some say the women were motivated by "patriotism." Others say it was a desire for excitement. One man, later a lieutenant colonel of Marines, recalls idly asking the question of three girls at a boardinghouse on 19th Street, N.W., and "all I received was three blank stares.")

Whatever their motivations, they were delightfully different and cracked the crust of what had traditionally been a staid old city. The small-town girls brought with them the informality of their home towns, and the city girls the swish of the big city. They wore sweaters revealing or deceiving of what blossomed underneath: they went about hatless; they clomped about in saddle shoes; they wore their hair in either an upsweep or down to their shoulders, and sported skirts slightly below the knees. Their faces were open and the eyes friendly, often starry. They appeared lacking in self-consciousness. They formed a habit of eating their lunches in good weather from paper bags on the steps of office buildings, or while sprawled on the grass in the parks.

With the war actually on, it was relieving to remember the good old days of that era called the Defense Program time. Handsome and sartorially impeccable Igor Cassini of the *Times-Herald,* on April 20, 1941, had delivered himself of a fast-paced look at the capital:

> The man standing near the State Department trying to persuade the tourists to come for a sight-seeing drive . . . The First Lady appearing in a pink dress at the [National] Theatre opening . . . Senator Wheeler mowing his cigar before delivering a speech . . . Mrs. Sol Bloom rushing to get her Representative hubby to go to the British Embassy . . . The Peruvian Ambassador sniffing cherry blossoms in his morning promenade . . . Justice Frank Murphy, who takes an early horseback ride before going to his desk at the Supreme Court . . . The boys and girls parked in cars along the Speedway, watching the twinkling lights of the capital . . . The people in rowboats crowding around the floating stage at the Watergate Symphonies . . . Alice Roosevelt Longworth running into the offices of the America First Committee . . . Mrs. Lester Buchanan and Coleman Jennings, the millionaire philanthropist, singing in jail at church services they organize for the prisoners . . . The corner table in the Mayflower main dining-room always reserved for Under Secretary of State Sumner

Welles . . . Georgetown—the paradox where only the richest or poorest can afford to live . . . The original parties at which people as different a Father Walsh, Liz Whitney, John L. Lewis, Wendell Willkie and Gene Autry can be found conversing . . . Chevy Chase Club, the snootiest club in the country; it takes seven years of waiting before one can be permitted to join . . . Rose Merriam, who has to draft the new recruits for Washington society—the debutantes . . . The noble expression of Chief Justice Hughes . . . The Soviet Ambassador Constantine Oumansky visiting all the antique shops to find rare objects and paintings . . . Jimmy Lake's Gayety, where solons and diplomats go to strip their minds from their heavy worries.

The girls didn't know any of the people mentioned; but the feeling that they were a part of the capital and even a part of these people, the sense of identification with them, was well worth the price of a newspaper.

But disillusionment soon affected thousands of the girls. From their homes, especially in the small towns, they had announced they were going to Washington as defense workers— a patriotic gesture. Their telephones had rung, and the voices had cried, "You're going to *Washington*?" They were instantly changed in all but name. Glamour had rubbed off on them: they were important. They would be where great men did great things, and they would be in some way a part of them. Goodbye parties were hastily arranged, and those remaining behind pleaded, "You won't forget us, now?"

Arriving in Washington, they had scant time to remember anything. Hours dragged as they filled out forms, and time passed in awaiting assignments. The babble of voices, the crowding into small offices, the absence of personal notice removed any sense of personal identity. Many were escorted off impersonally for duty in stenographic pools. Back home the people had paid more attention to kittens in a litter.

The crowding was inescapable—for everyone. It quickly became the city's number-one problem. The era of the square foot began. With the exactness of cost accountants, men with pinched eyes came into every office and with trained glances calculated how many people could squeeze in. It was a mathematical process, devoid of any personalization, except that the mandates for squeezing compelled the men and women frequently to rub against one another, accelerating morale but slowing the Defense Program.

An Associated Press reporter (as he remembered years later) overheard an argument over space in the Munitions Building. A long steel-faced row of filing cabinets bulged with records concerning the Spanish-American War, which the Spaniards amiably wanted to forget and which most Americans knew little about beyond an explosion which had torn the bowels from the Battleship Maine. Could these files be removed to make space for the girls or anything current? Word came down in triplicate that the documents could be removed if copies were made in duplicate.

As early as April 1941, the *Property Owner* characterized Washington as "the No. 1 boom town of the defense program as thousands of government workers pour monthly into the national capital." Washington, indeed, had become the nation's tenth largest city in population, pushing Pittsburgh aside.

Exactly how many people were in Washington, since no one checked trains, buses, airports, and bridges, only the god of battles and buildings could know. One account said that the capital's population, added to the numbers in Alexandria, other adjacent Virginia areas, and Maryland, totaled 962,472. Capital retailers were overjoyed. Business had risen ten percent during the preceding year, and, in April, promised more than a half billion dollars a year. Excluding the military—alert to the competition for the square foot with civilian agencies—the federal payroll reached $29 million a month.

Clay J. Guthridge, a government expert burdened with finding the square feet to accommodate all these workers, expressed the situation in formal governmentese: "The government is now resorting to conversion of warehouses and apartment houses into office buildings." The government then owned entirely 129 buildings containing a precious 17,300,000 square feet. Then came the soul-wrenching prediction that an additional 500,000 square feet of space would be needed within "a few months."

The government, prime property owner or user, took over 189 privately owned buildings, tapping the taxpayers some $6.2 million a year in rentals and maintenance. It became so bad that one girl was heard to remark toward nightfall, "I must hurry to my apartment building, because the government may have moved in."

The capital's housing enterprises patriotically joined the square-foot squirm, flushing estimates into the newspapers. So much was discussed statistically that reporters covering the housing beat preferred to write obituaries. Curiously, too little was said about the men and women, children, dogs, and cats that were cast into the streets as building after building was acquired by an impersonal something called the government.

Washington, never intended nor laid out for such a crisis, developed a severe case of building bellyache, accompanied by the groans and screams of the evicted residents. So the experts in square feet decided to grab the last remaining "temporary buildings" of World War I, and to erect others equally as unsightly on the Virginia side.

The problem, having benumbed the mind and confounded calculations and conferences, was tossed to that American catchall called the committee. Representative Everett McKinley Dirksen, born in Pekin, Illinois, where people had huge backyards to laze in and died in the homes of their birth, was shaken by the square-foot crisis. One manner of relieving a crisis was to growl it out of the way. So he considered the floating proposals of erecting temporary structures on federal acreage in the District of Columbia and its adjoining states. He brought matters to an uncertain head with the introduction of a House resolution creating an investigation by a subcommittee of the Appropriations Committee.

At the White House, President Roosevelt saw the space squeeze as being an inevitable part of that ultimate goal—the saving of every square foot of England, and, considering Hitler's madness, probably the United States itself. The disaster of Dunkirk lay in the memory, with its miracle of having saved 338,226 troops with 900 vessels; and London, lovely Coventry, and industrialized Birmingham had been blasted from the air.

As the newcomers battled hard within a lonely survival program of their own unwitting and unwilling creation, the newspapers reacted vocally to the unsettling changes. The *Washington Times-Herald* saw the capital as the center of the earth, and the conservative newspaper didn't much like it.

> The once sleepy southern city of charm and grace on the Potomac has burgeoned into the frenzied capital of the world. Where money pours, power reigns. Here is being enacted a spectacle of imperial waste. It is being enacted on a scale that would have been considered grandiose even in the days of Xerxes, most lavish of the kings of man.
>
> Out of the city pours a ceaseless stream of money at the rate of $175 million a day. If it keeps up, $63,875 billion will have poured out by this time next year. Not for routine costs of government, not for loans to the British or other nations, but all in the name of 'defense.'

The comings and goings irritated the anti-Roosevelt newspaper, closely allied by family and money ties to the *Chicago Tribune*. The *Times-Herald* disclosed:

> Into this city to direct, touch, fight for or carry away a bit of this money, now tumble 45,000 people a day by train, 1,000 by plane. An almost equal number tumble out again, many with a fistful of arms contracts, many with broken hopes and illusions. Here a conglomerate army of government workers holds forth. As armaments become more of an octopus, so the multitude swells. With this army of jobholders, who hurry down the streets and sidewalks morning, noon, and evening, is a camp-following of amazing proportions. Lobbyists, propagandists, experts of every species, wealthy industrialists, social climbers, inventors, ladies of uneasy virtue and pickpockets infest

the city. . . . During the chaotic days before the Civil War, a common Washington joke was that if a boy threw a stone on Pennsylvania Avenue he would hit three brigadier generals. Now he would hit at least two dollar-a-year men, an Office of Production Management official, and a defense contract that had been misplaced.

The *Washington Evening Star*, the sedate Old Lady of Eleventh Street, which could boast of having covered the Civil War and took all matters beyond the serious business of citizens' associations with calm maturity, maintained its composure; and the *Post*, accused of being ready to open a recruiting station at any moment in its frowzy lobby, continued to be exceedingly polite to the defense worker. Its Federal Diary column, devoted to little items about the government people, had previously held two contests—a dignified one to select a "Miss Civil Service," and a later one styled as a competition to choose a "Miss Beauty with Brains." The prize was a trip to the New York World's Fair. But upon her arrival, the reporters beset her with a series of questions which Einstein could not have solved in mathematics nor any Ph.D. in the area of his own discipline. It resulted in embarrassment, but the girl was pleased because nearly everyone agreed that she was pretty, and the whole affair was soon forgotten.

But Washington grew serious when Germany declared war on Russia on June 22, 1941. Among those most affected was Soviet Ambassador Constantine A. Oumansky. A man of tiny and humble appearance, he seemed to slide rather than walk to a destination, and he looked misplaced physically as master of his revolutionized country's affairs in the mighty United States. But he had seemed to fit perfectly into the old Pullman mansion, which housed the Embassy staff on lower Sixteenth Street, N.W. The hard marble aloof four-story building reflected Oumansky's personality. The windows projected steel grilles, and the interior lay secreted behind red curtains that were always drawn. But change in everything, including Oumansky, came with the declaration of war on his country. The short circular driveway at the Embassy door became busy with black limousines bearing diplomatic license plates. The red curtains parted, and the quick opening of the front door matched the incredible opening of the formerly furtive Ambassador's countenance.

The average young defense worker didn't know of Oumansky's sudden emergence into the sunlight of favor. That sort of thing was beyond his personal concern, but he felt a dislike and dread of Hitler's threat to what was commonly called "the free world," and his collaborations with the growing menace of Japan.

The President, of course, knew that nothing short of a world revolution was raging. Students in the capital's George Washington, Georgetown, American, and Catholic Universities knew it, too, as did the defense workers. But, like the President, they sought occasional release from their mood. If the President chose stamp albums, the comradeship of Hopkins, and the holding of unprecedented numbers of press conferences, the young men and women might escape their oppressive thoughts by the quickest way ever devised—a little pardonable hell-raising.

Moreover, they delighted in gossip. There was a story that unseemly conduct between man and woman occurred nightly too close to hallowed Arlington Cemetery—either in automobiles or on the grass. And one story went the rounds that an agile man and his girl had climbed a fence at Mount Vernon to perform an act upon the ground owned by the allegedly impotent Father of His Country. Soldiers guarding the reservoir against saboteurs out to kill everyone taking a drink of water heard a rustling in the woods (one remembers that it was an enthusiastic kind of sound). As the soldiers surrounded the dark Virginia bushes, out loped a man and a woman.

The servicemen were disinclined to let the civilians have all the pleasures traditionally afforded by an approaching war. One officer developed an unfailing ploy. He would buy a fifth of whisky and wander a hotel's corridors until he heard the sound of a party in a room. He would then knock on the door and hold out his bottle, saying, "I'm in a little jam here. Does

anyone have a knife or something I can open this bottle with?"
He was invariably invited in, and would score a dead-center
bull's-eye if some of the men were civilians. Women favored
uniforms, and someone in the assemblage went home woman-
less each time.

A newsman began wondering what the drinking situation was
like in the Congress. After an investigation (the depth of which
he failed to disclose in his account), he concluded that "there is
no more drinking among Congressmen than among any other
group of men in public life." How he arrived at this profound
conclusion is unknown, but he went on: "Out of the 435
Representatives and 96 Senators, only a dozen are what might
be called heavy drinkers; the others are either teetotalers or
social drinkers." A clergyman, left unnamed after a similar
inquiry, said that only on a "few occasions" in the past six
years had he seen any "dead soldiers" in or around the
legislative offices. (Employment requirements did not contain
such a clause, but the lowest-ranking member of female staffs
accepted the sly removal of bottles as part of her work.
Congressmen, too, can be lonely, and as poet Stephen Vincent
Benét said, "A little whisky is a comforting thing when men are
lonely.")

Fortunately, in the uproarious months preceding Pearl
Harbor, Washington's conglomerate population of New Eng-
landers, Westerners, Southerners, and foreigners gathered into a
harmonious whole—with the exception of the British (excluding
Lord Halifax) who were generally regarded as politely arrogant.
The people, as a whole, suggested the summer crowds at
Atlantic City, a place of pleasure but hardly one to be accepted
as home.

Very few had the foggiest notion of how the capital as a city
functioned officially. Washington appeared to be packaged in
something called The Government, the giant mechanism that
also ran The Nation. After a while, the people learned that the
ornate building standing off Pennsylvania Avenue's south side at
Fourteenth Street was the District Building, and a few seekers
after knowledge learned that the structure housed three District

Commissioners headed by a gaunt, melancholy, and kindly man named Melvin Hazen. The marble-pedestaled statue out front of a gentleman in a swallow-tail coat was somebody named Boss Shepherd, a one-time political controller of the capital's official life. They did not know that the Commissioners had to wrench the major portion of money for the operation of Washington from a highly conservative and fractious so-called District Committee in Congress.

Only the political-science-minded among the newcomers knew that few, if any, members of the Committee wanted to serve, because they could be—and were—accused back home of paying too much attention to "that place there and not enough attention to us."

"That place," in the minds of righteous Southerners, Puritan New Englanders, and suspicious Midwesterners, was a roost of thieves by day and a Sodom which revolved around Gomorrah by night.

But there was something about Washington, and tens of thousands knew inwardly that they were there to stay. This troubled one newsman, who, not looking beyond the contemporary scene, aligned himself with the statisticians to estimate that there were not enough men to go around. And the men were already doing the best they could. A generation of spinsters would result. Casting back to 1940, the observer recalled a condition of 91 men for every 100 women, and said that so lamentable a condition was unequaled anywhere else in the United States.

The women received much unjustified sympathy. An old army rule forbade officers from holding informal conversation with female subordinates. But had this been enforced, there would not have been sufficient square feet in the capital for the holding of courts-martial. One officer, indeed, emerged around daybreak from the immensity of the Wardman Park Hotel, at Connecticut Avenue and Woodley Road, far from his armchair of duty, exclaiming as he slumped into a taxicab, "My God, I'll be glad when this world crisis is finished."

Some of the girls, the matter of men aside, were accomplished

complainers about government and capital life in general. Their
insights were as sharp as their tongues. A female clerk in the
Reconstruction Finance Corporation became physically exhausted from signing out so many millions of dollars in checks.
Avoiding the danger of bottled emotion, she uncorked herself
to a newspaper reporter:

"Everybody in America except the DuPonts have been
borrowing money from us this year, and I guess they just hate
Roosevelt too much. Why, we have eighteen thousand telephone calls a day. I tell you, after a day of this, it just seems
silly to go home and try to budget my salary." She went on:

> No matter what salary you make in Washington, it takes
> half of it to eat and sleep. Just for creature comforts alone.
> The cost of living has gone up about fifteen percent, and
> no one really makes a lot even though it sounds like it
> when you first get it. The average girl makes $1,560 a year,
> and it doesn't go far here. I came up in 1940, and there
> were no vacancies. When I went around they'd say,
> 'Vacancies are made, you know.' It depended on whom
> you knew, and how prominent they were.
>
> Well, it was wonderful. You could find a job and have
> the most powerful politics in the world, and they still
> wouldn't want you. Then they'd give you an examination
> that all hell couldn't pass, so they could kick you out
> again. It was a racket pure and simple.

Then she whirled upon the capital of the earth presided over
by the three Commissioners and the Congressional Committee:

> Since March, there have been three sex murders within a
> radius of two blocks of where I live. It's a neighborhood of
> old homes, most of them filled with government clerks.
> It's just as dangerous as it can be. You lose respect for just
> about everything and everyone. But I'll tell you one thing
> Washington cures you of—the respect you had back home
> for Congressmen. If you went to the dime store to buy
> buttons by the dozen it would mean about as much.

The churches and the Y.W.C.A. felt concern about the morals

and moods of the girls and held programs to save their souls—such things as "activities" and get-togethers where nice young men might mingle. *The New York Times* of November 23, 1941, sighed, "But all this is not answering the long-term question of what in the end is going to happen to these young women." (The *Times* knew positively what was going to happen, but it only carries all the news that's fit to print.)

The looseness of morals, the loneliness in its numerous variations extending from the President's chambers to Meridian Place—where four girls through uncurtained windows visibly ironed their underpants and unlimbered their desk-wearied hips by performing somersaults on the floor at night—in no way dimmed the jubilation within the marketplace. Bank deposits on June 30, 1941, totaled a record $450,970,637.97. During the first six months of 1941, department store sales soared twenty percent over the same period of 1940, another all-time Washington high. But there came a growing shortage of salespeople, and the stores would not offer competitive salaries. The Chesapeake and Potomac Telephone Company counted the total telephones, including extensions and branches, as 321,924 by the end of the year. (The number would reach 364,354 by the same date in 1945.) Total main telephones, excluding all extensions and branches, numbered 141,746 on December 31, 1941 (and would reach 166,000 by December 31, 1945).

More than one hundred new restaurants appeared in likely places, which was anywhere, during the six months preceding Pearl Harbor, but they did not relieve the load on the old establishments. Many of the places were of the stand-up kind. And with the passing of days, the flagging waitresses—particularly during the rush hours of 11:45 A.M. to 2:00 P.M.—developed a characteristic previously unknown in leisurely, polite Washington. They would never look a customer in the eye. They dragged their feet behind the counter, and their eyes dragged along with the feet, or fixed upon the dishes or whatever was alongside their knees. Customers became hopeful when one of the girls shuffled in his direction, but only the body approached. When a customer uttered a soft and entreating

"Miss," there was no reply and no reaction in the eyes.

If a customer cried out when angered beyond control, it might as well have been to the rocks. The people strove for explanations, only to conclude (1) the waitresses knew they had more load than was manageable, and, in consequence, had surrendered; (2) they were shiftless to begin with, and incapable of any other conduct; (3) they disliked the customers, believing them to be affluent and in need of being put in their place; and (4) it was a manifestation of mass sadism.

There was even brusqueness in the fine old restaurants along Connecticut and Pennsylvania Avenues, G and F Streets. Unless the diner was recognized as among the political or business nobility, he could sense in both waiter and management a desire for him to eat, pay, and get out. Frequently, a plate was grabbed before the meal was entirely eaten. The waiter wanted the table in fast action for tips; the management wanted a fast turnover for profit. But the old-line Washingtonians could never believe it was happening. "This town has gone to hell in a hack," became a common outcry. People remembered a time when a man could sit down at noon and leave at 3 P.M. if he chose. The manager himself would stop by, or even pull up a chair to talk. And talk about all sorts of things: of what had happened to the Senators, and how there could never be another pitcher like Walter Johnson. Or wonder out loud if it were true that a beloved bootlegger during Prohibition had really kept a dozen bottles of corn liquor behind a bush on the South Lawn of the White House, within reach of his hand through the iron-fence bars when business required.

Reporter Gerald G. Gross of the *Post* lamented, "It makes some of the old-timers sad."

It is improbable that the newcomers understood what Gross said, because what they saw was all they knew of Washington, except that it had a Capitol and a very high monument. The reporter simply meant that Washington had once been a small town in everything but size; a place of rooted people living quietly within magnificent distances, familiar enough to be taken for granted. Even the accent of Washington families might have been dropped almost anywhere in Virginia or southern Maryland and gone unnoticed. And now there was a babble of voices, compounding all the other changes. George Vivian, Director of the Academy of the Theatre, divided the capital's talking habits into two classes—careless and cultivated.

"Most men speak back in their throats, and most women high in their heads, and the net result is most unpleasant," the authority said. The affected speech was as unbearable as the careless. "Washingtonians haven't learned to strike a happy medium."

But authoritative pronouncements aside, some of the female newcomers created a speech-form that must have originated in hell's torture chamber. They would talk along in a well-modulated tone about something neither serious, amusing, nor interesting, and, then, like a whiplash, scream a final phrase. And to impress this outrage upon the startled listener they would flash a smile both meaningless and vacant.

From all this travail, compounded by the threat of Hitler whom many believed might strike at the United States before Japan moved, hundreds of sensitive defense workers fled to nearby places of peace on Sunday, if they could get off from work. They traveled often by automobile past the pillared Lincoln Memorial with the names of the reunited states chiseled on its marble top. They went inside and stood before the heroic, brooding figure of Lincoln, sitting with his arms low and weary. The tips of his fingers expressed the strain that Washington and war had imposed. The newcomers read the chiseled lines:

IN THIS TEMPLE AS IN THE HEARTS OF THE PEOPLE
FOR WHOM HE SAVED THE UNION, THE MEMORY
OF ABRAHAM LINCOLN IS ENSHRINED FOREVER.

They drove across Memorial Bridge and looked up and down the wide green-brown river and ahead to a wooded hilltop and to a mansion with high white columns startling against the autumn death of the trees. Robert E. Lee had lived there once, and had caused Lincoln more troubles than his generals and his Administration. And now they faced each other in quiet, the carved figure and the great house.

Lincoln and Lee had both been torn in mind—the victims of war that neither had wanted. The newcomers looked down from the hilltop, and the Washington Monument rose slim and high, a memorial to a man who also had been torn by war, which he had wanted. The city lay flat and distant. There was no sound from the streets nor the buildings in panorama so far below. The dark, groomed roadways threaded ahead between tall and low white gravestones, with the names of well-known soldiers and some with just names. But they were all the residue of war. Was Washington, one wondered, a seat of government, or the symbol of a sword?

The newcomers seeking escape drove along to find a crowd of people standing silently before a low marble Tomb, and in front of which a soldier marched, stopped and turned with exactness, and marched back again with the precise motions of a minute hand on a watch. The newcomers stared at the Tomb, of which they had heard much. President Harding and the great men of the world had stood there when it was dedicated November 11, 1921, in an outpouring of emotion such as the nation had never experienced before. The lines on the Tomb were clearly seen:

HERE RESTS IN HONORED GLORY
AN AMERICAN SOLDIER KNOWN BUT TO GOD.

He had died for something, and they were in Washington now for maybe the same thing.

CHAPTER FOUR

CHURCHILL BRIGHTENS THE FIRST WAR CHRISTMAS

IN THE EARLY AFTERNOON of December 24, 1941—seventeen days after Pearl Harbor—some 20,000 Washington men and women put aside their last-minute Christmas shopping and little happinesses at home to go to the White House for the twentieth lighting of the National Christmas Tree. En route, they looked from streetcars, buses, and automobiles at store windows filled with fineries brightened by the colored lights and tinsel. Those walking along the crowded streets saw the clear sky and the sun slanting into the southwest and the Virginia uplands.

The people were edgy, and the kind of mood that bright sunshine scarcely lifts and the white of snow deepens cut below the spell of Christmas. By now, that damnable but necessary war overshadowed everything. They would see the tree (and the power of the Federal Government would make it beautiful to the last green stem and colored bulb) and they would see the President again and hear his familiar voice. He would talk, as always, on the upbeat—if conditions had been bad, and if conditions were worsening, all would yet be right in the end. He was a personality cut to a pattern, and it was easy to guess what he would say. It would be another Christmas Eve beside the tree—though this was the first time it had been placed on the South Lawn of the White House. (In other years, the tree had gleamed on the Ellipse south of the mansion grounds, or even farther to the east in Sherman Square.)

But now, more compelling than Christmas and more power-

ful than danger, deprivation, and death itself, was Winston
Churchill, Britain's Prime Minister, who seemed from his
pictures like a bulldog in human form, combat-ready, eager to
confront the impossible, restive, tough, and demanding that all
of life be as unyielding as he. The people would see him and
wonder whether such a personality could suddenly, by the mere
motion of standing near a Christmas tree on a late afternoon,
soften to the point of yielding to the power of a spiritual day.

(Around this time of day in Washington, night was down on
the Kentish coast of England. The houses were dark. Children
stood in the dark and sang carols, and some of them trembled
when the German long-range artillery shells burst over the white
cliffs of Dover. Far away from where the lonely voices trailed
through the night the bells of Bethlehem rang.)

At 4:05 P.M., the southwest and southeast gates of the White
House South Lawn were opened. Crisp commands of "No
cameras, no packages" came incessantly to the visitors, eyed by
the Secret Service, the White House police, and soldiers. The
army had raised a long tent across the street on the grass as a
package-checking station. But many people refused to go there
and lose their place in line. Rather, they laid their Christmas
bundles alongside the iron-picket fence. They jammed through
the two gates at the rate of four a minute. Some veterans of the
annual Easter Egg Rolling affrays (reputedly started during the
Andrew Johnson Administration) pushed toward the Easter Egg
Knoll, a vantage place near the portico.

The lawn filled quickly in the reddish glow of twilight.
Nearly three thousand persons stood outside the fence. Low in
the sky, a flight of birds passed silently within the roar of a
passing airplane.

In the guest stand were Supreme Court Justices Jackson and
Reed, and sharp-eyed Attorney General Francis Biddle. Massed
choristers and the Marine Band stood nearby. The band struck
up at 4:30 P.M., and the Christmas music faded into the traffic
of the streets. A few moments after 5 P.M., the bandsmen
stiffened, played "Hail to the Chief," and the fidgety crowd
tightened.

The President and Winston Churchill came slowly upon the portico and faced the people. Through the music they could hear the echoes of the sunset gun at Fort Myer. Churchill's eyes roamed every part of the crowd, and then strained toward the Washington Monument, where a tiny red light shone in a window 550 feet above the ground.

Roosevelt pressed a button, and the tree lights glowed in the near dark. On the portico were Mrs. Roosevelt, Crown Prince Olaf and Crown Princess Martha of Norway, refugee friends of the Roosevelts, and their three children. And there stood Harry Hopkins, a household name but an elusive figure. Few looked at him; the eyes were on the man from England, whose face did not seem hard. He stood in the center of a long silence, close beside the President. Slowly, his eyes fastened upon the Christmas tree.

The Most Reverend Joseph Corrigan, rector of Catholic University, began the invocation with, "Hear a united people, girded for battle, dedicate themselves to the peace of Christmas, nor find strangeness in our words. All the material resources with which Thou hast blessed our native land we consecrate to the dread tasks of war." He prayed for "all who hold power over human life."

The crowd began almost visibly to become restless when the President started speaking. The change of mood appeared in little ways—the shuffling of feet, low-pitched conversations, and the gaze at Churchill. The question could be seen in many eyes: What would he say of the war and what, if anything, of Christmas? For some it didn't matter; they had seen Winston Churchill, and that was good for a week of conversation and something to remember and hand down to their children.

The President reminded them of his Proclamation of January 1 as a Day of Prayer, "of asking forgiveness for our shortcomings of the past, of consecration to the tasks of the present, of asking God's help in days to come." The soothing voice continued: "It is in the spirit of peace and good will, and with particular thoughtfulness of those, our sons and brothers, who serve in our armed forces on land and sea, near and far—those who serve for us and endure for us—that we light our Christmas candles now across this continent from one coast to the other on this Christmas evening."

The words went to all in the United States and by shortwave abroad. The President spoke of Churchill. The Prime Minister had arrived in deepest secrecy at an air base and was met by the President. Now Churchill wanted to speak to Washington and to the world. For a moment Churchill seemed to tighten within himself, and the crowd tensed with him. Then his voice came out:

> I spend this anniversary and festival far from my country, far from my family, yet I cannot truthfully say that I feel far from home. Whether it be the ties of blood on my mother's side, or the friendships I have developed here over many years of active life, or the commanding sentiment of comradeship in the common cause of great peoples who speak the same language, who kneel at the same altars and, to a very large extent, pursue the same ideals, I cannot feel myself a stranger here in the centre and at the summit of the United States. I feel a sense of unity and fraternal association which, added to the kindliness of your welcome, convinces me that I have a right to sit at your firesides and share your Christmas joys.
>
> This is a strange Christmas Eve. Almost the whole world is locked in deadly struggle, and, with the most terrible weapons which science can devise, the nations advance upon each other. Ill would it be for us this Christmastide if we were not sure that no greed for the land or wealth of any other people, no vulgar ambition, no morbid lust for material gain at the expense of others has led us to the field. Here, in the midst of war, raging and roaring over all the lands and seas, creeping nearer to our hearts and homes, here, amid all the tumult, we have tonight the peace of the spirit in each cottage home and in every generous heart. Therefore, we may cast aside for this night at least the cares and dangers which beset us, and make for the children an evening of happiness in a world of storm. Here, then, for one night only, each home throughout the

English-speaking world should be a brightly-lighted island of happiness and peace.

Let the children have their night of fun and laughter. Let the gifts of Father Christmas delight their play. Let us grown-ups share to the full in their unstinted pleasures before we turn again to the stern task and the formidable years that lie before us, resolved that, by our sacrifice and daring, these same children shall not be robbed of their inheritance or denied their right to live in a free and decent world.

And so, in God's mercy, a happy Christmas to you all.

The gates drew open and the crowds pushed out upon the hundreds on the sidewalk where a man mumbled, "When I saw this mob I was just as glad that I didn't get inside." One who was inside said, "Now I know how a fellow feels to be let out of jail." But the crowd was more quiet than it had been upon its arrival. Walking in the crush became maddening; but overhead a crescent moon and one bold star lay peaceful in Roosevelt's and Churchill's and Washington's "world of storm."

Most of the people going into their homes that night undoubtedly felt the war shadows lessening. Churchill was here to see about the war. Few in Washington knew that a decision was firm to crush Hitler first and to hold Japan at bay until a combined might could be turned upon her. For the moment, Churchill, with Christmas in his heart but the weight of war upon his mind, was somewhere in the White House. It was impossible to know that from the talks would emerge a Joint Chiefs of Staff to guide the allied war effort.

Against the backdrop of war in his own land, the Englishman would later learn that on that Christmas Day the British forces in Hong Kong had climaxed a seven-day engagement with surrender.

Five thousand people stood in the damp when Churchill went to the Congress to deliver a fiercely eloquent address on December 26, "greatly honored that you should have invited me to enter the United States Senate Chamber and address the representatives of both branches of Congress." He was thunderously received, but the pixy side of his nature emerged whenever he was posed what Roosevelt would have called an "iffy" question.

"By the way," Churchill told the Congress, "I cannot help reflecting that if my father had been an American and my mother British, instead of the other way round, I might have got here on my own."

Churchill had assessed the public mood of Washington as accurately as any storekeeper on a corner. He was "impressed and encouraged by the breadth of view and sense of proportion which I have found in all quarters over here to which I have had access. Anyone who did not understand the size and solidarity of the foundations of the United States might easily have expected to find an excited, disturbed, self-centered atmosphere, with all minds fixed upon the novel, startling, and painful episodes of sudden war as they hit America. After all, the United States have been attacked and set upon by three most powerfully-armed dictator States. The greatest military power in Europe, the greatest military power in Asia—Germany and Japan, Italy, too—have all declared, and are making, war upon you, and a quarrel is opened, which can only end in their overthrow or yours. But here in Washington, in these memorable days, I have found an Olympian fortitude which, far from being based upon complacency, is only the mask of an inflexible purpose and the proof of a sure and well-grounded confidence in the final outcome. We in Britain had the same feeling in our darkest days. We, too, were sure in the end all would be well."

The Prime Minister ventured an explanation of what had so puzzled the people of Washington and everywhere else on Pearl Harbor Day: How did the Japanese find the audacity to strike the powerful United States? Churchill told the Congress:

Many people have been astonished that Japan should in a single day have plunged into war against the United States and the British Empire. We all wonder why, if this dark design, with all its laborious and intricate preparations, had been so long filling their secret minds, they did not choose our moment of weakness eighteen months ago. Viewed quite dispassionately, in spite of the losses we have suffered and the further punishment we shall have to take, it certainly appears to be an irrational act. It is, of course, only prudent to assume that they have made very careful calculations and think they see their way through. Nevertheless, there may be another explanation. We know that for many years past the policy of Japan has been dominated by secret societies of subalterns and junior offices of the Army and Navy, who have enforced their will upon successive Japanese Cabinets and Parliaments by the assassination of any Japanese statesman who opposed, or who did not sufficiently further, their aggressive policy. It may be that these societies, dazzled and dizzy with their own schemes of aggression and the prospect of early victories, have forced their country against its better judgment into war. They have certainly embarked upon a very considerable undertaking. For after the outrages they have committed upon us at Pearl Harbor, in the Pacific islands, in the Philippines, in Malaya, and in the Dutch East Indies, they must now know that the stakes for which they have decided to play are mortal.

The address concluded with a Churchillian burst of prose, envisioning an England and a United States walking "together side by side in majesty, in justice, and in peace."

The Congress roared approval. And soon Churchill made off for Ottawa, but quickly to return to Washington.

Entertaining Winston Churchill anywhere, with his disdain for sleep, was a questionable delight. In his role in Washington as the King's First Minister, he was not only entitled to White House accommodations but enjoyed every personal demonstration of warmth which the President could show, simply because he was as fond of the Englishman as Churchill was of him. So he was given the best, including a large bedroom off a usually quiet hall. The room lay across from one where Harry Hopkins dwelt—and this was a tactical blunder, not in the amenities of protocol but in the matter of preserving the peace. Hopkins also could go a long stretch without sleep, and he and Churchill became great chums.

Churchill liked to prowl around during the night to muse upon historical pieces of furniture and gaze at pictures on the walls, faces with eyes looking out from America's past. The historian in his soul appeared to move him ever backward while the compelling conference, carrying the code name ARCADIA, yanked him into the present and even hurled him into the future.

Roosevelt, on the other hand, liked to be in bed early. So Hopkins and Churchill would roam about, talking and shuffling along. With the White House aides who were compelled to be always on call, it was quite a bustling assemblage. To compound the nocturnal disturbance, someone had placed Christmas packages in the hallway, and Hopkins or the Prime Minister would frequently stumble upon them. When the two sat down to talk in the night, Roosevelt's uncontrollable curiosity would send him forth, breaking his sleep. Moreover, as this was Christmastime, the best of drinks flowed abundantly, making for Churchill a finest hour anywhere on the clock.

But there was no truth to the story heard thousands of times in Washington that Roosevelt once had entered Churchill's room to find the Prime Minister naked, drawing from the Prime Minister the quip, "The Prime Minister of Great Britain has nothing to conceal from the President of the United States." (This anecdote purportedly was originated by Hopkins.) Churchill branded the tale as "nonsense." He claimed that he certainly would have placed a bath towel around himself in such circumstances.

Churchill found the White House almost childless—saddening because even the Executive Mansion is a home. Six-year-old Diana Hopkins was the only child there. (No evidence exists, but conceivably it caused Churchill to speak so movingly about children that Christmas Eve.)

One of the things that Churchill wanted to do on his trip was to look deeply into America, and he set about it on January 1, 1942. The first inkling anyone outside of the White House had of his intentions was the arrival of Secret Servicemen at Christ Church in Alexandria. They talked with the Reverend Edward R. Welles, D.D., the rector and a biblical scholar, and then poked about through every part of the church. They were purposeful and shadowlike figures, moving among the purple and crimson glows of the stained windows and then quickly gone. The Secret Service, which guards the President's life, is obsessed with its mission. The shadows of antiquity within the brick of the church could not have meant anything to them, nor the date—1767—when the church was established. It was of no consequence that the Squire of Mount Vernon, George Washington, the wealthiest man in all those parts who lived a piece down the river, had worshiped there quite humble before a God larger than his own aspirations. And it was unimportant that Robert E. Lee, for whom God towered higher than even the Commonwealth of Virginia, had been perhaps the most humble and modest man among all the fashionable congregation.

The men who poked about would very soon know more of every nook and corner of the building than Washington, Lee, and Welles combined. They wanted no one in the church on The Day other than a hand-picked and certified 250 parishioners. The notification of these came according to a strange arrangement. Eight carefully selected young men of the parish were assembled at daybreak of January 1, and handed the Secret Service approved list. The eight fanned out as day broke across the sleeping city to raise the polished door knockers, and invite the astounded householders, rubbing sleep from their eyes, to attend special services at Christ Church at 11 A.M. (One person now says that he knew all about it the night before. He had heard at a party that the Secret Service had examined the church and knew that it could mean only one thing.) The parishioners were cautioned to hold their tongues. It was all very strange for a Thursday—but of course anything could happen with all those so-called defense workers or war workers or whatever they were who had descended upon a peaceful town that only wanted to be let alone.

Churchill, the President, Mrs. Roosevelt, Lord and Lady Halifax, and ox-bodied and amiable Major General Edwin "Pa" Watson, Roosevelt's military aide and buddy, arrived, the President entering the church on the arm of Watson. A light rain was falling, darkening the leafless January trees, but the melancholy gray of the morning was stained by the crimsons and purples of the lighted windows. People stood along wide Washington Street, the Old City's main street, staring. The drizzle dripped from the gravestones standing low on the grass between the street and the church.

Inside, the White House party was ushered to the hard-bottomed, square, box-like, and gate-enclosed pew which George Washington had once occupied, in the front of the church. For those outside there was silence, but soon soft music came through the windows. The people inside were singing "God of Our Fathers," and lost among the voices was the voice of Churchill.

And then, louder, came "The Battle Hymn of the Republic":

> Mine eyes have seen the glory of the coming of the Lord,
> He is trampling out the vintage where the grapes of wrath are stored;
> He hath loosed the fateful lightning of His terrible swift sword,
> His truth is marching on.

The Reverend Dr. Welles delivered himself of a militant sermon, leaving no doubt that the United States was in the war to stay. Churchill left the services with his features clamped. Everywhere he might have had a chance to look was a corner of a now-foreign field that once conspicuously was England. Down gently sloping hills lay the Old Town brooding above the Potomac, where bullheaded General Braddock had begun his ill-starred march to Fort Duquesne at present-day Pittsburgh—a trek that should have started at Philadelphia. Along Prince Street's time-polished cobblestones, placed by Britain's Hessian

troops, England murmured across the centuries. The flat
flounder houses and other enduring structures stood near the
river, reminders of the British and Scottish ship captains of the
eighteenth century.

The rain fell more heavily. The White House automobiles
reached the Mount Vernon Memorial Highway, built in 1932 to
link Washington's home to Alexandria and to commemorate the
bicentennial of the first President's birth. The highway wound
with the river's winding, and sometimes the river was lost to
view behind screens of trees. There were plots where flowers
must look lovely in summer. As Churchill passed by, it was too
early for the April extravaganzas of yellow forsythia, crabapple,
pear, hawthorn, and serviceberry. The Algonquin Indians had
lived along here, before the English came.

When the automobiles passed through the gate at Mount
Vernon within clear view of the mansion and the tilled fields
where crops are grown as in Washington's time, they slowed in
movement downhill toward the Washington Tomb. Washington
had wanted to be placed in death overlooking the river.
Churchill looked hard at the brick (he reputedly had a fancy for
old brick). The steel-barred gate of the Tomb had been opened.
Churchill stood for a moment beside the President, who was
protected from the rain by an umbrella. Then Churchill entered
the Tomb and placed a wreath of red-brown chrysanthemums
and blue iris, tied with a ribbon of red, white, and blue, against
the sarcophagus.

He walked out into the rain with his shoulders hunched, and
again his features were clamped. Newsmen pressed about him
(and one would remember that then, if ever, was a moment for
a great thought to burst forth with a lasting echo).

Churchill turned to Mrs. Roosevelt, while pencils poised
above note pads.

"A very wet day, isn't it?" he said.

"Yes it is, isn't it?" she replied.

At the mansion, the President and Churchill signed the
guestbook (the disfigurement of the rain drops still show on the
page). Charles C. Wall, the resident director, waved a farewell.

(Insofar as is known, these were the first signatures of Roosevelt and Churchill in the year 1942. Their names would be signed so many other times spelling out life or death for thousands.)

After Churchill had returned to England, Harry Hopkins wrote Mrs. Churchill: "You would have been quite proud of your husband on this trip. First, because he was ever so good natured. I didn't see him take anybody's head off, and he eats and drinks with his customary vigor, and still dislikes the same people. If he had half as good a time here as the President did having him about the White House, he surely will carry pleasant memories of the past three weeks."

One of the memories that Churchill carried with him was of the pictures he had gazed at on the walls. He cabled the President: "I was terribly sorry to have to leave you, and, what is more than those can say whose pictures are on the walls, there is not a moment of it that I did not enjoy."

CHAPTER FIVE

MUCH ADO ABOUT SOMETHING

JUST WHAT ALL the fighting and uproar were about became many things to many men, as indefinable as Truth, whose meaning has tantalized the ages. But there was really no great puzzle. The United States, embroiled in a world revolution bent upon its destruction, desired, in simplest terms, to keep its way of life, the way of life clearly expressed in the Constitution and by Thomas Jefferson in the Declaration of Independence.

Copies of the documents might be bought at any bookstore, but the invaluable originals were enshrined in the Library of Congress, testifying not only to the soul of the nation but to the seeming physical immortality of the documents as well. Each had taken wearing journeys at times under stress from the British. In December 1776, the Declaration was transported in a light wagon from Philadelphia to Baltimore, remained there for some two months, and was then hauled back to Philadelphia. A short while later it lay in the York, Pennsylvania, courthouse; still later it was taken to Annapolis; and subsequently to Trenton, New Jersey; and in 1785 found its way to the second story of New York's City Hall. The national government brought it back to Philadelphia in late 1790, and sheltered it first in a structure on Market Street, and later in one at 5th and Chestnut streets.

When the Federal City was established in a swampy mosquito and muskrat haven cheerfully released by Maryland and Virginia in 1800, the words that flamed like summer suns above the heights of Monticello came into custody of the new Department of State at what would become Washington, D.C. Thereupon, the documents bounced through three different locations—and the British became troublesome again. During the summer, Secretary of State James Monroe ordered evacuation, and the documents were jammed into a linen bag and kept overnight in a barn west of Chain Bridge not far up the Potomac from Washington. For the following few weeks, their resting place was in the home of a Reverend Mr. Littlejohn at Leesburg, Virginia. When the British menace concluded, Washington became their home again.

The Department of State during the Administration of President Harding feared the threat of fire to the great documents, and urged safekeeping in the Library of Congress. Harding, who himself was difficult to cool down on occasions, agreed.

The Washingtonians of World War II had little knowledge of the painstaking care given the enshrinement of the documents while they came, looked, grew awe-struck, and filed away something else to write home about—something indescribable, soul-wrenching.

The shrine had been dedicated on February 28, 1924, with President and Mrs. Coolidge, Secretary of State Hughes, and a scattering of Congressmen in the forefront. The occasion would remain clear in the memory of Dr. David C. Mearns, the assistant librarian: "Not a word was spoken. Mr. Putnam [Herbert Putnam, L.L.D., Librarian of Congress] stood upon the 'desk' and fitted the Declaration to its frame, then arranged the leaves of the Constitution, closed the lid, turned the locks, and the staff of the Library, assembled in the adjoining hall, sang two stanzas of 'America.' That was all. Yet the ceremony was as moving as it was outwardly austere; it seemed to Mr. Putnam that 'the impression upon the audience proved the emotional potency of documents animate with a great tradition.' "

The Library of Congress is a gigantic hulk of ornate architecture situated behind the Capitol and adorned with a symbolic torch. Its interior is slashed by corridors streaming off from one another to collide with others as though attempting to make the seekers of knowledge cry, To hell with it all. Along the byways are rare old prints and other memorabilia of such interest as to make the lost researcher pause and after a while forget momentarily his original purpose. Offices of various functionaries, sufficiently adorned with academic plumage to acquire their public trusts, line the hallways. Unlike those of officeholders in most other federal buildings, the librarians' eyes reveal interest, and something deeper than interest— concern; for they control the vastest pile of knowledge on earth, and it constantly pulsates in marvels of breadth continually extending.

In April 1941, Archibald MacLeish, ninth librarian since the Library of Congress's founding in 1802, a poet absorbed with flowers and earth and sky, with seashores and gulls and another morning, sat disturbed in his quiet-toned office. Hitler was trampling the civilizations of Europe and, as the Library would later report officially, "the progress of the Second World War suggested that the United States might become involved."

MacLeish worried about the precious documents in his charge and inquired of the Secretary of the Treasury "whether space might perhaps be found at [the Bullion Depository] Fort Knox for these materials, in the unlikely event that it becomes necessary to remove them from Washington." Secretary of the Treasury Morgenthau was agreeable.

The wheels began turning; more than sixty cubic feet were allocated. Sixteen days after Pearl Harbor, MacLeish and a hand-picked few watched the Declaration and the Constitution lifted from the shrine and set between two sheets of acid-free manila paper. The tedious procedure was described by Dr. Mearns: "The documents were then wrapped in a container stiffened at top and bottom with all-rag, neutral millboard and secured by Scotch tape, and inserted in a specially-designed bronze container, which had been scrupulously cleaned of (except for Scotch tape) other possible harmful elements, and heated for some six hours to a temperature of about 90°F to drive off any moisture. Empty space was then filled with sheets of all-rag, neutral millboard, and the top of the container was screwed tight over a cork gasket and locked with padlocks on each side. It was late in the evening when work was suspended."

Before the month ended, the bronze container was transferred to the carpenter shop in the building's depths and tightened with wire and a lead seal bearing block initials L.C. It was placed in rock wool in a metal-bound box 40 by 36 inches. The weight was about 150 pounds.

No one on the outside knew that this exercise in scientific packaging was underway. For once, the British weren't responsible for a round of traveling by the documents.

Congress would receive the details of the shipment later, but it is doubtful if many members minded them under the crush of war. At any rate, at 5 P.M., December 26, the documents and sundry other rare items were placed in a truck belonging to the Bureau of Engraving and Printing—a vehicle fiercely armed. Aboard it and riding alongside were guards with automatic weapons. The convoy pointed toward Union Station, separated from the Library by expanses of greenery and rows of trees. The train awaited the treasure. It was lifted into Compartment B, Car A-1. This was the Pullman sleeper Eastlake, National Limited of the Baltimore & Ohio Railroad. Secret Service agents took compartments on either side, and others roamed the corridor. When the last traces of the day limned the torch on the Library's dome and the train pulled away, the watch in the conductor's vest pocket showed 6:30 P.M.

In Louisville, Kentucky, early the next morning, four Secret Service agents and a troop of the 13th Armored Division waited for the car. At 10:30 A.M., the train groaned in. Verner W. Clapp, chief assistant librarian, oversaw the unloading. The documents were lifted into an army truck, a scout car swung ahead and was followed by another occupied by the agents. At the Bullion Depository, the materials were checked in by the chief clerk and placed in Compartment No. 24—an outer tier on the ground level. The vault closed. Everything is exact at Fort Knox: the hour was recorded as 12:07 P.M.

Move the governments from, say, Paris or London and a

self-sustaining economy would flow along. But the U.S. capital was (and remains) strictly what it was intended to be—the seat of government—and without it the city would disintegrate. Most of the inhabitants during World War II were government-minded because the federal payrolls directly or indirectly affected the livelihoods of a preponderance of the population. This was abnormal for an American city of considerable size. And across the decades, a self-consciousness developed, amounting to an inferiority complex where cultural concerns were involved. The arts, especially, were associated with Philadelphia, New York, and Boston, but many Washingtonians aspired to compete. By the late 1930's, the capital could show off some three notable art galleries. Among these was the Corcoran Gallery of Art, near the White House, filled with collections from Washington philanthropist and banker William Wilson Corcoran, and others from William Andrews Clark, a metal tycoon and United States Senator from Montana. A particular warmth and hospitality was always radiated at the Phillips Memorial Gallery at 1600 21st Street, N.W., an easy walk from downtown Washington. The Gallery was installed in the former home of the distinguished Washington family, which lent its name. Duncan Phillips incorporated the Gallery in 1918 to commemorate the lives of his father, mother, and brother, and the purpose was educational. One of the capital's most authoritative works says the "collection of modern art is one of the best in America." There was a symphony orchestra under the fiery and determined Dr. Hans Kindler. There were also four good universities—Georgetown, George Washington, Catholic, and American. These were strengthened by an influx of outside professors, some of whom moonlighted as government consultants.

But culture had been reached for more than randomly for nearly a century. And a touch of it had come in the mid-nineteenth century because of a bit of adultery in faraway England. A son was born to the Duke of Northumberland, a skilled philanderer. But James Smithson, who would elevate Washington's cultural sights, was born out of wedlock—a background he would later strongly object to. This precluded his wearing a noble title, though he was pampered and favored by a fortune. At twenty-one, Smithson was welcomed into the Royal Society of London and later became distinguished for researches in mineralogy. But the inner man remained frustrated, and he had no intention of bottling up his dissatisfaction.

"The best blood of England flows in my veins; on my father's side I am a Northumberland; on my mother's side I am related to kings, but this avails me naught," he once wrote. Then he reared up: "My name shall live in the memory of men, when the titles of the Northumberlands and the Percys are extinct and forgotten." James Smithson died in Genoa in 1829. In 1835 President Jackson informed Congress of a legacy from an Englishman, who, it was determined, had never even been to the United States. The funds would found an institution of science and related interests there. A few Congressmen exclaimed that such a gift would demean the nation. Senator Preston of South Carolina drawled loudly that if the donation were accepted, "every whippersnapper vagabond that had been traducing our country might think proper to have his name distinguished in the same way." But a more sensible view taken by John Quincy Adams prevailed.

The legacy in gold sovereigns was brought by ship to New York, to land in the center of a controversy: What did Smithson mean by saying that his bequest should be used "for the increase and diffusion of knowledge among men"? The fuss resolved itself into the creation of the Smithsonian Institution in 1846, grounded upon the $550,000 bequest, and Washington soon began nurturing an infant of culture. The Smithsonian, the word went around, was presenting paintings of Indians and wildlife, and mineral exhibits, and lectures on erudite subjects.

When the defense workers arrived they found not only the matured Smithsonian but one of the world's greatest art galleries in the making on Constitution Avenue, thanks to Andrew Mellon of Pittsburgh, financier and Secretary of the Treasury under Harding, Coolidge, and Hoover. Conscious that Washington lacked such art treasures as European capitals enjoyed, Mellon had proposed a gallery, contributing $15 million for the construction of the building as well as his priceless art collection.

On March 17, 1941, President Roosevelt formally opened the National Gallery of Art, which had been under construction since June 1937. As he stood before a nest of microphones, the lights shone on the President's face, and his eyes at the moment of a photographer's flash were raised toward the ceiling as if in reflection. Abreast of him sat Mrs. Roosevelt with her neck encircled by pearls; her hair was drawn tightly back. Vice President Wallace sat with a look of puzzlement in his eyes. Also present were Chief Justice Charles Evans Hughes, gray and austere; Paul Mellon, son of Andrew Mellon, and Samuel H. Kress, the donor of additional fabulous collections.

"The giver of this building," the familiar voice told the audience, "has matched the richness of his gift with the modesty of his spirit, stipulating that the gallery shall be known not by his name but by the nation's."

Andrew Mellon had been shrewd about the name for his structure; had it been called by his name—The Mellon Art Gallery—other possessors of great art might have become discouraged in making gifts. By giving it the name of the National Gallery of Art, the government now could say in truth, "Your contribution goes to the nation."

The fear of air attack in 1942, or more realistically the fear of sabotage to hurt morale, caused David E. Finley, gallery director, to take more than an esthetic look at the masterpieces in his stewardship. Among these were works by Van Dyck, Frans Hals, and Rembrandt, Raphael's "St. George and the Dragon" and the "Alba Madonna", the Botticelli "Adoration of the Magi", Perugino's "Crucifixion With Saints", Titian's "Venus With a Mirror", Veronese's "Finding of Moses", the Van Eyck "Annunciation", and the Velázquez "Study for Innocent."

The gallery security guards, uniformed and armed and attuned to alarm bells, eyed every square inch of the building with lectured understanding of the treasures they watched; but security was not tight enough for the director or his assistant,

John Walker (Harvard '30), a knowledgeable man among the masters, who never forgot that the Gallery belonged to everybody.

Finley and Walker, like MacLeish, decided that the treasures in their charge should be removed from Washington. From within the entire breadth of America, they selected Biltmore, a mansion built by George Vanderbilt near mountainous Asheville, North Carolina. In his own selection of a place to build a fabulous mansion, Vanderbilt undoubtedly had taken into account the high cool climate for summers, and the grandeur of the view. He had wanted a broad view, and, indeed, had removed wide areas of terrain to widen the vistas. His great gray mansion would become nearly as famous as the modest Asheville dwelling of Thomas Wolfe.

The art gallery authorities' main concern was for the safety of the masterpieces. Biltmore was remote, well-guarded, and the climate was favorable to the preservation of painted works. The pictures were quietly packed at the gallery in January, 1942, and transported by train to Asheville. Upon arrival at Asheville, the paintings were removed from the train at an obscure railroad siding and put inside heavy trucks.

Along the way to the estate was a steep and slippery hill. Suddenly one of the trucks lost its hold on the slippery road and started to tilt. Finley and Walker jumped from their trucks with outstretched arms and grabbed the side of the tilting vehicle. Later, Walker would say, "I wonder how we thought we could keep that truck from falling?" The treasures were placed in one of the wings of the house and the area was blocked off and guarded.

The removal of its historical documents and its art treasures did not significantly alter the lives of the people of Washington. Yet, strangely enough, these objects may have acquired even more meaning and value in their going than they had enjoyed while they were there. Their absence may have made people a little more aware that they were indeed involved in a war—and may even have suggested to them what, in part, they were working and fighting for.

CHAPTER SIX

A MONSTROUS WAR SEAT IS DECREED

WHEN ANYONE STOOD at 14th and F Streets, N.W., in January, 1942, an intersection famed for the Willard Hotel, the National Press Club, and Garfinckel's, whose labels ladies wished they might wear outwardly on hats and dresses, the southwesterly view was blocked by the Department of Commerce Building and the Washington Monument reaching high from its low green knoll. Beyond such physical obstacles prior to August 11, 1941, stretched an area variously called a wasteland, a swamp, or a dump. But a building was rising now from an idea that the armed services should have a common roof rather than be scattered across the square-foot-conscious capital.

It was generally believed that the War Department had sprung the idea and that some officials approved; but in other quarters it was called a piece of folly. The dissenters gasped, saying it would be the world's hugest office building, twice as big as the Merchandise Mart in Chicago, and with three times more space than New York's Empire State Building. In the common parlance, it was a monstrosity, the goddamnest thing ever seen. There would be five wedge-shaped sections, and the United States Capitol could slide into any one. Moreover, the unforgotten taxpayers, already financing a two-front war, would now have to claw out some $75 million to pay for a five-sided building.

People stopped to watch and ponder the operation. The

government, as time passed, poured five and a half million cubic yards of earth and noisily drove 41,492 concrete piles. Here was a statistician's heyday. Upon the mount, 680,000 tons of gravel and sand sucked from the Potomac River were processed into 435,000 cubic yards of concrete and molded into a pentagonal form. Few realized the speed behind the construction, the relentless pressure the government could apply when, as so infrequently, it chose to move.

The driver was Secretary of War Henry Stimson, who could also adore such drowsy quietudes as his great house, Woodley Oaks, at 3000 Cathedral Avenue, N.W., where the lawns invited leisure and the neighboring Cathedral of St. Peter and St. Paul invested the nice neighborhood with a cathedral's awesome timelessness.

Indeed, the prime contract was awarded August 11, 1941, the grading contract, September 24, 1941; construction began August 11, 1941, and the first occupants, three hundred employees from the Ordnance Department, stepped in wide-eyed on April 29, 1942. Then the reaction flared, the jokes began.

A virgin war worker, it was related, had entered the building, became lost in the maze of 17½ miles of corridors, 280 rest rooms, and 150 stairways, during the ordeal was seduced, and emerged, with child, nine months later for delivery. It was true that during the Pentagon's early period four babies were born in the building's medical centers, and another entered the world in a washroom.

There were two medical centers. One was operated by the Public Health Service, the other by the army. The former had a health education section, headed by Miss Bessie Boggess, formerly of Macon, Mississippi, functioning to make Pentagonians eat properly balanced meals. One day, Miss Boggess noticed a stenographer, a native of Minnesota, who seemed to be suffering from pellagra, a severe dietary disorder. The girl had been eating on forty cents a day. She ate no breakfast, consistently had coffee and doughnuts for lunch, and supper on whatever nickels were left. The girl had been sending nearly everything to a destitute family back home. In cases of such seriousness the government always moves.

Most of the hardships were not so dramatic. It was said that Pentagonians would demand portal-to-portal pay, because a half-mile or more lay between their parking places or bus stops and their desks. They complained of the building's location, calling it Hellangone; and old-line Arlington families saw another disfigurement of their hallowed ground. But, also desirous of winning the war, they indulged the intrusion, though not without a squint at the as yet unexploited expanses to be grabbed for sale before those Yankees and carpetbaggers could beat them to the federal moneybag.

There were other minor problems, most of which the higher authorities ignored, probably believing that someone down below oversaw such matters or that right, like might, would triumph in the end. Someone did become concerned over the condition of men going by mistake into ladies' washrooms and ladies going into the men's. There was a reason: the door signs, *Men*, or *Women*, would catch the glare of light off the tilings, creating the confusion. But the problem was ingeniously corrected. Soon the Pentagon signs read:

WOMEN
O
M
E
N

As the months of 1942 passed, important parts of the Pentagon were still in the building stage.

Secretary Stimson looked at his calendar in his entirely unsatisfactory quarters in the Munitions Building and centered on November 14. He would move the following week into the Pentagon. And certainly while no such thought had room in his generous mind, his accommodations would overshadow those of Secretary Ickes to such an extent that the Old Curmudgeon—a nickname alternating with Honest Harold—could believe himself enduring the privations of the Forgotten Man over whom he had fumed and labored in the good old days of the New Deal.

The luxurious furnishings and pastel tintings—with special interior decorating touches to the toilet—glorifying the Ickes spread had brought public outcries from a press which recalled that Ickes had built the South Interior Department Building with Public Works Administration funds. There was no dishonesty whatever involved: Ickes merely desired a public servant's due and considered that he had earned it. Certainly he had earned both nicknames; he reputedly knew the whereabouts of every box of paperclips in the Interior Department. And he had once secreted himself in the cafeteria around 10 A.M. to pounce forth with a Comanche yell at a swarm of employees malingering over coffee. He had grown tired as hell of that wasteful business of writing one-paragraph memos on long sheets of paper, and substituted short sheets. He was an arch-foe of fifth wheels and mumbo-jumbo in all their forms. Once his public relations men (dear to his heart) formally complained that the Department's attorneys were re-jiggering press releases into gobbledygook unintelligible to already harassed newspaper rewrite men. Once more the old man pounced, and the attorneys leaped through loopholes to correct the situation. Ickes was coldly capable, but he was also a human being, a fact he tried desperately to disguise.

He wouldn't have given a damn, if anyone had asked him, what kind of layout awaited his fellow Cabinet member Stimson. But little things seemed continually to bite his hurrying heels. One day, Walton Onslow, a Minnesotan of giant frame who had joined Ickes' writing stable by way of the Washington press corps, was minding his business on the seventh floor of the Interior Department. (The exact date is obscure, but it was during the early part of the war.)

Onslow remembers:

> There were considerable jitters in Washington, and especially in the government, that somehow, some way, the Germans would launch an air attack on us. How in the world that might have been accomplished I can't imagine,

unless the War Department figured the Nazis might get a submarine offshore and dispatch a small plane against the city. Anyway, guns were mounted on numerous government buildings, guns of the heavy machine-gun type. You could see them from the streets, with the little groups of soldiers standing by. We all knew a gun was atop our building, and my office was just under the roof. Some of the gun crew shifts came by elevator to the seventh floor and took the stairwell to the roof. This day, I heard a chuff, chuff, chuff from overhead, and I said to myself, "My God, they're firing that gun." It occurred to me that just maybe they were testing the thing with blanks. But the next thing we heard was that a frightened guard at the Lincoln Memorial had yelled into a telephone, "They're bombing the Memorial."

The guard was right, except that he had the wrong "they" and the bombs were bullets. The gun had gone off accidentally, and the bullets slapped the top section of the Memorial, with its interior reminder that "The world will little note nor long remember what we say here but it can never forget what they did here." Everything possible was done to keep the world from noting what had just been done. At the Pentagon, investigators sprang from arm chairs, and Ickes—who also as head man of the Park Service was responsible for the Memorial and the roof of his own building—howled. Who would pay for the damage? It was easier to bargain in the marketplaces of Casablanca than with Honest Harold, and, if reports were true, the army paid.

Stimson, an attorney by profession and now aging, had retained the sharp edge of his mind in a body worn hard by years. Like any lawyer, he preferred ten words to one, but began eventually to whittle away his verbiage through close contact with Marshall. Stimson was a late worker. When night came and the automobile lights danced toward Virginia's spreading developments and the people moved toward home, an aide would summon him to an unexpected conference. When he finally left for Woodley, he would be carrying homework in his hands. So the nation gave him a private dining room, kitchenette, bath, and emergency living quarters, sparing him the strain of long drives to distant conference sites.

A *Washington Star* reporter, after sneaking a view of the layouts, commented: "Both Mr. Stimson and General Marshall are among the most overworked officials in war-minded Washington—and time-saving is an element of utmost importance to the furtherance of war plans." Thus, confreres would sit at the dining room tables late into the night. For mere official entertaining, Stimson and Marshall could use their quarters rather than seek accommodations at the Mayflower, Shoreham, Carlton, or Wardman Park hotels.

The dining room and kitchen across the corridor from the Secretary of War's offices might have been showplaces. The two army chefs delighted in the electric fixtures and gadgets. A main pride was the electric steam table trundled in when the Secretary was too busy at his desk in his gray-toned office to use the dining room. The room decorations were suitably subdued to formal or informal occupancy. The white china bore the mark of the War Department. White linen-spread tables could accommodate 24 persons.

The offices of the Secretary and Chief of Staff adjoined as they had in the Munitions Building where a sign said, "This door is always open." The soldier and the civilian were friends, despite their individual viewpoints. The two came and went by private elevator, and its use was open to friendly Secretary of the Navy Knox, former newspaper publisher, who delighted in picking up government girls in his car while en route to work. His office was directly overhead. Knox, indeed, was charmed to be in the Pentagon, and had referred to his colleague's "generous offer" of inviting him under the roof.

Stimson could locate every important main road and waterway of the world by stepping up to maps fixed upon 12'x8' panels on his office walls. These did not disturb the decor; attached to runways, each map could be shunted from sight into recesses in the wall.

General Marshall's quarters lacked the spaciousness of Stimson's appointments. But he enjoyed a wardrobe room, large closet space, a chest of drawers, and a shower—a refreshing necessity sometimes missed for days by the lowlier war workers crowded out of their boardinghouse bathrooms. Not distant lay the offices of Under Secretary Robert Patterson, notable for their massive period furniture and the contract-seekers eager to get in on the expanding millions.

A problem arose at the start over how to keep people away from the harried Stimson and Patterson and others of high rank. Suave and impressively credentialed gentlemen approached the batteries of receptionists in the Pentagon lobby, murmuring casually and confidently, "I want to see Bob Patterson or Hank Stimson." The receptionists were schooled. They politely rejected the request that the caller be permitted to go without escort or wearing an identification badge. The receptionists would quietly inform the caller that a supervisor must be consulted, and before the supervisor arrived the two offices had been notified and were prepared, if so minded, to put off the men. Few were bold enough to want to see George Marshall, unless he had known about it some time in advance. Prestige meant nothing to him; enlisted men at Fort Myer remembered that he had often spoken informally and cordially to them; and a reporter recalled seeing him standing alone one day, as though in deep thought, and approaching him and engaging pleasantly in small talk for a while. But while doing his job, which was making war, he had no loose words for anybody, and, above all, he wanted no self-aggrandizement.

Marshall Andrews, Washington military writer, combat veteran of World War I, and highly respected by the military establishment, saw early in General Marshall what Roosevelt had assessed—a great soldier, and a superior man. Andrews had written a newspaper series about the new army in training, now he wanted to do a biography of the Chief of Staff. He put the request through channels. A communication went from Colonel William T. Sexton, who was Secretary of the War Department General Staff, to General Marshall, as follows:

Marshall Andrews (who wrote the good articles on

Army camps) is working on a biography of you. General
Surles [Army Information chief] believes that he will do a
creditable job, but the question immediately comes up of
the release of certain material.

Unless you wish to go the whole distance in releasing
your personal correspondence, etc., an indicated basis
appears to be that he be given everything which has been
released to the public (speeches, testimony before
Congress, messages which have been made public, etc.) and
the people in your office give him every possible
cooperation in assembling this data.

I understand Andrews is traveling now interviewing
several of your old friends.

W . T . S .
Sexton.

It is impossible to know what General Marshall really
thought, but he replied with 19 words to the 109 required to
tell him of the author's intentions. He scribbled across the top
of the memorandum: "If it is possible to avoid this I want it
done. Can't he be persuaded to drop the matter? G.C.M."

This was, indeed, a strange reaction to arise from Washington,
traditionally a roost of publicity seekers. It was scarcely
motivated by preoccupation with the war, or the fear of a word
slipped unwittingly in wartime. It was the instantaneous
decision of an individual who resisted public attention. (It is
difficult now, looking back, to name another official of wartime
Washington who would have refused an honest biography.)

Marshall, more than any other one man, created the World
War II army from a citizenry which, generally, did not want
war—as the General himself did not. In this respect he was much
like General Grant, who had conducted another war nearly a
century before. Though soldiers to the core, each, paradoxically, had disliked war. Grant's entire motivation had been to
end the conflict with victory and then to settle down to peace.
It is difficult not to appraise Marshall in the same light. Each
differed from General Lee—if one assertion he made reveals
him. He had said, in essence, that it was good that war was
so terrible or else we would come to like it.

CHAPTER SEVEN

A WHOLE PACK OF NUISANCES EMERGES

IN THE WHOLE of the Washington war extravaganza there were two persons whom no one knew exactly what to make of, though, paradoxically, opinions about them were rigidly fixed. One was Henry A. Wallace, the mystical Vice President, and the other was Mrs. Franklin D. Roosevelt. Each was detestable— even dangerous—to many minds; and perhaps to an equal number of others, each was a godsend. Even the most vehement detractors could not deny that both practiced their preachments of warmth and the common touch—but concerning the touch, the detractors believed each was employing it on the taxpayers' pockets to further socialism in the United States.

Mrs. Roosevelt may have been explainable, but no one ever understood the ways of Wallace, no doubt including Wallace himself, who dabbled in the occult, searching for something unknown—perhaps Wallace. He did strange little things. One morning he attended one of those seemingly endless luncheons at the Mayflower Hotel, listened indifferently to the vaporous talks, and at the end slipped out through the crowd into the foyer leading to the lobby. En route, he brushed against a news photographer carrying a camera in one hand and in the other a heavy black box full of equipment. Wallace mumbled something sounding like a shy "Hello," took the carrying case and lifted it through the lobby until, reaching the sidewalk outside, he set it down with a smile. An official of his rank, according to the manual of Washington amenities, was not obliged to reach for a telephone directory, much less to lift it. The action suggested a man who, though having reached the heights, was unable to abandon the manners of the farm, where if one man carries two buckets of chicken feed an unencumbered person by his side takes hold of one.

He enjoyed one blessing. He was unnoticed in a crowd and at will could fade equally unnoticed from the scene.

By contrast, there was never a woman who became more instantly visible in a crowd than Mrs. Roosevelt—who had learned to dress since she had first come to the White House. If she had not been born pretty, she learned along the way to compensate for nature's omission by wearing lovely attire with style. She was also blessed with a figure for clothes. Tall, stately, self-assured and well-groomed, unlike the poor she led like a lioness, her manner (if one looked only casually) was of supreme haughtiness buttressed by a strong will. Perhaps she could only find the strength she needed from a posture of power. In any event, her facial expressions would change as though in actress-like obedience to a script, but she would have failed on a stage because she reacted from within herself.

Once, on a late afternoon, Mrs. Roosevelt walked with a half dozen women down a corridor from one of those meetings she fluttered among incessantly. The women, noticeably stirred by the privilege of having heard an inspirational message from the President's wife, cackled competitively for her attention. A lone male reporter approaching the swishing onrush decided to experiment, to determine if the great lady who had mastered the common touch would speak to him—an unknown. When fully abreast of the group, he looked hard at Mrs. Roosevelt and caught her eyes, saying "How do you do, Mrs. Roosevelt." She stopped ever so slightly, and her eyes showed an interest she had not entirely given to her entourage. She returned the greeting and appeared about to say something else, but the other women looked at him severely and the reporter bowed and walked on.

She was accused of many faults, not the least of which was an uncontrollable enthusiasm causing an over-extension of herself into thinly-thought-out "projects," as the term was used from the start of the New Deal days. Her most disastrous fiasco originated before Pearl Harbor, when her husband and Harry Hopkins mulled the establishment of something to be called an Office of Civilian Defense. This dedicated but all-too-often harum-scarum army of civilians, who watched the skies for hostile aircraft and prowled the streets in early wartime yelling at householders during practice blackouts, was headed by Mayor Fiorello LaGuardia of New York—the first and whopping choice of Roosevelt and Hopkins. Many persons were considered for the post, but in every consideration the fiery mayor seemed best. There was only one drawback: the mayor wanted this job like a hole in his staccato-like oratory because it conflicted with his combustible nature and martial background. Robert Sherwood remembered the mayor's distaste for the words "civilian" and "defense," each abrasive when LaGuardia remembered his World War I service as a bomber pilot. Like Lyndon Johnson and "Happy" Chandler, the mayor wanted a slice of the action. He bombarded the War Department for a chance at any kind of real service. But in that uncomputerized era, the department could figure LaGuardia's age by mere finger-counting and recognized the need for him elsewhere. So the mayor had come in, and so had Mrs. Roosevelt. (Even from the perspective of this late day, it is inconceivable how a government involved in a war on two oceans and several islands permitted Mrs. Roosevelt to plunge into the OCD with such a fantastic title as leader of the Community and Volunteer Participation Service of the Physical Fitness Division, and all this while the head man in New York was depressed about the whole thing.)

But nothing could perturb Mrs. Roosevelt; beneath her finery lay a skin as thick as that protecting the rhinoceros in Washington's famed zoo. And if neither her husband nor anyone else could ever control her, she certainly shared one characteristic with the President, and that was a tendency to reach for old friends. The leader of CVPSPFD envisioned precisely how Mayris Chaney could adjust to an annual salary of $4,600 for directing a physical fitness program for youngsters.

At the time, Miss Chaney was half of the San Francisco ballroom dance attraction of Chaney and Fox. A frequent visitor to the White House during the New Deal era, Miss Chaney had warmed to the First Lady, and in appreciation of her kindness had contrived a dance titled "The Eleanor Glide." And, upon being invited to join the war service, Miss Chaney glided with considerable fanfare into the capital.

Congressmen well aware of the death-dance in the Pacific Theater became enraged. They turned their attention temporarily away from the topic of war to denounce the introduction into national affairs of a "strip teaser." The expression "fan dancer" brightened an otherwise grim front page—not quite accurately, as it happened—for Miss Chaney, however unnecessary her new role may have been, danced quite properly.

Mrs. Roosevelt could never let bad enough alone. In the midst of this uproar, she brought in good-looking Hollywood actor, Melvyn Douglas, as head man of the Arts Council; whereupon nothing but the sheer weight of metal kept the headdress of the Capitol's goddess from whirling away in the winds of denunciation. Douglas replied with schooled elocution that he was a dollar-a-year man. (There seldom was any such remuneration, in reality; many of those so dubbed were being paid from where they had come from.) But the protest did not subside. Douglas, it was claimed, was too far left of center. (Of course, the Russians were off-center also, but this was no time to quarrel with them.)

To the press—which sometimes reflects the public attitude—it was incredible that 62 (or, for that matter, one) coordinators for physical fitness were needed. These factotums were coordinating horseshoe pitching, ping-pong, and all manner of swing-your-partner folk dances. While advocating prayer three hours a week, Mrs. Roosevelt frequently pranced into the Dupont Circle Building, which had been commandeered by the government to become the seat of the programs, and bullhooked the OCD typists and the aspiring young men into folk dances during the coffee breaks. The opportunities for acquaintance and the ultimate results afforded by these occasions often became so exhausting they canceled out the benefits of the physical fitness program.

In time, the outcries drowned out the fiddles and the clinking of the horseshoes, and no amount of physical fitness nor the soothing touch of the arts can sustain the soul under such stress. Congress reviewed the situation and snapped off funds for "instructions in physical fitness by dancers, fan dancing, street shows, theatrical performances or other public entertainment." Mrs. Roosevelt, Miss Chaney, and Mr. Douglas retired, the latter two growling. But Mrs. Roosevelt's valedictory should, for its command of understatement, be included among the great expressions of the resigned spirit: "The whole episode was unfortunate," she said. LaGuardia finally succeeded in bowing out, and James M. Landis, former dean of the Harvard Law School and a scholar who could phrase the simplest thought in terms beyond human understanding, bowed confidently in. If his articulations were burdened with fandangles, he at least dispensed with them in an OCD, which he associated with war. He leaned more toward sand buckets and aggressive block wardens.

Perhaps there was an auxiliary reason for the hostility of the press to Mrs. Roosevelt's misguided appointments. Over the years the First Lady's press conferences had become exclusively limited to women reporters, who had been awarded the name of Mrs. Roosevelt's Press Conference Association. The women, of course, were passed for security by the Secret Service. Mrs. Roosevelt had, purportedly, two reasons for keeping her conferences exclusively feminine—to expatiate upon subjects of peculiar interest to women, and, by locking the conferences against men, to force the news media to hire women to get the tidings from her conferences. The scheme worked in a number of instances, notably in the case of Ruby Black, a skilled newspaperwoman, who was grabbed by the United Press.

The conferences were held generally in the Monroe Room on the second floor of the White House, with Mrs. Roosevelt seated and her social secretary, Edith Helm, at her side. If there were visiting royalty or other notables in town, Mrs. Roosevelt faithfully saw that they attended to expound on the feminine problems in the world.

The Association members at the start took the name of the "incense burners" because a shortage of chairs caused a few to sit on the floor gazing at the First Lady ritualistically. But chairs later were provided for the thirty or forty women in attendance. Mrs. Roosevelt believed that the conferences "dealt with questions of interest to women, from a woman's point of view," and that meant that men were not welcome. With the exception of Gordon Cole, Washington correspondent for New York's *PM* newspaper, who made formal application for admission to the First Lady's press conferences and was refused, no man ever contested the decision.

CHAPTER EIGHT

WASHINGTON AT PLAY

WASHINGTON HAD A RIGIDLY stratified society, and it persisted throughout the war. It differed from the society, say, of Boston, New York, Louisville, Richmond, Charleston, or New York, because the capital had Congress and the diplomatic set to adjust within its framework. There were the cave-dwellers of Georgetown, mostly elderly ladies and gentlemen conscious of breeding traceable from the days of Scottish merchant princes in the port of Georgetown when Washington was a swamp. There was the diplomatic corps, who would scratch a name from party lists upon the slightest hint of its lowering in prestige. There were the rich and the newly-rich in conflict with each other, the former claiming that the latter couldn't understand that it requires four generations to create a gentleman. And there was the Congressional society set with fairly good entrees. Of the entire crowd, the Negroes within their own society were the most class-conscious. Status among them relied largely upon their professions. Inventors of the phrase "poor white trash," they could look at a white man and tell whether he was something, and, indeed, they were experts in human behavior. They knew good manners instinctively, and practiced them. Their society was iron-ribbed, hard to crack. The old-line Negro families of Georgetown secretly resented the wartime influx of people lacking status credentials for the environment.

The restrictions of war and the involvement of people in the war effort had at least a quieting effect upon society. But parties continued, muted to prevent public and official criticism. As far back as August 1941, the social world had held expectations of brightness. Choice targets among the social-climber categories were the dollar-a-year men, obviously with status back home and certainly of importance in Washington. Contests were waged to ensnare them to parties. Marcia Winn wrote in the *Times-Herald*: "To corner this game, wealthy social climbers from all sections of the country are planning to take houses in Washington for the winter 'season.' One frankly said she is coming 'just to be in the swim for I couldn't bear to be so far away from all that excitement.' "

The word spread in excitement that Mrs. J. Borden Harriman, a social power and former Minister to Norway, was returning. A wealthy California woman bound for Washington hired a social secretary with orders to see to a Washington party for twenty or thirty people each week. Having one's fortune told became a rage throughout the social sets, and a soothsayer could almost name her price upon predicting a party which would leave every guest happy and soaked, along with the carpets, in champagne. A most desired prediction was for social success with the Latin Americans, who had become extraordinarily popular.

A matron exclaimed, "Everyone is passionate about them. From the head, not from the heart." But the Good Neighbors were often remarkably unreliable in the performance of the amenities. One socialite suffered every pleasurable agony in arranging a "Good Neighbor Party," only to discover that five important ones would fail to appear, though they did telephone regrets. Five P.M. came and the most important guest had neither arrived nor called. The hostess telephoned his Embassy to hear from his secretary, "You expect the Minister to dinner? Do not expect the Minister. He is suffering from the alcohol."

The socialites did not know they were toying with a stick of international wartime dynamite. Despite the Monroe Doctrine, so long taken seriously, Germany had for more than a quarter of a century eyed Paraguay, Argentina, Brazil, and Bolivia as potential holdings through infiltration and international and internal political intrigue.

Approximately 700,000 Germans had a foothold in the business and civic life of Argentina, Brazil, and Chile by 1939 when Hitler meditated his plunge into Poland. And just as ominous for the United States as this incursion—begun long before Hitler even came to power—was a chain of spies extending from Mexico City to South America's southern tip. The FBI would reveal years later that Hitler's agents went from their schooling in the Good Neighbor countries into the United States on specialized missions of espionage, relating largely to American industry and military preparedness. President Roosevelt's concern was shared by the Department of State and the defense establishments—a concern resulting in the creation of a Special Intelligence Service, with the FBI handling information outside the military area. In mid-July 1940, FBI operatives posing as salesmen, business executives, or workmen fanned across the spy-infested countries. Cooperation from the affected governments was obviously essential, and some actually placed FBI agents among police forces. One agent represented an American soap manufacturer, and his sales techniques were so brilliant that the franchise was expanded. The manufacturer did not know that its ace man had FBI connections. Another became a stockbroker, and his success was phenomenal, the envy of Argentinian financial experts. The dangers which many of them accepted transcended anything a "government employee" might be asked to experience. Platinum smugglers were tracked through Colombia's Choco jungle where every step, even in normal times, could be one more toward death. The FBI would disclose years later that some of the agents went in canoes up the Amazon's headwaters, potential targets for a bite by piranhas, a fractious fish favoring human flesh.

Don Whitehead, in his definitive *FBI Story*, asserts: "The United States' own 'soft underbelly' was exposed in a time of crisis unless the Americas stood together."

Whenever groups of South Americans arrived for conferences in Washington, State Department officials held luncheons at the Carlton Hotel with the most sophisticated tilting of fingers over coffee. The reasons behind the almost strained attentions paid the Latin American by the government in Washington are now clear. But what motivated Washington society beyond passing fad and caprice and the gaiety generated by the rhumba experts is impossible to resolve. *Esquire* magazine had long before notified American women that "Latins Are Lousy Lovers," so that allurement might be precluded.

In any event, Washington society by its fawning attentions probably aided the war effort, for they also serve who only stand and pass out champagne with dashes of charming chatter, all adding up to make the United States a nation worth aligning with.

The legations' business expanded and additions of space became commonplace. Pressures upon them for news of every kind grew unmanageable and press agents were employed, quickly to learn the twists of evasion. Crown Princess Martha of Norway, whose frequent visits to the White House were discussed in discerning circles, quit the city to dominate a $262,000 estate near Bethesda, Maryland. The President was a frequent guest at the royal home.

In that first war year, it is doubtful that a Thomas Paine could have looked about Washington and said, as he had of the days of Revolution, "These are the times that try men's souls." The absence of gloom in the capital seemed to result from a certainty that the war would be won. History was a determining factor: the United States had never lost a war. It was all a matter of sweating out the necessary months or years, of working hard as was demanded, and, when possible, of working together.

There was, for example, a corpulent reporter on the *Times-Herald* who nobly helped a newly arrived girl find a job as a receptionist in a nightspot near 14th and K Streets. The nobility within her rose rapidly to meet her benefactor's own. Whenever the reporter entered the music-drenched club, the girl would point to a table saying, "There's one sitting over there and I think she's ready," and she would seat her friend nearby. Such an isolated incident could be multiplied many times to prove the esprit de corps among Washingtonians in helping one another in little ways to sustain the stresses.

The people, generally, were friendly toward one another and almost entirely lacking in the suspicion so rampant during the first World War, when a German sympathizer lurked behind every plate of sauerkraut—a name which, fantastically, was changed to "liberty cabbage." Dachshunds, regarded with suspicion during World War I, remained unsuspect even into 1945. So deep was the confidence in draft boards that rejected young men could walk about, unhappy in instances, but without self-consciousness or fear of becoming targets of abuse.

Hundreds of men and women escaped the tiger that was Washington, with its appetite for innocence and raking claws for everyone, through a natural camaraderie. It shows better now through their recollections. One resident of the city, who had come from Ohio, later recalled:

When I came to Washington ten months before Pearl Harbor I found the most economical form of living to be a boarding club. There were then about eight large ones in existence, and the rates were practically the same, i.e., $40 per month for three-in-a-room, $45 per month for a two-bed room, and $60 if one were lucky (and rich) enough to get a single. The rates included two meals a day, breakfast and evening dinner. The one I first entered comprised some eight different houses with a central dining room for all the residents. The room accommodations and food were not like what we were used to at home but wide friendships were made (some lasting until this day), and because we all shared the common bond of being from distant states it may rightly be said that we stayed because of each other. There were companions for any activities—the boat trips down the river at night, the concerts, galleries, riding clubs, picnics, and parties.

The Saturday night parties never varied. Only the faces changed at intervals. There was a bathtub full of ice and beer, a record player, dancing, and, if we were affluent enough, food. The dining room food rarely sufficed in quantity and quality and constantly needed supplementing. To cut down on costs, I moved after a while to another club. It was concentrated in one building, but the quantity and quality of the food were much the same. I shared quarters in the basement with two first-year medical students, a situation which had its good and bad points. They were good companions but their long hours of study made the basement quarters off-limits socially. Once they brought home a disassembled skeleton for study. The club proprietors owned a small dog that roamed the house, and the dog developed a curiosity about the box full of bones, and got into it. A girl entertaining her boy friend in the lounge on the first floor became upset when the dog passed through dragging half of a skull.

The club had an antiquated water system that frequently failed. Sometimes for three days running there was no hot water. This, along with other inconveniences, caused me to move to yet another club called the Mar-Leeta, which was quite ornate and had an elevator. The boys, however, were assigned to basement rooms. The girls had the rooms above the first floor. Each of their rooms had a fireplace, and we had many social gatherings beside blazing fires. On my very first night, I was invited by one of the girls to go for a walk. What I didn't know was that she was supposed to get me out of the house so that the other men could wire up my room. They placed a loudspeaker in my empty suitcase beneath the bed, ran the connection through the switchboard directly overhead, and were planning to make frightening noises after I went to bed. The girl kept her promise not to tell me. But she liked me well enough to keep me out so late that the boys gave up and went to bed.

When anyone in the club became ill there were plenty of friends to look after him. One boy got appendicitis and was taken to the hospital by so many people it looked like an invasion. When anyone received a box of pastries or candy from home—not too often because of the sugar rationing—it was always shared with others.

Thirty-two marriages resulted from meetings at the Mar-Leeta, and the proprietor himself gave away many of the brides. Because of the restrictions on wartime travel and the seven-day work week in the defense agencies, they hadn't been able to go home for the weddings.

With everyone far from their childhood homes and parental supervision, it was amazing that so many went to church on Sundays despite the late hours on Saturday nights. After church, we would go to the Riverside Stables for horses to ride in Rock Creek Park. There was never a problem of what to do; rather a question of which one of a number of things.

Not everyone regarded the general camaraderie with equanimity. A skilled psychiatrist and administrator brooded about the general situation. Like everyone else, he was confident about the war's outcome, but he was equally certain about its aftermath—a prospect which troubled him.

Dr. Winfred Overholser, a bulky balding man, was superintendent of St. Elizabeth's (mental) Hospital. He liked people and, consequently, knew more about them than most members of his profession. He was a joy to newspaper reporters because he said what was on his mind, and what was on his mind was the current Washington scene:

"A period of lax morals and undress exceeding even the riotous living of the twenties will follow this war. The loosening of morals started after World War I has continued and is reaching a new high now as evidenced by the soaring tide of illegitimacy."

The doctor went on:

"I foresee no early return to the Victorian era in the United States." The present promiscuity was due not so much "to predatory activities of soldiers and sailors as it is to the fact that so many young girls, whose parents are working, are unsupervised. When girls are willing, immorality cannot be considered rape or a sex crime. Cynics say there is no reason to commit rape here in Washington."

Then the doctor, more hopefully, reflected that "we are gaining a broader attitude toward sex and a more reasonable approach toward life in general." But he was distrustful of hit-and-run war marriages, believing these would fall apart.

The discerning doctor undoubtedly knew, aside from what he might personally observe, that home-front carrying-on was as much a part of any war as ammunition and agony at the fronts. Indeed, during the Civil War, when daily existence was endangered by rowdies and barroom brawls which spilled into the streets, the muddy thoroughfares were thronged with prostitutes. Civil War statistics generally are inexact, but in such an important matter as these women, the number is known to have been five hundred when the war began and five thousand (excluding the competition intruding from Alexandria) when General Lee called a halt to the war and attendant festivities at Appomattox. Such a vast industry did not exist in Washington during World War II, though some houses existed quietly.

It is an injustice to label the nocturnal pastimes as immoral. It was all a form of utterly necessary release. Word spread around that the men at the fighting fronts felt a contempt for the war workers back home. The complainants couldn't look into some of the cheaper lunch rooms near the government buildings. During the evenings as the war progressed, government girls sat on the counter stools hunched over plates of the first thing they could think of to order without thinking, because thinking hurt. Many raised their forks or spoons slowly. The stains of ink from typewriters discolored their fingers. The fingernails were unattended, and their hair straggly. The eyes were staring. Outside, the night turned bronze under dimmed street lights. To the girls, the night was a time of day, and the day wasn't ended. This was war, and they felt themselves in it, but they didn't know exactly what it was all about except that the Japanese had attacked the United States. And they didn't know exactly what they, as individuals, were doing about it. They were doing what they were told to do, and it would have been impossible to relate what they were doing to the total war machinery. They knew they were tired, and something screamed for release of the mind and the body. A few broke under the strain. Others stepped into their places, and little was made of it beyond murmurings.

Some of them had heard that a man named Henry F. Pringle, author and one-time reporter on the *New York World*, had proposed a government slogan, "Exhaustion is not enough."

It became rough all over—from the expansive offices of the Pentagon's upper echelons to the crowded boardinghouses, to the inner rooms of the White House.

Robert E. Sherwood, playwright, Roosevelt speech writer, veteran of World War I, watched Roosevelt live what Pringle had demanded. Sherwood would remember that Mrs. Roosevelt once telephoned the Cabinet Room at 3 A.M. to say that the hour was too late, but without mentioning that she herself was working. He remembered the days standing with Judge Rosenman beside French windows near the colonnade and hearing the bells give notice that the President was nearing. The President would pass along seated in a cushionless wheelchair pushed by Chief Petty Officer Arthur Prettyman, the Negro valet. In front, beside, and behind the chair walked the expressionless Secret Servicemen. Some carried wire baskets filled with materials the President had worked on during the night. Some of it had been read when he awakened from sleep. The face, fixed, pitched forward, already was showing the two terms of the killing job, and part of a third.

And what the face showed would deepen in coming months under pressures where exhaustion was no boundary.

CHAPTER NINE

NEWS FROM HELL BEFORE BREAKFAST

THE PEOPLE'S MOODS rose and fell with victories and setbacks, though too many had no understanding that any war is a patchwork of ups and downs, neither entirely forecasting the final score of the awful game. It appeared that there had been nothing but setbacks since Pearl Harbor—until one day in mid-April 1942, when word came that United States fliers had bombed Japan and, most wonderful of all, Tokyo itself. Of all the places on earth, Tokyo had seemed the most remote and untouchable, but the most desirable of all places to drop with explosive force the weight of America's wrath. There followed an instantaneous rise of spirits, and people on streets and in offices told the news excitedly to one another as though it weren't already known. But the excitement was mixed with perplexity: How had such a feat—something beyond imagining—been accomplished? President Roosevelt would say only that the airmen had taken off on the mission from Shangri-la, which, of course, didn't exist, except in James Hilton's book *Lost Horizon*.

It wasn't until late May 1942, that people learned the identity of the man who had led the midday attack on Japan on April 18, a man they already knew of and liked. He was Brigadier General James H. Doolittle, who combined such characteristics as modesty, aggressiveness, and scholarship. On May 19, Doolittle received the Congressional Medal of Honor from President Roosevelt. Roosevelt, obviously in high spirits, laughingly remarked, in an apparent reference to Drew Pearson, that not even a columnist had known who had led the raid on Japan. The facts emerged—some a long time later. Sixteen B-25s and eighty pilots and crewmen had taken off from the carrier "Hornet" 688 miles from Tokyo by sea. From thirteen of the planes, 500-pound bombs were dropped upon Tokyo, and Nagoya and Kobe were hit by explosives tumbling from the low-flying aircraft. The fliers might, indeed, have destroyed the palace of Emperor Hirohito, but inflexible orders had been given against striking directly at the man considered by the Japanese to be a god. The losses would later be learned. Eight airmen fell into Japanese hands off the China coast; three were executed, and the others imprisoned. The raid, in a final count, brought death to nine of the fliers. But the immediate effect of the announcement was that the civilian spirit was immeasurably lifted. It had the effect of making everyone want to do more to speed actions that now really were under way.

Sometimes, however, what it was that they were doing wasn't exactly clear to Washingtonians. The soldiers, sailors, and airmen banded in exclusive comradeship apart from the civilians, were disciplined and indoctrinated to "do your bit." The war workers had little indoctrination beyond the speeches and slogans inspired by the bombs that had fallen on Pearl Harbor. But they, too, acted on orders without understanding the final effect of their actions on the complex design of the war. The name a girl might indifferently type on a slip of paper could mean the life or death of the man who chanced to bear it.

Perhaps the most perplexed of all groups among the population were the newspaper reporters. They had always been exposed to pressure, but never any as intense as this. Many reporters had entered the service, and this extended down to the copyboys who, stretching their ages, put on uniforms. News rooms became strange sights. The copygirl came into being; and it was impossible for the remaining male reporters to concentrate when the old shout, "Boy!" from the city desk brought a young girl forward. And swarms of girl reporters, to whom this situation spelled golden opportunity, descended to replace the absent men, bringing with them despair to the editors—to say nothing of inhibiting the normally tough language of the city rooms. Old men scratched their heads and observed that "the business" and the world had gone to hell.

The scarcity was made even more acute by the Marine Corps, which had brought many of the best of the young and healthy and competent newsmen into its ranks through a plan that had been evolved by Brigadier General Robert L. Denig, USMC. After 36 years of service, General Denig had been recalled to Washington in late June 1941. He had known Major General Commandant Thomas Holcomb in France during World War I, and upon entering Holcomb's office was greeted with, "Well, Denig, what do you know about public relations?" Denig stood there, a stout-bodied man with a determined chin and hair that sloped from the back of his head.

"I don't know anything about it, never heard of it. What is it?" The commandant replied, "You had better learn about it because that's what you're going to be."

Denig entered his new office and looked about. The office was a dark inner room formerly used as a gear locker. The only illumination came from a soiled and unshaded light. Denig's staff stood up: First Sergeant Walter J. Shipman—at thirty-one, young for his rank in the Marines—and two civilian clerks, Lorene Lomax and Helen Draper. (None of them could have imagined that within four years the public relations force overseas and at Headquarters would number 268 officers and enlisted marines.) Denig looked sharply around at his working gear—circulars and material on football games and nondescript pamphlets, all of it known as publicity. But for the next five months his job was to concentrate on recruitment. For assistance, Denig brought in George Van der Hoef, who had headed screen and radio publicity at the Federal Housing Administration. He was commissioned a major in the Reserves. Later came Second Lieutenant John W. Thomason III, son of the famed biographer and artist and himself a marine. Then came Second Lieutenants William P. McCahill and Eugene M. Key. These two alone of those in the office had newspaper experience.

After awhile, with war inevitably approaching, it became clear that the division should keep the press, radio, motion pictures, and citizens generally informed concerning the part marines traditionally take in the nation's service. There followed a number of abortive plans revolving around the recruitment of young reporters for public relations work, as sergeants with boot-camp training. But out of conferences generated by Denig emerged the idea of the battle-hardened Combat Correspondent—news-trained marines on the actual scene through whom the American people could learn what was going on.

The flimsiness of news from the embattled garrison on Wake Island was a compelling motivation as Denig's plan took shape. It was later to be observed: "There was a story on Wake to be written but there was no one there to write it. All that arrived in Washington were dry, dispassionate, routine messages which had to be converted into communiqués for general release. Denig told Holcomb that he wanted a hundred young newspapermen, and was told the idea must be submitted to the Division of Plans and Policies for concurrence—which meant a 'study.' The decision eventually came back. He could have ten men. If he could find the ten, he could have ten more. A more frustrating example of Washington thinking would be difficult to find."

Denig and Shipman went directly to the newspaper city rooms of Washington. Shipman would remember: " . . . I prepared for this mission by putting on my blues . . . my decorations, and then went to the city editors for permission to talk to their personnel, and got it in each case. We just gathered around a desk and I told my story. Then I was subjected to a session of questions from men trained to get the meat of a story, and I did my best. The big thing, probably the only thing, was the complete assurance of their getting into combat."

Sam Stavisky, assistant city editor of the *Post*, would remember: " . . . by word of mouth it went around town that a man by the name of Shipman was trying to recruit newspapermen for CCs for the Marine Corps, and the idea sounded good.

Shipman to me represented gung ho, China Marines, and all that. He was a very intelligent, articulate fellow. I liked him. . . ." Stavisky went.

The first ten were recruited. General Holcomb asked, "Where did you get them?" and Denig explained, "Oh, I just sent Sergeant Shipman around town."

Historian Benis M. Frank later would recall: "Hardest hit were the ranks of the *Times-Herald*, whose owner, Cissie Patterson, raised the kind of hell that only she was capable of raising. First she complained to President Roosevelt about the loss of her reporters. FDR passed the matter on to General Holcomb, who called in Denig. Shipman later commented: "Damned if I didn't have to see the Commandant. Holcomb in civvies looked like a contented farmer, including the pipe. But underneath that disguise was a will of firmness that, when expressed, increased your stance of rigid attention practically to immobility. However, he just reiterated his orders to General Denig, which were to canvass for Combat Correspondents elsewhere than D.C."

The actual recruitment of the CCs had begun in Washington in late March and early April, but no nationwide notice came until the commandant put the capital off limits for the recruiting. The Associated Press of June 6, 1942, spread the word:

> Lieutenant General Thomas A. Holcomb . . . announced today that newspaper reporters of not less than five years experience are being accepted for enlistment as combat correspondents. After six weeks training as fighting troops, they will be given the rank of sergeant and sent overseas with combat units. General Holcomb said the Marine Corps is sacrificing none of its high standards, and combat correspondents must meet all physical requirements for regular marines.

The newspapers, like show business, went on, but nowhere nearly as well. The little men and the little women and the "important" people in the capital had no idea what the reporters underwent to put together, too often in patchwork fashion, the news they read, which was all they knew.

Nearly all the news, directly or indirectly (barring crime) related to the war, but the news too often lacked depth, creating elation, despair, or confusion in the public mind.

News flowed torrentially from the "war activities" of the citizens' associations, the state societies where men and women from the 48 states met to dance, talk of back home, and meet a representative or senator often appearing as guest of honor. News issued from the Board of Trade; from police headquarters—the city-side stuff of peacetime. These stories were handled by women and the younger reporters, who were generally let alone by the editors. The lash lay on the men covering the Pentagon, the White House, the Department of State, and the pyramiding agencies which oversaw everything from allocations of steel to the fighting forces and necessary wartime industries (whose Washington representatives fought like demons for their share) to the so-called hardware for women, meaning allocations of material for girdles and other attire.

News from the Pentagon was the hardest to get. On this matter a controversy persists to this day. Army and intelligence people contended that the enemy could splice together small bits of information into a revealing whole. But reporters knew that much information which couldn't be threaded into anything significant was withheld on the old army and government theory that if-you-don't-say-nothing-you-can't-get-in-no-trouble. Trivialities were fussed over, and passed along endlessly to censors.

One of the major problems was the unwillingness to tell the people any bad news. It was strange, this reluctance to tell the American people of setbacks; for the public, historically, has never cried quits at adversity. The Revolutionary War had produced little for jubilation besides Trenton, Saratoga, and Yorktown; during the Civil War, news of the retreat from Bull Run produced little reaction beyond slouching or drinking in the streets. But for some reason the firmness of the national backbone was held in doubt.

In the Pentagon was a public relations setup of enormous physical size. It was filled with officers, many of whom were former newspapermen who had obtained commissions. Now they found themselves on the other side. Long trained and hardened in getting news, they now had to use all their ingenuity to bamboozle their former colleagues. It is probable that they didn't know very much anyway. The knowledge of what was occurring at the fronts lay at the top, and was issued in carefully-worded communiqués. These were often pieced together by the news desks with what the newspapers received from censored correspondents at the fronts.

The problem was to get the top to talk beyond what the communiqués hinted at, and what the correspondents reported. In 1942 the lid was so tight that the ghastly sinking of United States oil tankers off the south Atlantic coast, spreading oil slicks as far north as Virginia Beach, was unknown in any detail for a long time.

Sometimes, as a result of the lack of hard news, reporters were given some fantastic assignments. A day city editor, new to the job but an old hand in the business, beckoned one slow afternoon to a reporter. The dialogue went something like this:

"I overheard on a streetcar this morning that the Navy WAVES are getting tattoo artists to put battleships across their breasts. See what you can find out about it."

"I don't believe a goddamn word of it," the reporter answered. "They'd be thrown out of the service. You can hear anything on a streetcar."

"Just see what you can get on it," the editor insisted, rubbing his bald head fringed with gray.

Rain poured outside. The reporter walked out into it. If there were any tattoo artists in town, one might be found on 9th Street. The reporter roamed the thoroughfare of penny-arcades and pitchmen who had enough sense that day to come in out of the rain, and finally spoke with Jimmy Lake, renowned for his Gayety Theatre and title of Mayor of 9th Street. This authority on bosoms said that he had never heard tell of such carryings-on (for he had an old-fashioned side). The reporter found a tattoo man in a nearby barbershop. When presented with the story, he shook his head piously. There was no truth in the tale.

The city editor said little upon hearing this, but his thoughts showed through a frown—reporters were no good these days. But he had an easier assignment for the reporter. He was ordered to the White House to interview one of the squirrels.

"Interview a squirrel about what?" he asked.

"About the general situation, the war, current events. You know."

"Like hell I know. A squirrel can't talk. Although there are some two-legged ones there who know everything." But the city editor was firm: "I mean squirrels," he insisted.

The reporter informed him that that kind of journalism had ended around 1902, gave two weeks' notice and then left, though not without a backward look through the door where the bust of John Philip Sousa stood covered by dust, a marble face among all the remembered faces. It was just damn sentimentality he thought, but nearly everyone had gone. There remained Edward T. Folliard, the greatest reporter of them all, but later he would be gone to cover the fighting in Europe. There was somebody at the desk where Johnny Oakes had sat (John Bertram Oakes, now editorial page editor of *The New York Times*). His incisive mind had been hidden by his great sense of fun. A woman sat intently pecking at a typewriter not so long ago used by Hedley Donovan (now editor-in-chief of *Time, Life,* and *Fortune*). Donovan was using his fine mind and, hopefully, his wry humor in the Navy. And Marshall Andrews, the best military analyst the capital had produced, was there, though he was aching to return to the Army, and eventually did, winding up in France where he had been in 1918.

Outside, the city visibly throbbed. But it was different from a short time before. The victories of the Coral Sea and Midway had been won. And when the news of Midway was proclaimed by the press, a group of men who were huddled over a pile of papers in a 14th Street drugstore smiled. One of them said,

"Great! God knows we need these." He meant victories. But he didn't know the depth of his meaning. The people needed to know, and to understand, both the good news and the bad.

Of all the publications in Washington, with the possible exception of *The New York Times*, *Time* magazine had the most inside contacts. Its correspondents, occupying about half of the eighth floor at 815 15th Street, N.W., and headed by Felix Belair, Jr., a veteran and tough-minded reporter himself, were not permitted to get stories by telephone. Apparently Belair believed that Alexander Graham Bell had invented the telephone for reporters' appointments and housewives' gossip. And he growlingly rejected any suggestion that a story be obtained through a government or any other public relations person. News had to emanate from the top, and the top frequently was a Cabinet member. This could be accomplished only because of the magazine's towering prestige; and there was another factor: vanity, of which Washington had an overload. The highly placed officials somehow believed, with the wistful expectation of children, that an interview by a *Time* man guaranteed a notice and perhaps a picture . . . or, in the farthest reaches of hope, a picture on the cover.

These interviews were tortures. When probing questions came, the official had no answers. And this was understandable because the full operations below where he sat were impossible to contain in the one bag of his mind. So he summoned experts on the subject, sometimes consuming hours. The correspondent would return to his cubbyhole often to write two thousand or more words for the New York editors (the actual writers) who wanted everything in a rush beyond human capacity. Meanwhile, the official who was interviewed waited impatiently for the next issue of the magazine. More often than not, he would see two or three paragraphs—from which he would learn that he had wide-set dreamy eyes, wore a blue-and-white-striped necktie, and had neglected to have his trousers pressed—all the gleaming detail that made *Time* famous, along with the original idea that a story could be told without toppling over from weight of type.

But it played hell with the correspondents whom Belair had hand-picked, and who were his monument. (He had the finest staff in Washington and the best directed, but it was not at that time appreciated in New York and eventually was capriciously dispersed.) The correspondents without exception had been by-line men who had commanded respect on a telephone by their name, not by a magazine's reputation. They were stung by the anonymity; they resented seeing shapely and detailed copy they had written "processed" (as the late Henry R. Luce, *Time*'s tense-faced, fidgety, and sedate-necktie-wearing owner, described the editorial system) and fleeced down into two paragraphs. Worst of all was the eventual distrust shown by the news sources—the upper officials of government. The question came: "Do you really want a story or a paragraph or nothing?"

Time and its sister *Life* operated somewhat like driving sales managers; they asked for the impossible, knowing that if it didn't produce the moon, the correspondents, at the least, would bring in a star. Someone in New York heard that a high official in the Department of State had adjoining bath tubs—one for his wife and one for himself, with the probability that they bathed simultaneously. The editors asked for pictures. Word was teletyped back that it wasn't true, but even if true it was doubtful that the diplomat, schooled in not revealing his inner thoughts, would expose his outer self, or that his wife would want her measurements known. The command came back to try for a rear view.

Some of the staff got foreign assignments, and all wanted to be sent to the fighting fronts to keep from going crazy. But there was one consolation. They talked with the war makers on a non-attribution basis, purely as background for the New York editors. The best of these contacts was Bernard Baruch, who stayed frequently at the Carlton Hotel. The reception room of his suite was generally filled with people. But he appeared to know of the pressure harassing the *Time* reporters (he was a close friend of Luce, the originator of that sort of pressure) and always gave them preference. He often looked gray and tired; and sometimes he talked while reclining on his bed. He was a repository of facts, and had an interpretation for every one of them.

Within two weeks after the attack on Pearl Harbor, Roosevelt had selected Byron Price, executive editor of the Associated Press in New York, to direct an Office of Censorship. Whether a knowledgeable choice or one of those impetuous decisions of which the President was capable, the choice was excellent for three reasons: (1) Price was respected by newspapermen, (2) he could count 22 years' experience as a Washington correspondent and knew the thickets within which bureaucrats weaved and dodged, and (3) he had the newspaperman's ingrained dislike of censorship.

Perhaps psychiatrists, who blame nearly everything on a bruising childhood experience, would have quickly spotted the reason for Price's distaste for the role he was yanked into. When commanded into the job, he said with resignation, "Censorship is nothing new to me." And in his quiet manner, he told how at the age of ten he decided that his home town of Topeka, Indiana, needed another newspaper, so he had published one. But his father clamped down after reading items Byron had written about his relatives.

Roosevelt had reached for his long cigarette holder and manipulated it upon the edge of his desk as he told the news conference that the heavy-set quiet man with the steel-rimmed glasses would be their court of voluntary resort. There would be no more attempts, as in World War I, to operate a joint censorship-propaganda agency. The office now would censor mail and cables entering and leaving the country, and would urge the press, voluntarily, to withhold information useful to the enemy.

Approximately 14,000 mail and cable censors were required. But, says Price, " ... It was the second responsibility which carried the dynamite. In any democratic country the press censor's house can be built only on sand. He can rely only on the shifting possibilities of mutual understanding; no barrier to free expression will be tolerated by free people if they believe it imposes senseless restraints."

Newsmen later entering Price's office were impressed by his unshakable calm; by the desk that was clear of any clutter—indeed, there often was nothing on the desk but a telephone; and by the staff of known newspapermen, creating a comfortable feeling of familiarity. The number of Price's personal aides never exceeded a dozen at any one time, probably the most extraordinary restraint ever shown by a government executive.

Decisions of a Yes or No nature (and Price made very few in the latter category) came quickly. He early foresaw, however, a danger in comic strips. The imaginative creators of the science-type strips might quite innocently venture into the realm of physics, more than hinting at the explosive potential in atoms.

Price would recall: "Editors were asked to be cautious about stories involving certain minerals in the atomic table and their compounds, including several having no connection with the bomb and a few phonies which the resourceful and imaginative Nat Howard [Nathaniel R. Howard, editor of the *Cleveland News*, on loan to head the Press Division] said later he threw in gratuitously in the admonitory note to editors 'just to confuse the enemy.' "

(An unsung hero of the war effort except among newsmen, Price would close his office upon his own request within 24 hours after Japan surrendered. Whatever bored gods presided over Washington bureaucracy must have raised a stein to dear old Byron and given absolute clearance to the Valhalla press to ring his praise.)

Neither in Washington nor throughout the nation was it known how trustworthy the vast segments of the news media had been. Throughout the war many correspondents wore worried faces because of the things they knew. Price, who knew most about what they knew, would later say: "Neither the first landing in Africa in November 1942, nor D-Day at Normandy in June 1944, nor the development of The Bomb, nor any other major military project had been disclosed prematurely. In no single case was evidence produced that any newspaper or

magazine had violated deliberately any request of the Office of
Censorship. And in the end the press emerged as free as it had
been before."

It could be said that the press had matured, and the coming
of age had required nearly a century. Correspondents during the
Civil War had nearly driven General William T. Sherman crazy, a
condition from which many said he already suffered. Prowling
through the tensed camps, the correspondents easily discerned
the next movement of forces and spelled it out to their
newspapers, often with dangerous accuracy. The Confederates
got hold of the newspapers which were transmitted into silver
platters bearing intelligence. Furious, Sherman wrote to his wife
from Vicksburg, Mississippi, April 10, 1863: "... the
newspaper correspondents, encouraged by the political generals,
and even President Lincoln, having full swing in this and all
camps, report all news, secret and otherwise.... all persons
who don't have to fight must be kept out of camp, else secrecy,
a great element of military success, is an impossibility." A story
spread that one day Sherman was told that an exploding shell
had killed a correspondent. The general leaped from his camp
stool shouting, "Good! Now we shall have all the news from
hell before breakfast."

Is it possible that many within the military establishment
emerged from World War II with a different impression of
newsmen? Despite everything, it is highly doubtful.

It was a godsend to the spirit of the people that some of the
happenings in Washington were kept under wraps. They did not
know for example—and this is perhaps the first time it has been
written—that somebody, identity now unknown, sometime in
early 1942, had hatched the idea of creating a secret body to be
called the Interdepartmental Security Committee. The purpose
of the ghostly gang was to coordinate security problems with all
of the so-called war agencies, including the Navy, Army, Air
Force, and, indeed, the major federal departments. The idea
reached the President, and he appointed Attorney General
Francis Biddle as the committee's chairman.

In Washington at the time was a lieutenant, USNR, performing a highly specialized task for the Office of Naval Intelligence—the finest intelligence service the nation had. The lieutenant was stationed in the Apex Building at Pennsylvania and Constitution Avenues, serving under the late Captain H. K. ("Bunny") Fenn, of ONI, who reported to Byron Price, who, in turn, reported to the President. The lieutenant was selected because of his specialization to serve on the secret "coordinating" committee, with instructions from Price to observe "and use my judgment in all matters before the committee," and to report anything of major importance to Price himself.

The committee crept furtively once a week into a large and chandeliered room in the Department of Justice Building. In the best traditions of bureaucratese, several weeks passed in organizing a "secretariat," and just what a secretariat was is unknown except that one was believed to be needed. Some twenty bureaucrats mulled the problem over while the lieutenant became convinced that his time was being wasted. But finally the secretariat was created. During the general rubbing of hands at a job well done, a young committeeman moved that the first order of business should be an analysis of the techniques used by Naval Intelligence. This young man represented the Department of State.

Before the motion could be seconded, the lieutenant got the floor on a point of order and informed the chairman that it was unlawful for anyone outside of ONI, including the President, to know anything about ONI activities and procedures. He was further emboldened to move that the committee adjourn and never meet again.

"Captain, you can't be serious," Biddle exclaimed, unwittingly jumping the lieutenant three grades in rank. Growing more determined, the lieutenant told the chairman that he had never been more serious, and, furthermore, according to Navy Intelligence standards, none of the others present could meet the security requirements.

The lieutenant walked across the room, picked up his cap and walked out, leaving in his wake a flurry of astonished jabbering. Back at the Apex Building, he wrote a one-sentence memorandum to Price stating that he had moved for abolishment of the committee on security grounds. Price sent for him and heard the details. He got the President on his "hot line," to say that the committee was insecure and should be abolished. The President gave the order, and the committee died that day.

CHAPTER TEN

THE FIRST WAR SUMMER

WASHINGTON, AS USUAL, was hot in the summer of 1942. People who had time showered twice a day to rid their bodies of the sticky humidity. Talk went around that the British officials in Washington drew "tropical post pay," and curiously enough the loudest complaints about the heat came from southerners who may innocently have believed that upon moving to Washington they were going into the cool north. People in homes with front steps sat there limply in the evenings fanning themselves with afternoon newspapers, or went to the parks and sprawled upon the hot grass. Sinus attacks, attributed to the awful climate, bedeviled untold thousands, and the ailment again struck President Roosevelt. It was no relief to the sinuses, but he took more and more to the comfort of white palm-beach suits.

If the people had known the truth about the war, the heat would have seemed a minor irritation. On June 21, a Japanese submarine had shelled Fort Stevens, Oregon, a minor incident but revealing of the slyness of Japanese aggression. More ominously, the Nazis, who had stormed into Tobruk powered by planes and tanks, showed their great strength in North Africa when that city fell and 25,000 troops surrendered. Meanwhile, in Europe the shouts grew louder from ally Russia for a second front to lift the pressure off her stubbornly battling armies. General Eisenhower arrived in London June 24 to prepare for a storming of Europe, but few in authority could see it materialize in under two years. The name Eisenhower suggested to the old-line Washingtonians the dapper young major who, with almost a show of indifference, had helped General MacArthur chase the Bonus Marchers from Washington in 1932. How fast the years moved; how swiftly some young officers advanced while others didn't.

Churchill had arrived at Hyde Park June 18, and the British Chiefs of Staff had come to Washington. In the dark of June 20, Roosevelt and Churchill, with Harry Hopkins, entrained for the capital, and the next day conferred with the Chiefs until late into the night, resuming talks the following day with Eisenhower, Stimson, Knox, General Mark Clark, and Dr. T. V. Soong, the impeccable, popular Chinese Foreign Minister.

The United States, through the strength of its soldiers, sailors, airmen, and marines, poised to pursue the Japanese in a bloody but determined island-capturing effort in the Pacific. No one was told that the victory road would be short and smooth, but there did exude from somewhere at the top an almost devil-may-care optimism, and it was infectious. Dr. Soong, in the course of a meeting of the Pacific War Council, learned that his embattled country would receive all sorts of help. Churchill, "sipping water and champing a dead cigar" (according to *Time*) told Congressional leaders that Egypt would hold, that Alexandria and Suez would be inviolate. (Headlines on June 25 would proclaim "Rommel 60 Miles in Egypt." The next day, "Rommel 100 Miles in Egypt.")

The group posed for a photograph, with Roosevelt attired in white linen and Churchill wearing a garment too hot for the Washington summer. There followed a joint statement affirming that "we have taken full cognizance of our disadvantages as well as our advantages. Transportation of the fighting forces, together with transportation of munitions of war and supplies still constitutes the major problem." But it was believed that "coming operations, which were discussed in detail," would divert German strength from the attack on Russia.

A fat luncheon preceded Churchill's departure by bomber on June 25, a smiling talkative fest attended by Lord Halifax, Dr.

Soong, Prime Minister Mackenzie King of Canada, and others. Hopkins had found a moment during the conference interludes to inform the Prime Minister and the President that he would marry Mrs. Louise Macy. The lady, whom Hopkins had known only a short time, had served as a nurse's aide in the New York City war effort. Mutual friends had arranged the introduction. Churchill sprang up to express his delight, and the President conveyed his pleasure.

As a form of backdrop to the festivities, elements generally regarded as left-wing placed picket lines in front of the District Building, with placards demanding the immediate opening of a second front to help Russia. A more unlikely place for the demonstration is unimaginable, since the politically-castrated commissioners could scarcely open a sewer for repair without a deep study of their skimpy budget. Congressmen were already angry enough because kitchen matters related to their bellies were out of control.

During a June lunchtime, members found the waiters on strike, an unprecedented development in a place where precedent rules. In the kitchens, bean soup lay in vast pots on the stoves with no one to serve it. (Bean soup was traditional in the Capitol; no man could be a real good fellow unless, after a visit to the restaurant as a guest, he could say back home, "I have eaten Capitol bean soup." Long years before, Speaker Joe Cannon of Illinois had in disappointment exclaimed, "By God, we are going to have bean soup in here everyday." And since then unrecorded gallons had simmered on the Capitol restaurant stoves.) A few Congressmen tried to wait on themselves, something even more unprecedented. Money was the problem. The waiters averaged $55 a month, including tips, for their three-and-a-half-hour day. Ten to $15 more came from the Senate restaurants. The trouble ended three days later when the politicians made some promises.

This was far from Egypt, where the Germans took Matruh on June 29. It was far from Sevastopol, the Russians' great Black Sea naval base, which the Germans were poised to capture; and far from the place where on Independence Day they crossed the English Channel to drop loads of explosives on Holland ports. Four of the six U.S. bombers would return. The loss wasn't known in Washington, but everyone knew, because they had been told, that there would always be an England.

In the meantime there was the exciting news that Clark Gable had come to town to take his physical examination at Bolling Field for service in the Army Air Force. Also, Yugoslavia's King Peter had arrived, all the more enchanting because he was only 18 years old. A brunette boy with prominent eyebrows, he was photographed riding a bicycle, but somehow didn't appear to be enjoying the sport. He had come by plane and wanted to talk with President Roosevelt, play baseball, observe airplane production, and drive a jeep. He would find everybody terribly busy. Indeed, 2,011,848 persons twenty years old and over were working one way or another (excluding the military) for the government all across the land. Royalty frequently came and went. Only the work remained.

The work and bothersome problem of shortages, which was scarcely relieved when the War Department, anxious to show its own cooperation, announced that it had contributed hundreds of rubber stamps to the scrap-rubber campaign, bringing from Lieutenant General Brehon B. Somervell, commanding the Service of Supply, the observation, "There goes the curse of the Army."

The most acute shortage was that of sugar. Men wanted it in their coffee; women for their pies. Older residents remembered the same thing happening in World War I. The sugar refiners reached full cry, urging the Office of Price Administration and other regulatory agencies to loosen the flow of sugar. The refiners knew that warehouses bulged at their sweetened seams, and more was arriving from Hawaii. Puerto Rico and Cuba held surpluses. A Gulf Coast refinery had shooed off an incoming load for lack of storage space. It seemed to make no sense to anybody. But OPA had a reason, just as the planners had a reason for removing the cuffs from men's trousers (which later proved to be absolutely senseless).

The United States, it was announced, imported seventy percent of its sugar. It was feared that ships engaged in its transport might at any time be diverted to war use. Black marketeers, like bootleggers back in Prohibition, were delighted at the turn of events.

There were other vexing scarcities. Women began looking at themselves, and, as they had concluded since the time of Eve, didn't entirely admire what they saw. Their clothes were getting old, and new attire, while still randomly available, lacked quality. But austerity was the word, and it was synonymous with patriotism. While servicemen were suffering and dying, it would be unbecoming for women to strut like fashionplates amidst what was literally a time of national mourning. Elegance, like steel and explosives, had gone to war, and everyone had been made aware by the impatient store clerks that there was a war going on. And the fashion designers cooperated in, if they didn't promote, this program of austerity.

As early as June 1942, word went by telephone, over backyard fences, and across kitchen tables over morning coffee that the designers had decreed that autumn fashions would be stripped of every "extra." There would be restrictions on dyes, slide fasteners, and the quality of materials. Clothes-conscious strollers along Connecticut Avenue's brittle-bright environs or Georgetown's historic brick streets would wear peg-topped dresses with skirts draped to disguise skimpy cuts. There would be spool-shaped coats, and suits with shorter jackets. Patch pockets would be gone, replaced by the slash. Moreover, there would be kick-pleat instead of box-pleat skirts. The women went along gamely.

Stocks of basic dyes were frozen; they were required for service uniforms. So the brilliant shades faded away like Washington's famed sunsets above the statue of General Sherman, who had once said that war was hell.

There were many mystifying shortages, which the government remained either unwilling or uninclined to explain. There was the rationing of gasoline, which would send OPA headman Leon Henderson skittering through the streets on a bicycle to prove his cooperation, and the disappearance of nylon for hosiery, causing a near mass-panic among women. These things, it was said, had gone to war. The women who accepted other shortages gracefully, found it hard to tolerate the lack of nylon hosiery. About such an important matter it was not unpatriotic to raise unshirted hell. Beer eventually became rationed in the bars, causing people to go from one bar to another in the course of an evening. And soon to get a tube of toothpaste one had to turn in an empty tube. But an envisioned shortage of cigarettes became probably the most demoralizing factor in Washington and throughout the United States, so far as nearly everybody was concerned.

But at least, there were still ways of forgetting the war and its worrisome demands, if only for a time. Reading, for instance, popular and war-packed books like the lingering *Reveille in Washington*, describing a capital really in a mess; *Dialogue with Death*, and *Paul Revere and the World He Lived In*. And there was music of a gentleness and fierceness to deepen dreams through the dark of night. The open-air concert season was on, as exciting in Washington as in Philadelphia, New York, and Cleveland. The National Symphony Orchestra, which numbered some 65 musicians, performed under the baton of Dr. Hans Kindler, a huge man with blue arrow eyes and an emotional apparatus easily triggered by a wrong word or a misinterpreted passage in the score. He had been waylaid in the United States from his native Holland by the First World War and soon became a distinguished cellist in the Philadelphia Symphony, and later a soloist. Music lovers gave him credit for coming to Washington and wandering the thickets of cultural indifference until driblets of money brought the National Symphony into being, largely through his perseverance. His Sunset Symphonies were performed on a "shell" (or covered barge) drawn against the shore near the foot of a high flight of stone steps near the Lincoln Memorial. Crowds variously estimated from 10,000 to 30,000 sat on the steps or the grass around the top of the steps or in rows of chairs lined before the barge—which had been built in the middle 1930's by the New Deal Works Progress Administration, when it was probably termed another boondoggle. The musicians in the soft-lit barge appeared to ride crests of music carried on the waters of the river. The turbulent *Fourth Symphony* of Tchaikovsky, or his *1812 Overture*—the latter with off-stage cannon roars—tumbled across the night and the dancing glows of starlight on the water. In the interludes the silence became unreal, and the troubles of Washington were, for the moment, forgotten.

CHAPTER ELEVEN

DEATH WAS THEIR BUSINESS, AND END

A JULY IN WASHINGTON is a difficult month for anyone to find an interest in anything. On many mornings, persons standing on the hill where Connecticut Avenue rises from Dupont Circle looked northeastward where the Capitol dome stands so sharply and distantly in winter air, and if they saw the dome at all through the July humidity it resembled a pale emblem on a light blue cushion. A war was raging, but people talked of the heat and of summer clothes wearing thin and the scarcity of new and attractive wear. Despite the war and the excitement war generally brings, life had become monotonous.

But there came a mild flurry in the beginning of July 1942 over the impending trial of eight saboteurs, who, incredibly, had traveled secretly from Germany to the United States in order to cripple and panic the country. The news of their capture had been broken by the FBI on June 27, but little information had been given about the saboteurs, and none about how they had been captured. It was not till years later that the facts emerged.

Hitler, Himmler, and Goering, even in 1942, were confident of air and ground power in Europe, but feared the strength of United States industries. Moreover, the high command lacked satisfactory intelligence about what actually was developing within American industry. Abwehr 2 (Intelligence-2) fidgeted while Hitler fumed. German secret agents were known to the FBI, and important ones were in custody, while suspected ones moved under close surveillance.

(The Bureau later would reveal: "In 1939, the activities of
the Japanese and Germans, including diplomatic representatives,
became so obnoxious that something had to be done to
counteract their brazen abuse of hospitality and diplomatic
immunity. The countermove was a directive from the President,
who instructed the FBI 'to take charge of investigative work in
matters relating to espionage, sabotage, and violations of the
neutrality regulations.' All law enforcement officers were
directed to refer such matters to the FBI. Beginning
immediately, Special Agents surveyed strategic plants which
were pouring out defense material. Recommendations for
changes to increase their security against spies and saboteurs
were made in 2,350 instances. . . . During the entire wartime
emergency there was no single successful act of foreign-directed
sabotage. . . . As a result of FBI investigations, 603 persons have
been convicted in state and federal courts.")

In its frustration, the Abwehr reached for eight men,
Germans who had at some time lived in the United States and
could speak the language. They were to implement a plot that
was a testament to Teutonic thoroughness—except for the
unpredictable human element. These men would be trained in
sabotage and espionage, with special attention to the
destruction of aluminum and magnesium plants. They would
blast bridges, railroad stations, a great coal-carrying railroad,
while the shattering explosions detonating in stores would rock
the public morale and convince Americans that Hitler's war,
successful to date, could span an ocean and rake its iron claws
across the United States. And it would not be known how the
perpetrators had managed to escape the FBI, and that in itself
would generate panic.

Each of the men chosen for training in the sabotage school at
Quenz Lake—a place resembling a well-kept farm not far from
Berlin—was chosen after long deliberation over meticulously
kept official records, and after interviews, the purpose of which
the tentative selectees were ignorant. Outstanding among them
was George John Dasch, square-shouldered, thin-faced, with the
eyes of a soldier constantly at attention. Born in 1903, he had

joined the German army at the age of 14, and served in the north of France. Five years later he entered the United States as a stowaway, but returned to Germany in order legally to enter the United States. During one interlude, he served as a private in the American army for a year. Dasch mostly supported himself as a waiter in the New York area restaurants and hotels, where he envied the manners and affluence of the patrons. His entire life betrayed a loose-footed restlessness easily equatable with emotional instability, and how this escaped Abwehr in one of its most sensitive examinations leaves a question. He had left New York in March 1941, for Germany by way of Japan, courtesy of the German Consulate. Arriving in Berlin in May, Dasch joined the German Foreign Office to monitor foreign language broadcasts. He came under the eye of Walter Kappe, head of the sabotage operation, in November or December 1941. He had the makings for a murderous enterprise, and strode into the Quenz Lake sabotage school in April 1942.

There was nothing of submerged derring-do in the oval placid face of Ernest Peter Burger, a man with eyes so indifferent to life as to make them scarcely his own. Burger had been born in 1906, and worked as a machinist until 1927, when he had come to the United States on an immigrant quota visa. He worked in machine shops in Detroit and Milwaukee, where he took the oath of allegiance as a citizen in February 1933. During the interim, one visit had been made to his homeland. In the summer of 1933, Burger returned to Germany.

Burger's adulthood was pockmarked by politics. He had been a member of the National Socialist Party as early as 1923 in Augsburg, and there was suspicion that his first excursion to the United States had Party motivations. So in 1933 the Party embraced him and he went to work in its division of journalism and propaganda. There were ups and downs awaiting him. Hitler loosed a blood purge inside the Nazi Party, and SA leader Ernst Roehm, to whose staff Burger was attached, was executed. Although escaping the killings, Burger was arrested by the Gestapo in March 1940, for criticizing party politics, and spent seventeen months in a concentration camp. Upon his release, the Army tossed him into the ranks as a private soldier—a discipline he would never forget. Some old Party members didn't turn their backs on him, and brought him and Kappe together. Thus he became a member of the enterprise concealed under the code name OPERATION PASTORIUS—the sabotage plan to paralyze the 48 states.

At Quenz Lake, the trainees enjoyed interludes of bicycling, banter, and pinochle, but their deadly game dominated their attention. The professional staff ranked high in the specialties. These included general chemistry; easily-ignited incendiaries; explosives; detonators and primers; mechanical, chemical, and electrical timing devices; the concealment of identity in the United States; secret writing, and the adoption of appropriate backgrounds and personal histories. Studies advanced from theory into ofttimes resounding practice. This mastered, the eight were taken to German aluminum and magnesium plants, river locks, and canals to learn the most vulnerable points of attack.

A basic principle was impressed on the trainees: the American people would not be mystified about the havoc; they would know it was the result of Nazi penetrations, and the destruction and accompanying deaths would continue for about two years.

In May, the graduates were escorted to the submarines at Lorient in conquered France. There were two submarines, and two teams of four men each. Led by Dasch, Team No. 1 consisted of Burger, Heinrich Heinck, thirty-four, and Richard Quirin, thirty-four. They would travel on U-202 with a northern destination and would land at Amagansett, Long Island. Edward Kerling, thirty-two, a square-faced man with bushy parted hair, would lead Team No. 2, overseeing Herman Neubauer, thirty-two, Werner Thiel, thirty-five, and Herbert Haupt, twenty-two. They would make the crossing on U-584, and land in Florida.

Few expeditions ever began with a stronger basis for self-sufficiency. Each group carried four waterproof cases of high explosives, bombs constructed to resemble chunks of coal, fuses, detonators, primers, and chemical and mechanical timing devices. There was abrasive material to ruin railroad engines.

They had more money than was needed. The leaders carried $50,000 each as a general fund. Each saboteur had $9,000, $5,000 of which the group leader held. In addition, every man was given $400 for his immediate use. There was no counterfeit. (The renowned German expertise proved subject to oversight. Included in the currency were American gold notes removed from circulation in 1933. But this was corrected after last-minute examinations.) Men having no American clothing received attire from countries other than Germany.

Secrecy shrouded everything. Not even the crews of the submarines—proud members of the wolf packs harassing American and British shipping in the lonely Atlantic—understood the mission of their strange compatriots. No one in the United States had been alerted to aid the landings (a circumstance which later would lead the FBI to believe its wartime dragnets had swept widely and well).

Team No. 2 left Lorient in the dark of May 26, and some 48 hours later former waiter-wanderer Dasch and his three began their journey aboard U-202. Two weeks and two days passed. Finally, near midnight of June 12, the crewmen quickly inflated a rubber boat, and, with the agents aboard attired in Navy fatigues, headed for the fog-obscured beach fifty yards away. The boat was additionally burdened by four heavy boxes of explosives and the other death-dealing devices. After the boat reached the shore, the seamen rejoined their commander.

Dasch was the first to see a light weaving through the fog. John Cullen of the Amagansett, Long Island Coast Guard Station was walking a lone patrol, unarmed. Dasch, presumably prepared for anything, froze momentarily, then recovered. He walked into the light to confront Cullen.

Cullen asked him who he was, and Dasch replied that they were fishermen from Southampton who had run ashore, but that they would be all right after sunrise. Cullen reminded Dasch that daylight was four hours away, and the party might better spend the rest of the night at the station. Dasch knew that it would be nearly impossible to escape detection there, and refused.

When he admitted that he had no fishing permit nor proper identification, Cullen grabbed his arm. Dasch flung it off, saying, "You don't know what this is all about."

At this point Burger drew near, dragging a heavy bag and, believing his leader was talking to a fellow agent, spoke out in German. Dasch silenced him with a loud, "Shut up, you damn fool." Heinck and Quirin were obscured in fog, sipping at a bottle of brandy. Burger obeyed the command.

Cullen then realized his inability to handle a possibly large number of suspicious men. He wanted to hasten to his station and make a report. Dasch threatened him, then attempted to bribe him, pressing on Cullen what he said was $300. Cullen took the money, backed away, and disappeared into the fog. Dasch assured his men that he had fixed everything. The Germans began burying the boxes.

At the station, Cullen hurriedly related the strange occurrence and showed the money. (Actually, Dasch had given him $260.) Coast Guardsmen raced to the scene of the landing. There was nothing but the sound of a motor near shore. Other Coast Guardsmen came at daybreak, and following the footprints discovered the buried boxes.

The FBI was informed of the landing twelve hours later. The currency underwent laboratory examination. The Navy and Coast Guard agreed that the FBI should handle the case.

After reaching New York City on the Long Island Railroad, Dasch and Burger joined up at the Governor Clinton Hotel, while Quirin and Heinck found accommodations at the Martinique.

U-584 nosed off Ponte Vedra, Florida, the night of June 16. The Germans landed, buried their boxes, and then went into Jacksonville by bus. The four spent the night, and the next day Kerling and Thiel boarded a train for New York. Neubauer and Haupt traveled to Chicago. The United States was penetrated, secretly at least, six months after Pearl Harbor.

There are numerous speculations about what so quickly broke the resolve in Dasch and how it infected Burger. But at some point, Dasch decided to betray the most important sabotage effort that Abwehr-2 had ever conceived.

The conversation between the group leader and Burger was held in Dasch's 13th-floor room the day following the inauspicious landing. The leader said, "I'm going to notify the FBI. I'm going to Washington and tell them everything," Burger's soldier-discipline purportedly broke, and he fell in line. Dasch phoned the New York FBI office, saying he was Franz Daniel Pastorius and he would be in touch with the headquarters in Washington four days later, a Thursday.

"I have some important information," he said. This was nothing new to FBI operatives because someone frequently has "important information" rooted in spite, rumor, or fancy. But the call was recorded. And all was real except the name, and even that was meaningful—"Pastorius."

The Washington Union Station around 7 P.M. on Thursday, June 18, was filled with men, women, and children milling about in the bright and shadowy places, their voices mingling with no sign of communion or human relationship. The one common factor of war lay submerged in their minds, for it was war that jammed every public place with people and robbed everyone of his good manners and made people push about like nervous cattle. They pushed against the train gates in the domed concourse, looking through the barriers at the trains which either stood agonizingly quiet or appeared about to move away, and at the people already crowded into the trains, the lucky ones.

It is improbable that anyone there would reach his destination with a fixed impression of any face. Time hung in suspension, related alone to the movement of trains. The day was dying; and in the dimly lighted spots uptown the musicians would be shuffling in, carrying those black cases of clarinets and trumpets. But a train was arriving from New York (or so the bulletin board said if anyone paid attention to schedules any more).

A broad line of people jostled upon the walkway leading into the concourse. And these were people, too, with no common concern except their places in the war shadow. They pushed through the waiting crowds and disappeared.

Dasch squirmed through the crowd, and the crowd, beyond doubt, was meaningless to him. His New York hotel had arranged accommodations for him at the Mayflower Hotel, famed for its clientele, renowned as the gathering place of contract seekers and other important people. Dasch, the waiter who had always wanted to be more, may have felt his status rise. And among many uncertainties there was one certainty: a hero's future awaited him. His revelations of impending sabotage and his disclosure that he never had been a Nazi at heart but a lover of democracy as exemplified by the United States would rank him high among the nation's historic patriots. If his word was doubted, there was Burger to substantiate the claim.

A Mayflower clerk assigned him Room 351, with occupancy limited to the following Monday. Dasch settled down, momentarily—and here was a perfect instance of Washington life in June 1942. Scarcely anyone except the old Washington families knew who had moved next door nor did they care as long as order was maintained. Certainly, the hotel went about its routine. Downstairs, contracts were spawned in the lounges; lobbyists and government officials and military officers walked expectantly to elevators with girl friends; innately honest guests swiped items of silverware from the dining-room tables to take home as souvenirs of the fashionable hotel; and the almost incessant cries of page boys—older men, now—disturbed the loungers.

The day after registering, Dasch phoned the FBI, speaking to Agent Duane L. Traynor, who knew of the New York call and the discoveries at Amagansett. Traynor told Dasch that he would be met at his room within half an hour. Later at FBI headquarters, Dasch told a rambling story of Abwehr and Quenz Lake, submarines, and of the landings—a tale fogged and diffused by claims of personal good intentions, and of Burger's goodwill. When the five-day-long interview ended, the FBI had 254 typewritten pages, had arrested five of the Nazis, and was observing the other two. Heavily guarded and in "protective custody," Dasch lived luxuriously in the Mayflower. But any notion that he was a hero was gone.

The FBI was aided by a handkerchief Dasch produced, concealing in invisible writing (to which ammonia was the key) the names of contacts in the United States. The entire roundup after Amagansett required 14 days.

And not a word had leaked to the public in Washington's life where war signified work and sorrow and fun, love and disillusionment, ambition and frustration, and unheard gunfire—a war without the beat of drums except in occasional parades, a conflict without banners except the flags raised in the early morning and lowered at sunset.

The FBI concealed its merited jubilation. Franklin D. Roosevelt, at Hyde Park, was equally pleased when he learned of the roundup from Attorney General Francis Biddle. Roosevelt said that it should be made public to discourage the Germans from any further incursions. FBI Director Hoover went to New York City and summoned the press to the Bureau's office in the federal courthouse. He told very little, considering the breadth and importance of the case. Reporters picked up pictures and biographies of the saboteurs, learned where they had landed, the ingeniousness of their weapons, and their projected targets. The headlines flared the next day across the nation. And an outcry rose for the death penalty. The prisoners were brought to the Washington jail.

The saboteurs were awaiting trial in the sweltering heat of Washington's jail, where the temperature sometimes rose to 110. There, the archaic architecture and accoutrements could provide for any form of execution: the condemned might be stood against one of the walls to die in wraiths of rifle smoke; an electric chair was handy, a product of the carpentry shop; and the high ceiling of the dining room had beams for the hoisting of ropes.

The saboteurs would unquestionably be condemned to death. But what kind of death? There were several methods of execution—electrocution, for one, supposedly quick and painless. A firing squad was somehow related to wartime, but so many honorable men had felt the crash of bullets for their country that it seemed too heroic a death for the eight who had appeared in civilian attire to murder Americans and wreck their plants. Hanging, traditionally, was considered the most ignominious form, and the one designated for spies.

The screams from the press and public for the death penalty grew louder and angrier than any heard since President Lincoln's assassination. But for the officials, calmness was essential. A question plagued the legal mind: Should the rag-tag conspirators be tried by civilian rather than military process? Attorney General Francis Biddle and the War Department leaned toward a military commission to function under the fixed guidelines of courts-martial. This would assure secrecy, withholding from the Nazi government the methods used in breaking the plot, and the death penalty would be almost certain. Roosevelt, showing the toughness of mind concealed below the Groton-Harvard polish, wanted penalties so severe that they would be a deterrent to the German government. He agreed with Biddle and the Department, and on July 2 told the nation:

> Whereas the safety of the United States demands that all enemies who have entered upon the territory as part of an invasion or predatory incursion ... should be promptly tried in accordance with the Law of War; now, therefore, I, Franklin D. Roosevelt ... do hereby proclaim that all persons who are subjects, citizens of any nation at war with the United States or who give obedience to or act under the direction of any such nation, and who during time of war enter or attempt to enter the United States or any territory or possession thereof, through coastal or boundary defenses, and are charged with committing or attempting or preparing to commit sabotage, espionage, hostile or warlike acts, or violations of the law of war, shall be subject to the law of war and to the jurisdiction of military tribunals; and that such persons shall not be privileged to seek any remedy or maintain any proceeding, directly or indirectly, or to have any such remedy or pro-

ceeding sought on their behalf, in the courts of the United
States. . . .

This was legalistic phraseology with a clear meaning. It meant
that spies and saboteurs would receive a military trial. For once,
the law did not delay. The trial of the saboteurs would begin on
July 8, 1942. Three major generals and three brigadier generals
under the presidency of Major General Frank R. McCoy would
compose the commission. Biddle would spearhead the prosecution, assisted by the Army's Judge Advocate General, Major
General Myron Cramer. History would remark that counsel
chosen for the defense were competent and dedicated to the
American tradition that every man, despite the hideousness of
his crime, is entitled under law to able counsel. The defense
lawyers were Colonel Cassius M. Dowell of the Regular Army,
and Colonel Kenneth C. Royall, a temporary officer in the
Army.

Military trials are notoriously efficient, necessarily so to
maintain discipline. Such a procedure was accepted by the public, who felt that any treatment was too good for the Germans.
The press generally was favorable but complained bitterly
against the secrecy; and the fuming was abetted by Hoosier-
voiced long-time radio commentator Elmer Davis, less than a
month on the job as head of the Office of War Information (an
agency which vigorously recruited Washington's already dwindling reporter ranks). Davis believed that OWI should report the
trial with copy screened by the military. The proposal provoked
a personal row with Stimson in which Roosevelt had to inter-
vene. But Davis and the press won a half-loaf of concession: The
commission agreed to issue daily communiqués. As it turned
out, the press might as well have said, We'd rather have nothing.
For nothing was what they got. The public, through the press
and radio, learned the hours of opening and closing of sessions.
Witnesses were heard, but were not named. From a trial reaching into Constitutional law and loaded with drama, one communiqué related that "George Washington, an attorney on the
staff of Assistant Solicitor General Oscar Cox, of the

Department of Justice, is the First President's nearest living collateral descendant."

Another concession yielded as much. A dozen reporters were shepherded into the chamber of the Justice Department Building with freedom to write what they saw. They saw a room about 20x100 feet; heavy curtains; the judges; the lawyers; the prisoners; a few witnesses, and various prosecution exhibits. Over all hung a funereal silence, and a deadline. Only fifteen minutes were allowed for the coverage. The failure to give information had the inevitable effect—the reporters began digging. And Thomas F. Reynolds of the *Chicago Sun* came up with the Coast Guard's confrontation with Dasch on the beach, and a little of the aftermath.

On the opening day the prisoners, now under military custody, were taken from individual cells at the jail and placed in two covered black vans for transport to the Justice Department Building. FBI agents led the procession, peering from their automobiles; and behind them two machine guns poked from an Army scout car toward the vans where the saboteurs sat—all of them but Dasch and Burger knowing little. The troops manning the guns wore steel helmets and looked at the vans rather than at the streets. These troops were reinforced by soldiers in back of them holding Tommy guns. The vans rolled with a rhythm suggesting the smoothness of Washington's famed sightseeing buses. A soldier rode the rear platform of each van. The crowd stared at the procession.

It was just before 9 A.M., and the heat could be felt on the sidewalks. People were entering the neighboring buildings for work; others were hurrying into the dining room of the Willard Hotel farther down the Avenue for breakfast; and many in the Press Club were already eating breakfast. Hundreds of people in the street didn't know what the procession meant, because Washington was always one procession after another. But somebody shouted, "There go the spies," and the crowds chased after the vans.

Inside the tightly-guarded chamber the witnesses swore not to relate what had occurred "until released from your obligation by proper authority." The events of the eighteen-day trial went undisclosed for some eighteen years. The transcript filled about three thousand pages.

There were moments of drama. Coast Guardsman Cullen confronted Nazi Dasch (or was he a Nazi, if his claim could be believed?). Cullen, the first witness, answered Biddle's questions as relaxed as though talking to the boys at his station.

"I think so, sir," he replied when asked if he recognized the man in the court who had emerged from the Amagansett fog. Upon request, he stood and pointed toward Dasch. Then Cullen asked a question: "Would he mind saying a few words?" He wanted to hear the voice that had broken the quiet that night. Dasch said, "What is your name?" The betrayer of the plot was cooperating. Cullen spoke to Biddle: "Yes, sir." The attorney general asked, "What do you mean by 'Yes, sir'?" Cullen replied, "That's the man."

Dasch stood upon his only tenable ground: He had gone to the FBI to reveal the plot. Foolish and insensitive though he was, it may have finally crossed his mind that he was as guilty of plotting against the United States as any of the three who came in with him. So in his testimony (the record would show) he rambled uncertainly.

As a student of the trial later wrote, "The result was foreseeable to all but Dasch; he gave the impression of protesting too much."

Biddle struck into Dasch with the question, "Why didn't you go right away to the FBI?" Dasch wanted to give three reasons. " . . . first of all I was a mental and nervous wreck. I was so glad that I was here. And, second of all, I had to be human, and that is mainly—I had to be human." Biddle pressed him for the third reason, and he started rambling again. "Just one second," Dasch said. "Why I had to be human—I have got to explain that to the commission. I knew why I came. I studied every other possible one to find out a reason why they came here. I knew this boy—what's his name here?" He was told the name was Burger. "Burger," Dasch picked up, "why he came here—but I wasn't quite sure why this little kid Haupt came here, a boy who has remained in Germany only four or five months, who had his mother here and had lived here in America. I didn't know why he came here. I could not at any time run to the police and at the same time take this chance away from the kid to prove why he came here. That would have been merely for the sake of my own self-protection. That would have been the rottenest thing in the world. To be a real decent person I had to wait. I had to give every person a chance to say what I had to say. That's the reason."

Burger said he was disillusioned with the Nazi Party, had wanted to return to the United States by legal means. The submarines were an opportunity. Any other leavetaking would have brought trouble on his family in Germany. And, lastly, Dasch, who was his leader, had originated the plan to summon the FBI. The commission drew from Burger the statement that Kappe had advised each saboteur that, in one sense, he was on his own. "Do you remember," McCoy asked, "whether or not Kappe told you to confess in case one or all of you were caught?" The reply was quick: "No, sir. On the contrary, in case anyone got caught we were not to tell anything. . . . That was understood from the beginning."

Millions of persons had been moved by the solemnity of the Supreme Court Building. Man reaching for majesty in expression had perhaps achieved it in the high-columned pile of white and shadowy marbles from many lands, manifesting the great law it shelters. No one thought of the material cost which had reached $9,740,000, but rather felt the symbol and basic belief that liberty exists best under law. The building stands to the east of the Capitol grounds, and in the middle 1930's one of the Justices had observed to Harlan Fiske Stone, as they studied the rising magnificence, that the Justices in their robes would resemble nine black beetles in the Temple of Karnak. Stone, who previously had demonstrated a near ferocity while cleaning out the mess in the Department of Justice when he was attorney general, wryly suggested that they place the Chief Justice astride an elephant and move in Oriental procession to the grand opening.

Now, in the oppression of the Washington summer, the Court was in adjournment, with the Justices scattered across the land—Douglas, indeed, as distant as Oregon. But they were hastening to Washington for the rare exercise of a special session, a coup accomplished by Defense Counsel Royall. The Court would decide whether the commission trial was constitutional and whether the President was empowered to deny the defendants a hearing in civil court. Royall relied upon an 1866 precedent that a civilian could be tried by the military only when martial law prevailed or civil courts lay in disbandment.

The date was set for Wednesday, July 29. One Washington correspondent viewed the defendants as "merely guinea pigs in a great laboratory of jurisprudence." With the word out, Washingtonians foresaw drama in the making. For Royall and Dowell, it was an exercise in faith. Letters came from lawyers complimenting them on fulfilling the ethic of defending—and so skillfully—defendants so hated.

The session would open at noon, but people gathered at 9 A.M., and the chamber's capacity of three hundred was quickly filled. Then the big letdown came: The defendants did not appear. Most of the crowd drifted away.

The arguments continued for two days. Then the decision came in two typewritten pages: "The court holds that the charges preferred against petitioners . . . allege an offense or offenses which the President is authorized to order tried before a military commission. That the military commission was lawfully constituted. That petitioners are held in lawful custody for trial before the military commission and have not shown cause for being discharged by writ of *habeas corpus*. The motions for leave to file petitions for writs of *habeas corpus* are denied."

Royall said only, "The Supreme Court has spoken." Biddle was noticeably pleased. The bronze doors of the Supreme Court Building closed. Next day the war workers talked about what had happened. The last few days of the commission trial ground along. And when it was finished the report was sent to the President, who would say only that he had a report and a verdict.

But what kind of execution? The newspapers wondered, and the people guessed. The President, resorting to seersucker trousers in the heat, told a conference that he was "reviewing the evidence." In the end, the reporters learned that the Attorney General, the Judge Advocate General of the Army, and the Commission had agreed that, though guilty, Dasch's and Burger's lives should be spared by Presidential commutation. And the President had approved the commission's view that death should come for the others by electrocution. Burger would be imprisoned for life, and Dasch would serve thirty years at hard labor. For the condemned six, Roosevelt desired death by hanging, and he was determined to withhold word of the execution hour to keep crowds away from the jail.

How Haupt, Thiel, Quirin, Heinck, Neubauer, and Kerling spent their last hours was unknown to the newsmen who watched the prison for any signs—especially the dimming of lights in the execution wing. A dimming, they understood, would indicate that the chair was being used. A small crowd gathered, and among them were a British sailor and three United States soldiers who asked to serve as a firing squad "to save the government some money on electricity."

On the early gloomy morning of Saturday, August 8, military officials, Army doctors, the city coroner, Army ambulances, and a chaplain arrived, moving quickly and saying nothing. At the White House, Steve Early kept saying, "There is still no news for you."

But it had leaked that the six Germans had eaten bacon, scrambled eggs, and toast at a 7 A.M. breakfast. At noon while a practice air raid siren blew, the first man went to the chair. No one was told the order in which the names fell into the slot of death, but each execution required fourteen minutes.

The six were buried in Washington's potter's field. The capital forgot very soon. Nothing was remembered long in August 1942 except that faraway islands with little-known names were under attack, and more and more words spread in neighborhoods that a boy so well liked by everybody was wounded, or killed.

Only the cold stars on clear nights lingered on the six graves, and by day the scorch of August sun.

CHAPTER TWELVE

INTO THE BREACH

FRANKLIN D. ROOSEVELT bore upon his afflicted body and harassed mind the most appalling burdens that any war President had ever carried, with the exception of Abraham Lincoln. He had entered office in 1933 when the nation seemed to be falling into a bottomless pit, when men out of work sold apples on corners, and when the cruel joke went around about stock market suicides: "My father was wiped out of business in the Wall Street crash; someone jumped from a 15th floor window and landed on his pushcart." The Duchess County aristocrat had come to office on a wave of national discontent deepening into despair, and used his finest gift, his vocal cords, to quiet the people. Assuring them that there was nothing to fear but fear itself (and the hell there wasn't) he proposed a New Deal—all in one speech, widely said to have been a collaboration of Roosevelt, Judge Rosenman, and the skilled political publicist, Charley Mickelson. The New Deal was a revolutionary method of putting people to work and spreading money. But as in every revolution, including the Colonies' revolt against England, there arose a wide opposition, and in Roosevelt's revolution it lay mainly among industrialists and conservative advocates of the old order. They complained that the nation was in transformation toward socialism, that nothing really had been done to adjust the economy, that the jobs provided by such agencies as the National Youth Administration and the Civilian Conservation Corps, and the writers', dramatists', and artists' projects were boondoggles financed entirely from teetering public funds. And worse yet, the dissenters complained that woolly-haired professors and others who had never met a payroll were theorists at best and communists at worst, weaving their schemes in cloisters by night, schemes built on the basis of tax and tax, spend and spend, elect and elect. There was no middle ground for divided public opinion.

There was one man weaving through Democratic politics with a firm opinion about the whole thing. He was Bob Hannegan of St. Louis who believed there was only one judgment day—that of Election Day. A wartime chairman of the Democratic National Committee, he was a strongly-built man with an easy smile and an old gaslight-era notion about elections. The only way to win one was by knocking on doors down at the precinct level. So what now in 1942 caused all the controversy to continue? There had been three judgment days in 1932, 1936, and 1940, when the President had won an unprecedented third term.

But the schism would not close, and to compound his troubles, Roosevelt in 1942 and before had been compelled by the war's exigencies to bring to Washington phalanxes of industrial executives "drafted" from the very top of the forces which most bitterly opposed his liberal policies. These men never abandoned the opinion that while the war would crush Nazi and Japanese aggression, the victory would in no wise halt the designs of the New Deal. A war of blood would be won; that of ideology lost.

"This war cannot possibly be won—ever—and may be irrevocably lost this year unless there is an immediate and extremely far-reaching reversal of policy and direction by our government," Thomas J. Wallner, president of the Southern States Industrial Council, had growled in March 1942. Enlarging the outward expression of his inner conviction, Wallner said, "America is losing the war for one fundamental reason and only one; our government . . . still stubbornly persists in the attempt simultaneously to fight a foreign war and wage an internal economic revolution—and wars are not, never were, and never can be won that way."

To make matters worse, the *Baltimore Sun* probed into neglected corners of the New Deal and found ten thousand machines and other hardware stored in 124 National Youth Administration training centers, materiel it claimed was needed for men in the Pacific theater or the war effort at home. Here was something unanswerable—a wasteful overlapping of the boondoggles into the crisis of national survival. Senator Kenneth McKellar of Tennessee, a competent man who would look at a dawn twice before believing the Bible's assertion that the sun also rises, drummed in his aides and drafted legislation to abolish the NYA and the Civilian Conservation Corps to boot. But a nerve was touched: the so-called boondoggles, which few expected or desired to last forever, had lifted the lives and spirits of thousands of young people. And at the very moment of the disclosure, thousands of these previously dispirited youths, drawn from idleness on city streets and in desolate small towns to toughen their muscles and gain a new grab on life, were competent members of the armed services. Was the nation now to ignore itself within while saving itself from without? The assault brought out busy union executive Sidney Hillman, who was already overwhelmed by the need to find trained factory workers—an area in which the NYA had been useful. And it cost the precious time of Donald Nelson, striving to allocate needed materiel both to the armed services and industries serving the war. They satisfactorily explained to Congress that the machines in question were usable in basic training but were outmoded for the requirements of the moment. Moreover, the defense authorities had encouraged the training of young men for specialized industry through the NYA. There had to be somebody at home to supply the fighting men.

There were other irritating disturbances. One of these affected an Indianian by birth, once described as "a slim, trim-rigged, facile, quiet-spoken gentleman," named Lowell Mellett, who was accused of being Roosevelt's propagandist.

The correspondents at White House press conferences did look at him and wonder if he was really happy in his abnormal role as one of perhaps a half-dozen men closest to the decisions of the President. They saw him obviously attempting to obscure himself at the conferences; but he was noticeable there sitting in the background at the edge of a green velvet couch a few feet from the President's desk. This was a long way from the smell of printer's ink Mellett first had inhaled in Indiana. No man in Washington had a more respected newspaper background. He was a good writer as well as a fine reporter. In World War I, Mellett had been a correspondent with the United States, French, and British armies, and in 1921 became editor of the *Washington Daily News*—a newspaper renowned locally for its exposés and which saw the talent in Ernie Pyle when the later great war writer was scarcely known in Washington.

Then Mellett had entered the war effort. He headed the bureau of motion pictures in the Office of War Information and also became director of the Office of Government Reports, making handy to federal officials pertinent newspaper and magazine opinions. He also became embroiled in one of Washington's endless controversies.

Who initiated original ideas in Washington was generally hard to pin down. They might come from an underling, fresh back from lunch, full of martinis and inspiration. Or they might be the product of casual words dropped during conferences. At any rate, someone had noticed a triangular spread of grass between the Willard Hotel at 14th Street and the Avenue, the Commerce Department to the south, and the equestrian statue of General William Tecumseh Sherman to the west. The greensward was a lovely emerald in summer, but the observer felt it should be employed for the purposes of war.

Untold thousands of businessmen were coming to Washington for urgent reasons relating to the war and had no idea whom they should see or where they should go in the capital's crazy-house maze of building corridors, or in the miles of temporary structures. (This now seems incredible. Any businessman worth the title should, through advance correspondence,

have established his contact and the location.) So an information center was placed in the triangle, an ugly brownish-gray
frame structure fronting on the Avenue. But nothing could
retain its original function in Washington. Men whose jobs
elsewhere were endangered by the information center soon used
the establishment as a general information outlet. And the
operation, being under Mellett, soon brought complaints that
here was another flambeau lighting the philosophies of Roosevelt socialism. Worse, the twisting hallways smelling of plywood
and floor soap were pockmarked by large and small offices
staffed with question-answerers from the Civil Service Commission, the Department of Commerce, the Treasury Department,
OPA, WPB, and other alphabetical agencies not only incom-
prehensible to the outsider but growing so rapidly and
displacing one another with such abandon that even their own
staffs hardly got to know some of them. Typewriters clattered
amid babbles of voices, and it was never easy for one to find
where he wanted to go in this source of information itself.

One man brought the enterprise into its original disrepute.
The office of Alexander F. Jones, managing editor of the *Post*
was on the southwest side of his building. The hammering and
banging by carpenters erecting the information center had
disturbed Jones' never-placid nerves, and, in any case, he
believed the project was a piece of foolishness. One day, in
anger, he wrote a tirade with a headline, "Mellett's Madhouse,"
and spread it on the front page. The name stuck; and people
thereafter said they were going to "the Madhouse" as auto-
matically as they might have referred to so unoffending a place
as the Bureau of Fisheries. But the center was heavily used, as
was everything that had a door that would open.

Mellett was not the only member of Roosevelt's intimate
circle to come under attack. The critics next turned their fire on
Harry Hopkins, and on the unlikely occasion of his marriage to
Louise Macy, thirty-six, socialite on the east coast, the west
coast, and abroad, and a brunettish demure-faced Madison
Avenue ideal of glowing health. She had, indeed, once posed for

a recruiting poster for civilian defense, and had sponsored fashion-showings. Weeks before the wedding, word of the impending marriage had monopolized the circles of society in which Hopkins moved (perhaps the diplomatic and upper-level official set), and nearly everyone wondered why in his declining state of health he would combine the rigors of wedlock with the exertions demanded by the war and internal politics. The fifty-one-year-old Hopkins was shown in a photograph seated beside Miss Macy on a sofa; the face was a whitened mask of drawn flesh, and the fixed stare in the eyes reflected a detachment from life. Perhaps the cameraman had caught him at the wrong emotional moment, for there was a great difference between this Hopkins and the man Washington had known for so long. The earlier pictures showed a slicked-down curve of dark hair; a wide, high, and unwrinkled forehead; eyes blazing in a look toward something attainable; firm cheeks, and an upthrust chin.

By 1942, Hopkins had almost worked himself to death. But he had created a legend, not only as a devious opportunist or a great man, according to the point of view, but in all truth as a devil-may-care fellow. He was familiar at race tracks, and Roosevelt's enemies nicknamed him "Horseyard Harry." Brilliant parties enchanted him, especially when these were attended by witty, gay, and talented people of renown. He posed for all to see a tormenting contradiction of purpose: His fame rested, aside from his intimacy with the Roosevelts, upon his dedication to the New Deal, the underprivileged, the Forgotten Man. But he loved equally well the lavish life, and thus his sincerity was questioned. It was easy to see the empathy with Roosevelt because they seemed of a similar pattern, with the exception that Roosevelt was to the manor born while Hopkins was one of five children of a humble Sioux City, Iowa, harness maker—an honorable origin he stubbornly refused to ignore or stop harping upon, to everyone's annoyance. He was perplexed (or so he claimed) that he could have come all this way. He had come by way of Roosevelt, whom he had casually met while the two were campaigning for Al Smith for President. And he later would serve Roosevelt as a social worker in New York State. Hopkins, simply put, had hung on, to emerge importantly into the New Deal.

And when he was married, on July 30, 1942, in the White House, the President served as best man. Witnessing the ceremony as gathered in the sight of God and man at noon in the Oval Study were Mrs. Roosevelt, and the groom's and the bride's immediate families. Also present were General Marshall, Admiral King, Sam Rosenman, and Robert Sherwood. The Reverend Russell Clinchy had come from Hartford, Connecticut, to perform the ceremony. Then the bridal couple disappeared.

But even in so joyous a time, the Hopkins-haters would not lie still. Soon, from Capitol Hill came a complaint that the honeymooners were cruising on the Great Lakes aboard a yacht which a wealthy Michigander had turned over to the Navy, but which had never been converted because of its immediate need by Hopkins for pleasure purposes. Someone elaborated on the story by adding that the yacht actually had been in use by its owner off New London, Connecticut, when the Coast Guard climbed aboard, chased off the owner and his family, and ensconced Mr. and Mrs. Hopkins in the vessel. Before the unexciting truth was discovered, the Secretary of the Navy, high Coast Guard officials, and the FBI spent uncounted hours tracing the transactions of the yacht's sale to the Coast Guard, its whereabouts at the time of the fuss—it was on Coast Guard business—and the location of Mr. and Mrs. Hopkins during the period.

Less than two weeks after their departure, the couple returned to Washington, with pleasant memories of a honeymoon on a small Connecticut farm. But precious time had been wasted by valuable men in Washington.

Roosevelt remained outwardly unaffected by the furor. He appeared to have a facility for ignoring or smiling off little and sometimes big complaints. He differed, fortunately, from Lincoln in that when Roosevelt went to bed at night he went to sleep. Lincoln had paced the floor and brooded in the shadows, and sometimes had had bad dreams of a shapeless ship speeding toward a shapeless shore. Roosevelt read detective stories and watched the newspapers for little things which many may have regarded as trivia. Once he sent to the *Washington Post* for several copies of an issue which carried the headline, "F.D.R. Takes to Bed with Co-Ed," while "cold" of course was meant. He wanted to send a copy to Churchill.

Scholars, political scientists, sociologists, and psychiatrists have had their say about Roosevelt, and some have said that he had a thick skin, while others believe that he was hypersensitive. Certainly, human foibles did not appear to bother him. He must have been aware that lovely Lafayette Park in front of the Executive Mansion was a national convention center for homosexuals. There is no record of any comment on it. He could shrug off everything except the war.

CHAPTER THIRTEEN

WOMEN GO TO WAR

OVETA CULP HOBBY, an important name in the big state of Texas, was scarcely noticed when she arrived in Washington during July 1941 as a dollar-a-year public relations executive in the War Department. But it would not be long before she became a household word and a uniformed lady for thousands to march behind with a swing of arms quite unfeminine—though any marching actually done by Mrs. Hobby would have been scarcely enough to bother her purported varicose veins. The role of commander of the Women's Auxiliary Army Corps (WAAC) seemed particularly appropriate to Major Hobby, or Mrs. Hobby as the civilians for some reason persistently called her, because she had commanded every environment and circumstance she had graced since childhood. No one believed she would be a mother to her army, simply because running a military establishment is a business, and Oveta Hobby's orientation came from a man's world. And if she herself could meet the rigorous demands of high standards, the same self-discipline and adaptability would be demanded of her skirted soldiers.

General Marshall had spotted her while she was working as head of the War Department's Women's Interest Section. The General knew her background. She was born in Killeen, Texas (population less than three hundred) January 19, 1905, the second of seven children, and when she reached fame, the people naturally began remembering little things about her. Oddly, she hadn't liked games, but whenever she did join in, she won. She played to win by the use of her brains rather than by strength or fleetness of limb. She was slight of build, solemn, moody, and studious. She showed an early interest in politics, law, and the actions of men in public life, which was curious in a girl of fourteeen. She had packed up and followed her father to Austin upon his election to the Legislature in 1919.

Oveta appeared to relish the sometimes tiresome complexities of law. She studied law at the University of Texas; served as parliamentarian of the Legislature at the age of twenty, then as an assistant city attorney in Houston; and later wrote a book, *Mr. Chairman*, concerning parliamentary law. The book was successful. She wrote as she had played in childhood—to win.

In 1931, she had married William Pettus Hobby, governor of Texas and publisher of the *Houston Post*. She was a pretty young woman and conscious of it, as shown in her finicky selection of hats, hairdos, and almost frivolous attire, all outward adornments concealing a firmness and drive amounting to an obsession. Her husband greatly admired her brainpower, remarking once in Texas homespun language that "anyone with as many ideas as you have is bound to hit a good one now and then." She threw her ideas at the newspaper, moving from literary critic to associate editor and executive vice president, a position which empowered her, as was remarked on the premises, to do what she was going to do anyway. Formats were changed, and she concentrated, with an insight into women which few knew she possessed, on the women's departments. She wanted women handling women's news, asserting, that "sometimes a man's nose gets out of joint on women's news."

She must have felt well at home in Washington. The capital at war had so many different sides, and so did she. Her marriage prospered. Someone had once asked her how such a hectic career and a fine home life could possibly blend. She gave the answer in Houston, but wherever it might have come from it was true to her nature: "It is not so difficult to combine matrimony and a career in a small city like Houston. I can reach home in fifteen minutes and always have lunch with my little boy when he comes from school."

She was appointed commander of the WAACs in September 1941, when Marshall asked her to blueprint the plans. On March 17, 1942, Representative Edith Nourse Rogers of Massachusetts presented a bill to create the organization, which passed the House, and on May 12, the Senate favored it by 38 to 27. Three days later, the elongated signature of Roosevelt was added.

Everybody was pleased. *Time* said, "Since last August she [Mrs. Hobby] filled the job (WIS) so ably that there was never much doubt she would get the WAAC post." Secretary Stimson brightened his face to swear her in on May 16 with the rank of major; and along with the gold oak leaf insignia she would receive $3,000 in salary and perquisites. Her husband watched the ceremony with a studied expression, causing George Dixon of the *New York Daily News* to write, "If ever a man looked as if he was saying to himself what-the-hell-am-I-doing-here? it was Mr. Hobby."

The War Department knew what it had done. It wanted a clean house of combat-fit soldiers presently drumming typewriters, baking bread, operating switchboards, and shuffling papers; indeed the generals listed 54 jobs the women could perform. The rest required imagination and thought, to Major Hobby.

There was a bothersome rule against pregnancy for unmarried women soldiers; the infraction brought a dishonorable discharge. But Major Hobby, skilled from her legal training in finding loopholes, argued that male soldiers should come under a parallel punishment. This proposal caused the generals great pain, because getting some woman in trouble had traditionally been one of those little personal problems the gal would have to solve. And it was unbecoming in officers and gentlemen to intrude too deeply into a lady's privacy—unless, of course, a Congressman, who seldom meant it, wrote in asking for an investigation. So Major Hobby's decision that the unfortunate WAAC should be released without stigma prevailed.

Nothing seemed to ruffle Mrs. Hobby, not even her first press conference. There was nothing deadlier than a Washington wartime press conference with women reporters interviewing a woman about other women. Through some mysterious feminine motivation, their backs were up and their claws extended. What, they asked, would Major Hobby do about WAAC make-up, nail polish, girdles? Could married enlistees have babies? Could WAAC enlistees date army officers? Could WAAC officers date army enlistees? It would appear that Mrs. Hobby had been commissioned solely to operate a love nest. And there were not precedents for her to pattern her answers on. Mrs Hobby replied that in all matters the traditions of the army would be relied upon. "In the Army, I believe, the fraternizing of officers with enlisted personnel is frowned upon," she said, and not in a Texas drawl, which she had trained herself to eliminate from her speech. She had no objection to inconspicuous make-up. The age limits of the women would be twenty-one to forty-five, inclusive, and the criteria would be character, personality, appearance, bearing, and adaptibility.

Then came one heavily-loaded question: What about Negroes in the WAAC? Mrs. Hobby, a southerner, replied that they would be recruited in proportion to their numbers in the population. Consequently, of the 450 candidates chosen for officer training at Fort Des Moines, Iowa, 40 were Negroes. The first group of commissions was awarded in September 1942, after two months of training.

Later on, the uniformed women contributed a briskness as they strode evenings in pairs or groups among the work-slouched civilians on the streets and in the parks. The WAACs had a model to imitate—the impeccable Major Hobby. An outside designer had dreamed up the WAAC uniform. (There was a widely held belief that Major Hobby had stood over the designer. A former WAAC officer who trained at Fort Des Moines now says: "Put it this way. If *you* were the commander of the WAAC and very clothes-conscious, what would you have done?" It was evidence enough that Major Hobby "had more than a hand in the design.")

What the women liked best about the uniform was the WAAC cap. It was made of dark olive-drab covert cloth, with semi-stiff visor and crown, and a soft chin strap. There was a bright eagle insignia of gold coloring for officers; a brass disc for enlisted women. Major Hobby, of course, wore such a cap, and it so became her that it was known throughout the ranks by her name. For example, a WAAC hurrying into dress might exclaim, "Now, where is my Hobby cap?" (The cap was worn less as the war progressed and the so-called overseas cap became popular. Some years later a surplus-goods entrepreneur in Chicago bought the Hobby caps by the thousands and sold them to African natives who, besides liking their flair, found the visor helpful against the sun.)

The WAAC winter uniform for officers was of dark olive-drab covert cloth. The jacket was single-breasted, with four bright buttons. There were three-inch shoulder straps, and a six-gored flared skirt in both light and dark drab. The same olive-drab colors worn by army enlisted men were issued the enlistees. The officers' summer uniforms were of gabardine or cotton twill in khaki coloring. Enlistees wore water-repellent cotton twill in hot weather. Hosiery varied: rayon stockings for dress occasions, mercerized cotton lisle for utility. The shade uniformly was suntan. Khaki-colored cotton anklets were issued.

All of this was accepted, despite the feminine notion about individualized clothing. But the shoes were a sore spot. The issue were oxfords in golden-brown calfskin for dress wear, and the better known athletic oxfords made of white canvas with black soles. Despite the Major's discipline, some of the WAACs owned contraband shoes and would wear them for a mere moment's satisfaction when out of sight of their superiors. Major Hobby herself sometimes improvised in her attire. (One former WAAC recalls the commander debarking from an airplane wearing a fetching yellow scarf. Innocently, the onlookers tried to follow the mode but soon learned they couldn't.)

Mrs. Hobby's personality was never clearly defined. While the war and all the complexities of Washington confounded most

people's memories for names, the very sight of a WAAC on the
street brought Major Hobby's name to mind. She was a center
of interest. The newspapers dwelt upon her, relating her career
from childhood on. The reasons for the attention were obscure.
The world is full of serious little girls and even frivolous little
girls who became important; there was nothing extraordinary in
this respect about Mrs. Hobby. And there was another curious
aspect: attention ordinarily focuses on the "personality" men
and women. Mrs. Roosevelt, for instance, could capture
attention anywhere; and there was "Hap" Arnold of the Air
Force; Bernard Baruch (an alluring personality even in his
quietudes), and Tommy "The Cork" Corcoran of the old New
Deal circle, still strongly remembered though he had largely
withdrawn from public view by this time. Nor is there evidence
that Mrs. Hobby, a pusher by nature, ever sought or desired to
assume importance in the capital's status structure, though she
was showered with invitations as a person having everything—
status back home, rank in Washington, and wealth to boot. One
answer may be that she was pioneering and visibly succeeding in
an experiment that many had believed could never reach an
enduring fruition. The very idea of a women's army had been
resisted just as the notion of women's suffrage a half century
and longer before. A basic objection was the individuality of
women. If they didn't openly defy uniformity of dress and
orders, they would at least simply go through the motions.
Obviously, that view was not shared by General Marshall or Mrs.
Hobby, who was convinced that (1) women should replace men
in non-combat duties; (2) carefully selected women could
perform the non-combatant duties, and, if necessary, fight, and
(3) women could be as disciplined as men, and, more, exhibit an
esprit de corps equalling any the Army could display. She never
had any intention of mothering the WAACs. A civilian woman
recently said, hesitantly, "Somehow . . . she seemed like a
martinet." Another, who had served closely with Mrs. Hobby in
uniform, disagreed. "She did the almost impossible. She took
thousands of women from every stratum of society and instilled
in them a pride that goes on to this day . . . goes on into a

tradition. She was nothing like a martinet. She simply lived by the book."

She once expressed a view of herself and her scattered interests—army, home, and personal business. She was keeping an "eagle eye" on "what's going on back in Houston." But "I'm giving up all other responsibilities to concentrate on the WAAC." Many of her army perhaps never saw her. They had only heard that she was an attractive woman, rather small with prematurely graying hair and a fairly quick smile when everything was going right. She was liked by photographers. She asked them not to take her picture smiling because it would detract from the seriousness of her image.

By December 1942, her army would total 10,000, and it was estimated that it would reach 56,000 by July 1943, with a maximum of 150,000 in 1944. The women would serve nearly everywhere the Army went, and endure the discomforts and some of the dangers. One of them would say later: the service toughened them to life when life, otherwise, might have destroyed many of them. A wide sampling was interviewed, and the moment the word WAAC was spoken a pride came into the voice precisely the same as a marine's when the Corps was mentioned. Mrs. Hobby had gone beyond "the book," to reach for the spirit. There was something rare about Mrs. Hobby, or else she had an extraordinary collection of women to mold, and it could have been a little of both.

For her contribution, Colonel Hobby became the first woman to receive the Distinguished Service Medal.

With passing months, Washington streets were a splash of WAAC olive drab, the blue of the Navy WAVES and the Coast Guard SPARS, the olive drab of the Army Air Force WAFS, and the forest green of the Lady Marines, who wore lipstick to match the vivid red of the braid on their caps. These visibly prideful women seemed, on the whole, younger than the WAACs. But their missions were exactly the same.

The dragnet of war reached into odd places to gather materials of the gentlest fibers for its harsh purposes. It swept across the calm of Wellesley, bringing to Washington as Commander of the WAVES the famed institution's seventh president, Mildred Helen McAfee. Lieutenant Commander McAfee, born in Parkville, Missouri, was the product of several generations of educators and could name a few ancestors who fought with Commodore Oliver Hazard Perry in 1812. She liked hockey and baseball and debating and young women who minded their manners and their studies—and while she was commander no radical innovations would be introduced.

In August, 1942, she became head of the Women Appointed for Volunteer Emergency Service, and worked hard with the Bureau of Naval Personnel on plans for the Women's Reserve. As head of the WAVES—sworn in on August 3, 1942—she established hard rules. There would be dates only when on leave; only enough make-up "to look human"; no smoking on the streets, and there would be the same drinking regulations as applied to Navy men (though how this could be defined, God in heaven would only know). She herself neither drank, smoked, nor played cards, though she liked dancing, the movies, and detective stories. Slender, curly-haired, and properly vivacious, she was a popular woman.

But she built a strong organization and ran a tight ship. By mid-May 1944, at Navy headquarters in Washington, almost half of the uniformed personnel were women. The Navy said without embellishment that in one bureau 158 WAVES had filled the jobs of 163 men.

The Lady Marines were a proud lot, chosen with a cold precision. Ruth Cheney Streeter, a tremendously capable woman, commanded 12,023 enlisted personnel and 515 officers. The authorized enrollment would be 18,000 enlisted women and 1,000 officers by July 1, 1944. By December 1943, some fifty percent of the Lady Marines were performing tasks formerly held by men of the Corps. Many of the women served the aviation branch as photographic technicians, aerographers; they operated control towers, packed parachutes, and drove trucks. Lady buglers even released the Marine "field musics" for more dangerous duty. It appeared that Mrs. Hobby's conviction that women could be as able, disciplined, and tightly knit as men when the need arose had been justified.

CHAPTER FOURTEEN

A CALM WITHIN THE STORM

THE FACE OF AMERICA showed that war, a sickening business, was raging. It could smile, but the eyes were concerned. It knew that both life and death were important, and that one had to be endured even in extremity and the other accepted without ignoring the requirements of life. There was no possible escape from the war. It hovered over everything, even expectations, the most uncertain of all things. It even was felt, as hot as an animal's breath, within the close of the Cathedral of St. Peter and St. Paul on Wisconsin Avenue, main thoroughfare leading north from Georgetown, and it came there because the Cathedral wanted to "do its bit," as the inspirational phrase went.

War or no war, it would have radiated the images of men closely identified with battle. It had begun with George Washington. There are paintings of him in prayer at Valley Forge where the snow and the sky and the trees were nature's walls enclosing the national conscience. When the war ended and the farmer-general-President helped plan the capital, he desired a church not for a doctrine or creed but for all to use in service to themselves and the new nation. A long-winded controversy arose over whether a national church might controvene the doctrine of the separation of church and state. But this was resolved when Congress in 1893 created the

Protestant Episcopal Cathedral Foundation for the promotion of religion, education, and charity.

Then came another warrior: fresh from his battles of blood and bluster, Teddy Roosevelt stood as solemnly as he was capable of upon the speakers' stand when the foundation stone was dedicated in 1907. Prominent Washingtonians peeked at him from behind the insurmountable barricades of women's hats. The Gothic structure soon began to form on Mount St. Alban—four hundred feet above the distant Potomac and about as close to the sky as is possible in Washington.

Woodrow Wilson's body was buried within the walls. And in the World War II years he was once again surrounded by uniforms—of soldiers, sailors, airmen, marines, and, strangely, of women. Little had changed. The autumn winds of the 1940's were like the autumn winds of 1917 and 1918, blowing across the crest of Mount St. Alban.

The visitors during these years watched the growing pains of the 14th-century Gothic-style church, bandaged in places with scaffoldings which did not obscure the upheaval of gray stones between the trees like transplants of the cathedrals they had seen in picture books or abroad.

The uniformed men and women felt a peculiar empathy with the Cathedral, the realization of a soldier's desire, especially while in the Holy Spirit Chapel, where candles burned around the clock and men and women came to meditate. But many would never see the late spring Massing of the Colors—a long procession of flags carried by Boy Scouts, Red Cross personnel, veterans' organizations, and others in a fluttering of color moving from the grounds into the building. Periodic special services were held for the various branches of the armed forces. For the Navy came its hymn:

> *"Eternal Father, strong to save,*
> *Whose arm has bound the restless wave,*
> *Who biddest the mighty ocean deep*
> *Its own appointed limits keep;*
> *O hear us when we cry to Thee*
> *For those in peril on the Sea!"*

Everyone felt a warmth of welcome. Though a Protestant Episcopal edifice, the Cathedral belonged to all Americans. In the past, Syrian Orthodox, Russian Orthodox, and Jewish congregations had worshiped there, each in their own manner. An appeal lay in the Cathedral's national purpose and created unexpected relationships. When the United Daughters of the Confederacy announced that they would erect two bays with stained glass windows to the memory of Lee and Jackson, a telegram came from New York: "The decision for Lee Memorial appeals to us as statesmanlike, fraternal and highly desirable. Therefore, a group of damn-Yankees sends $250 to start the ball rolling in a challenge to the sons of Dixie to match contributions." And the British would express their appreciation for the Cathedral's hospitality to its servicemen in Washington.

There stood a statue of Lincoln in prayer, placed just inside the parclose. A Pennsylvanian had seen the war President in precisely that posture in a field near Gettysburg, and the image had come down to the man's sculptor grandson. And just overhead was a symbolic array of state flags. There were exquisite carvings to see—some of church mice done in whimsy. But other carvings showed the heads of fighter pilots, soldiers, sailors, and marines—all created to place twentieth-century heroism in union with the saints in ancient struggle and sacrifice.

Another embattled personage had left his imprint. A prayer had been said at the Cathedral for the well-being of Emperor Haile Selassie, Conquering Lion of Judah and commander of Ethiopia's army, navy and air force, upon his coronation in 1930. Appreciative of this attention, the Emperor had sent an elaborate silver and gold cross. (Selassie visited the Cathedral in May 1954, and saw the cross carried in the processional. Quite unobtrusively, he gave another cross—this one of solid gold—and walked solemnly to the Bishop's Garden and planted a rose bush.)

And over all was God. A visitor one day stared at a stone mason forming a tiny intricate head within a mass of chiselings.

From any distance the head appeared to be minute and unimportant. The visitor asked, "Why do you take such pains on the back of the head? Nobody can see back there."

"God can see back there," the carver explained.

It was all something to see and *feel* and write home about, and to try, if it was possible in God's mercy, to disentangle from the war.

If anyone chose to look, the physical footnotes of wars past could be seen along Wisconsin Avenue on the ride back downtown. Behind a stone abutment stood Mount Alto Hospital for veterans, many still feeling the effect of machine-gun and artillery fire of World War I. It had the gentle appearance of a rest home sheltered by tall trees.

Through the front windows of the streetcars could be seen stores and shops, some four or five stories high, dabs of pastel or merely time-worn faded brick. "This is not a street," a wartime visiting New Yorker exclaimed upon his first sight of the avenue. "It is a painting of a nineteenth-century small-town main street." But the displays of antiques in the shops, the good foods in exclusive grocery stores, the imported tweeds in the haberdasheries—though these things were in scant quantity now—told the reputation of Georgetown. Up the hill during the mid-1860's, Union infantry had marched and artillery clattered toward the forts guarding the capital. Not far westerly from the corner where Wisconsin Avenue joins M Street stood a house where Francis Scott Key—who had never regarded himself as anything more than a jingle composer—had lived. On August 24, 1814, he had participated in the disastrous test between the raw American militia and the British regulars at Bladensburg, Maryland. And on that night he had agonized as the broken remnants of the militia howled and fled past his fashionable home. He had no notion that a short while later he would be aboard a British ship beside other ships bombarding Baltimore's Fort McHenry, and would write the lyrics set to an old British tune which would bring millions of Americans to their feet. Farther along, Washington Circle held a rearing bronze horse with George Washington in uniform sitting capably astride.

And, past that, at 1651 Pennsylvania Avenue, and diagonally across from the White House stood the brick Blair House where Robert E. Lee, a West Pointer, and of the regular service, had respectfully declined on April 18, 1861, the command of the Union army. The house was now used exclusively to accommodate visiting foreign dignitaries.

The Blair House had been a site that Washingtonians for generations had paused beside momentarily because its simple architectural beauty brought a stillness to the setting near the gleaming White House and the architectural confusion of the old State, War, and Navy Building across the Avenue. And there was always something engaging about the antics of the squirrels which appeared to own the house in their proprietary prancings upon the ten stone steps and their settling down upon the narrow entrance way. The house properly belonged in Georgetown or among the remaining fine old homes on Capitol Hill. But that was one of the delights of Washington; however well planned, the capital abounded in seemingly misplaced beauty.

For President Roosevelt the time had come when he could not accommodate the throngs of very important visitors from abroad; the White House from top to bottom was heavily engaged. So the President prevailed upon Congress to buy the Blair House, and by July 1942, it became known as the Chief Guest House of the nation. Some $150,000 was wrenched from Congress for the purchase from the Blair Estate, and for an additional $30,000 the priceless furnishings were acquired. In the dining room was a full set of Lowestoft china of blue and gold pattern impossible to duplicate. If some had feared that royalty and dignitaries might be offended by being routed not to the White House but to a nearby house they were mistaken. The visitors were in Washington on the war's grim business and they wanted privacy and more freedom of movement, furtive or otherwise, than the White House could offer. King Peter of Yugoslavia adored the house. Youthful, he worked hard at finding what he wanted to hear on a radio, and read the comics, favoring "Blondie." King George of Greece was more solemn. And there was the mysterious "Mr. Brown," who aroused wide curiosity until he left and it became known that he was the Russian Molotov.

The balance to be struck was a difficult one: the house had to be elegant and at the same time homey—based, probably, on the correct conclusion by the State Department that kings are human. They were used to palaces; a stay at the Blair House, a slumber in a room called the King's Room with a highboy and fine maple desk and an old four-poster bed, was a rare experience for them.

Blair House had been built by Dr. Joseph Lovell, first surgeon general of the United States, in 1824—27, when the Avenue beyond the doorway was a mudtrack leading to Georgetown, and some of the trees on the White House lawn were young. The name came down from the second owner, politically inclined Francis Preston Blair, a publicist who knew just about everybody and a one-time editor of the *Congressional Globe*. He had acquired the property for $6,500 in 1836, and just before the Civil War the adjoining Blair-Lee House was built for Elizabeth, his only daughter. The Roosevelt Administration took over this property in 1941, and reconditioned it for purposes of state in 1943.

There was a subtle, if overlooked, lesson in all of this. The United States was minding its little domestic matters as though no threat overhung its continued existence. It was really a notice to whom it might concern that the nation was intent upon doing business at the same old stand for a long time to come.

Sixteenth Street was endowed with a personality, a quiet flair and a cultivated beauty. And this was fortunate, because but for the intervention of Lafayette Park, Pennsylvania Avenue, an iron fence and a width of lawn, it would have streamed through the front door of the White House. It was admired because of its aloof composition, and the first thing that knowledgeable people said was "Sixteenth Street? That is . . . or *was* the street of the Embassies." That might have been enough, but not entirely. Streets are not buildings or museums but the people who breathe the spirit into them.

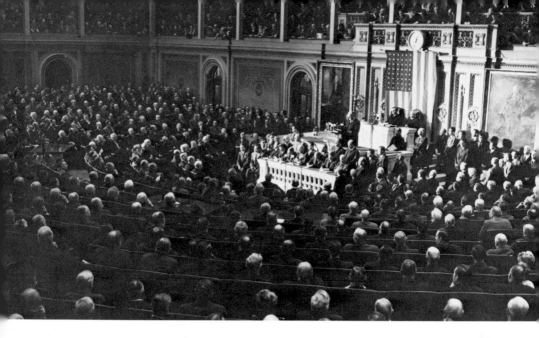

President Roosevelt addressing Congress and the nation on December 8, 1941, the day following the Japanese attack on Pearl Harbor. The President asked the Congress to declare that "a state of war . . . existed between the United States and the Japanese Empire." *(Wide World Photos)*

The Capitol on the night of December 9, when the lights disappeared from the dome. The Capitol remained dark until the surrender of Germany. *(Wide World Photos)*

Mrs. Eleanor Roosevelt, in her role as assistant director of the Office of Civilian Defense, with Miss Mary Beard, American Red Cross Nursing Director, at a luncheon for women defense heads in December, 1941. *(Wide World Photos)*

"The world's largest office building," the Pentagon under construction in March, 1942. The building was completed a month later. *(Wide World Photos)*

President Roosevelt, in an address to the nation on February 12, 1943, from a dinner at the White House Correspondents Association. He declared that "great and decisive actions" would be taken to smash Japan together with "constant and unrelenting pressure" on Germany and Italy. *(Wide World Photos)*

The look of Union Station during wartime—servicemen and civilians waiting patiently for trains, wondering when they will arrive and if there will be room for them when they do. *(Library of Congress)*

The zoot suit on display at the Uline Arena during a Woody Herman Orchestra engagement. Wartime restrictions on cloth dictated the end of the style's two-year career. *(Library of Congress)*

A Southwest Washington resident watching how her victory garden grows. The two stars in the window denote two men in the service. *(Library of Congress)*

The nearly completed Jefferson Memorial as seen through a hole in an ornamental stonework bridge over a nearby canal. *(Wide World Photos)*

Mrs. Oveta Culp Hobby, director of the Women's Army Auxiliary Corps, in the summer officer's uniform of gabardine. Although Mrs. Hobby wore a colonel's eagle on her shoulders, her rank actually corresponded to that of major. *(Wide World Photos)*

Vice President Henry Wallace on his way to the White House to see the President. *(Wide World Photos)*

The flag-draped coffin of President Roosevelt on Delaware Avenue en route to the White House for the funeral services on April 14, 1945. In the background is the Capitol. *(Wide World Photos)*

General Dwight D. Eisenhower, hands clasped in victory, acknowledging the cheers of Washington during his triumphal parade on June 18, 1945. *(Wide World Photos)*

T.Sgt. Jake W. Lindsey, of Lucedale, Mississippi, receiving the Congressional Medal of Honor for heroism in Germany in May, 1945. President Truman looks on while General George C. Marshall reads the official citation. *(U.S. Army Photograph)*

Crowds swarming before the White House on August 14, 1945, the day of the announcement of Japan's surrender. President Truman later addressed the people from the porch. *(Wide World Photos)*

Every President since James Madison had attended historic (it appeared impossible to remove the unnecessary adjective) St. John's Episcopal Church with its six white columns fronting on 16th at H Streets. When Abraham Lincoln arrived in Washington in February 1861, he walked in dark attire into the church to sit for a while. Franklin D. Roosevelt was in frequent attendance and here he was in his class because the church—despite denials—registered a fashionable membership.

Just across the street stood the Hay-Adams Hotel, one of the few remaining places of time-mellowed panelings and polished brass. Few people in Washington knew, until *Reveille in Washington* was published, that on the hotel's approximate site had stood the small home of Mrs. Rose O'Neal Greenhow, dark and stately society leader who scarcely concealed her Southern sympathies and was later jailed as a spy, a hideous appellation which didn't disturb her composure in the least, though it had terrified many Union officers and Congressmen who had talked too freely with her.

A few blocks north stood the Carlton Hotel, distinguished and making no secret of its impressive clientele. Mr. Baruch and Mr. Hull often passed through its lobby, attracting looks but never stares—an impropriety in the Carlton. Across K Street, the new Statler was the rallying place of lobbyists and contract-seekers. And farther up 16th Street was the Soviet Embassy, which rumor held was continually watched from nearby windows. Farther along were red brick dwellings, many transformed into boardinghouses. Nocturnal traipsings about from room to room were regarded as none of the landlord's (generally absentee) business, inasmuch as these gentlemen had not agreed to become the tenants' moral guardians.

As the street climbed beyond R (in the lettered category) it passed an open ground of large dimensions which sloped up from the sidewalk. Set far back on it was a huge and turreted redstone house, awesome to the eye among the surrounding greenery. The house had been built by Senator John B. Henderson of Missouri in 1888, and had become known as "Henderson's Castle," presided over by Mrs. Henderson (née

Mary N. Foote), a lady with a flair for social life, and ever eager for flings at real estate ventures. Under expert architectural guidance, Mrs. Henderson was involved in the construction of about twelve costly residences in the general vicinity of her castle. She had an eye for the housing of foreign embassies and legations. There resulted, among other handsome structures, the former French Embassy of stone at the southwest corner of 16th Street and Kalorama Road; on 15th Street, three buildings fronted upon a park—No. 2401, formerly the Egyptian, Persian, and Nicaraguan Legations. The former Brazilian Embassy stood at 2437, and nearby was the Legation of The Netherlands. And there was the "Pink Palace," just north of Meridian Hill Park near the castle. There was, too, the Spanish Embassy in the immediate vicinity. Mrs. Henderson had tried to sell this building to the U.S. government as a home for Vice Presidents, who resided wherever fancy dictated. Built in 1923, the residence was untenanted until the Spanish government bought it in 1926. Conscious of what she had accomplished, Mrs. Henderson hounded Congress to rename 16th Street the "Avenue of the Presidents," and this came about by Congressional Act of March 4, 1913. But the name was reconsidered and found inappropriate, so the Congress by an Act of July 21, 1914, restored the name to 16th Street. It was all just something to talk about by those who knew a little of the capital's past, while strolling.

Nearby, the hill was ornamented by Hotel 2400, built during an era when the affluent wanted both spaciousness and graciousness in living. The lobby was long, wide, and high-ceilinged, and there were marble stairways wide enough for four people to walk abreast. The larger suites had balconies. A few blocks along, where 16th Street reached a crest, rose the place of worship of the Congregation of Latter Day Saints, a tall edifice of shadowy and color-streaked stone brought block by block from Utah. It was topped by a steeple high and sharp, and upon the steeple was a golden figure with a summoning golden horn.

Here were a few sights for the war workers and for the women in uniform to see and to remember after they had arrived in the capital in large numbers and wandered its by-ways. The women took a great fancy to Meridian Hill Park across the street from Hotel 2400. The park took its name because one of the first stones designating Washington's meridian stood on the line of 16th Street, just north of Florida Avenue. The park slanted downward like an Italian Renaissance garden. The women climbed the high terraces and looked down upon the capital that in the distance was like a picture postcard tourists bought for a dime at the Pennsylvania Avenue novelty shops. Water splashed in controlled downward cascades, and in it the sunlight wove rainbows.

There was a small monument in the park to the memory of President Buchanan who had counted the days when he could flee the White House and leave an inevitable war to somebody named Abraham Lincoln—who seemed to believe that bursts of prose and common sense could quiet the madness in the regions across the river.

The women generally took a long look at the reproduction of the bronze Joan of Arc statue, a work of Paul Dubois. The original stood in Rheims; the one in the park was a gift to the women of America from the *Société des Femmes de France* of New York. Here was the only equestrian statue of a woman in Washington, though that really didn't matter. What mattered was that France had been beaten to the ground, and only the United States could raise her. Some of the women in uniform would scarcely believe that before the war ended they would wander to so remote a place as France.

CHAPTER FIFTEEN

A SMALL WINDOW OPENS

DESPITE FULLER COVERAGE from the war correspondents, after word reached Washington of the North African landings, there remained the hard job of learning all that was safe to print concerning the overall strategy. On November 7, 1942, paratroopers from England led the Allied invasion of French North Africa. American and British soldiers landed on the Mediterranean and Atlantic coasts of the French colonies of Morocco and Algeria, with Lieutenant General Dwight D. Eisenhower in supreme command. Here was one of the turning points in the morale of the capital; although details were lacking, it was a move toward Berlin, and, hopefully, the end. But the problem, which would dog the war, was once more: how much can be told?

The National Press Club card room, the sinking of three United States and one Australian cruisers, and a man named Neely Bull combined to penetrate somewhat the Navy's reticence. The card room was a place where poor members could lose any amount of money to visiting lobbyist-guests, who could draw on heavy expense accounts. Tradition held that the card room had never been inactive, day or night, since the club's founding in 1908 on the top floor of a jewelry store at 1205 F Street, N.W. The sunken United States cruisers were the "Vincennes," "Quincy," and "Astoria;" the "Canberra" was Australian—all victims of a Japanese night assault off Savo Island. The announcement came October 12, 1942, nine weeks after the disaster. Between cerebrations as to which card to play next, the reporters talked about the news suppressions, and Neely Bull listened.

Bull was related by marriage to Admiral Ernest J. King, chief of naval operations, and probably knew more of what was going on than did the others at the table. He certainly knew more about the admiral. Lyle C. Wilson, late chief of Washington's United Press bureau, had written that "King was counted among the roughest skippers in the Navy, whether aboard ship or on his land bridge." He nurtured a strong distaste for reserve officers, and a stronger one for the company of newsmen. (On the other hand, a prominent Washington correspondent says now that "King was really one of the sweetest men who ever lived.") At any rate, Bull told the admiral about the complaints and asked him bluntly if he would hold one secret meeting with selected correspondents. King refused. But Bull hammered away until the admiral gave in.

The first meeting occurred in Bull's home on an unrecorded date in November 1942. There were other meetings, well-spaced; and one correspondent saw the human side of King when he brought out a map that looked like one schoolchildren use, and crouched over it on his knees on the floor—tracing with a finger the island-hopping approach to Japan so widely credited now to MacArthur. (There was one difference: King pointed to Formosa along the distant way.)

The meetings continued in Neely Bull's home until his death, and then were held at the suburban residence of Phelps H. Adams, Washington correspondent of the *New York Sun*. Eventually—and it didn't take him long—King realized what every politician in the capital knew instinctively: the press could be a useful tool not only for "trial balloons" but for bringing to the public a sound viewpoint.

King learned that Roosevelt through bad judgment or worse advice was considering sending General Marshall to a European command, or as an alternative, "elevating" him to global control of the fighting—in essence, diffusing the capabilities of a general of whom Robert Sherwood remarked, "There can be

few people of any allied nation who came in contact with
Marshall during the war who would question the statement
made to him by Secretary Stimson on the day of Germany's
unconditional surrender: 'I have seen a great many soldiers in
my day and you, sir, are the finest soldier I have ever known.' "
Apparently, Admiral King would have concurred. Historically,
he leaped into the breach, bringing for support his new friends
of the press. The Washington correspondents had turned out
not to be devils, after all. And the admiral showed his goodwill
toward them on one occasion by accepting an invitation to a
testimonial dinner. He sat stiffly in uniform beside the white
linen spread, looking straight ahead, and surrounded by such
luminaries of the craft as Folliard and Barney Nover of the *Post*;
Lyle Wilson, and others whom he called friends.

A story, perhaps apocryphal, went the rounds that Marshall
once complained in his polite way that some off-the-record
background given at his conferences had leaked. Soon, it was
said, he complained that his complaint of the leaks had leaked.
Once, certainly, as the war progressed, he told of both the
United States and Russian battle order in the West. He was
quick to add that if the Russians knew of the hint they might
become quite angry, or worse.

The off-the-record conferences had one deep effect: they
largely dispelled the guessing games in which newsmen had
indulged in the early months of the war. The focal point of
these armchair speculations had been the Press Club bar (where
years later it was early decided that Dewey would beat
Truman—a wet conclusion that influenced millions of people
across the nation). The movement of troops flowed with the
thirty-cent bourbon across the bar until a consensus of sorts was
reached, later to be swallowed with ice and stirrer by the public.
And often in the early days of the war there was no agreement
and reams of conflicting views spread outward from the
"interpretive" correspondents. Such loose-jointed guessing may
have influenced both Marshall and King in their attempts to give
background facts. Roosevelt, who held more press conferences
than any other President had ever done, frequently used the

press for his trial balloons, and had no hesitancy in shifting position if the public reacted unfavorably. He was master of repartee at his conferences and with the swiftness of a fencer would dodge with "that is an iffy question." Marshall and King, on the other hand, talked facts.

Few in the crowded capital knew the inner turmoil endured by the upper echelons of the correspondents—not even, entirely, the lower echelons in the newsrooms. Perhaps of all the top ranking generals in the nation's history, Marshall had the clearest understanding that reporters, like himself, had a job to perform within bounds. And yet, allowing for individual opinions, many will contend that King reached the newsmen more deeply. In any case, not a word of his deepest confidences was ever violated.

CHAPTER SIXTEEN

RETREAT INTO WILDLIFE

ON NOVEMBER 10, 1942, EISENHOWER'S forces captured Oran; and word came that Casablanca was entered—all good news. On the heels of this, Hitler's army was ordered to move into unoccupied France and Corsica "to repel a possible American or British landing."

In Washington a brunette war worker thought about the past summer months with its unseasonable heat and abrasive routine. She had been at loose ends, particularly on Sundays, and had wandered the Zoo from the Lion House where the tan beasts shuffled and roared, to the cages where polar bears splashed in pools to keep cool, and other bears, to a command of "stand up" slouched back on their haunches for a payment in peanuts. The girl reflected in her loneliness, "It's surprising how much attention the animals pay to you."

It was scarcely surprising how much attention was given the animals. The National Zoological Park was almost as well known nationally as the Smithsonian and the Washington Monument. Long before the war transformed the park into an off-hours gathering place of service people who merged their regard for animals with needed relaxation, the Zoo was a favorite outing ground of Washingtonians. The 175 acres topped by oaks and pines and slashed by a charging creek, was in the vicinity of the Wardman Park Hotel and easily accessible by streetcar or even on foot, as many of the war workers who were young and strong and penny-conscious chose to move.

Here was an ideal place to muse on beast and bird, to hold picnics on the stout wooden tables under the trees, or merely to walk about unbothered in open courtship.

The Zoo had a peculiar appeal for the new dwellers in the capital. Years before, many had been brought there by their parents from distant places, or had come in visiting school groups, and the memory of certain animals had persisted through the intervening years. They looked all about now for the remembered animals, and sometimes found them and sometimes didn't because of deaths or the exchange of animals from one zoo to another.

To Washington city-side newsmen, the Zoo was a respectable and sought-after "beat." Now, with almost every story some-how related to the war, the birth of a baby lion or the antics of the goats on the twenty-foot-high simulated rock pile became a reminder of Washington's quiet and small-town good old days. The reporters knew where to get the stories. Two officials of the Zoo—neither ever on a newspaper—had marvelous news instincts. One was Dr. William M. Mann, the Director. He was a twinkly person of medium height with a fixed pleasantness on his round face, and his fingers were stained yellow from chain smoking. He gave the impression of being everywhere at once in the Zoo. He had a marked stoop, probably developed from years of hunching forward beside animal cages or looking at ant hills—one of his professional specialties. When he talked, it was crisp and to the point, and he knew more about the animals and birds and ants than they knew about themselves.

The other was a sturdily-built man named Edgar Roy. At forty-three, he was the chief clerk with an eighteen-year service at the park. He knew every time a seal learned a new flip, and often watched the Zoo's births and deaths with feeling. On December 4, 1942, while an edgy new hydrax was under close observation and a baby elk was borning on a hillside, a reporter phoned and was told, "Mr. Roy isn't here any more. He has gone into the Army." Dr. Mann said only, "He was a grand guy; I'm going to miss him like the devil." He was losing many men, but the Zoo had to do its bit, and sometimes in little ways. A 700-pound outmoded bear cage was ripped apart to give iron to the District of Columbia scrap metal drive. But the greatest contribution it made was immeasurable: the pleasure and relaxation it brought to a war town.

The town people took the Zoo for granted, but the servicemen wanted to show their appreciation, which was hard to do in a place with no admission charge. Many of them sought out Dr. Mann to ask what small animals he needed because, hopefully, they might find some in foreign lands and send them to the Zoo. They asked what kind of animals they might encounter on Pacific islands or in Europe. The servicemen weren't alone in asking questions. Representative Bell of Missouri had once inquired if the animals enjoyed seeing people as much as people liked watching the animals.

"Some of them are quite curious about people," the doctor replied. "But try to catch a tiger's eye and see the snooty treatment you get."

The doctor was well prepared for his severest task—maintaining a zoo under war conditions. He had been educated at Staunton Military Academy in Virginia, the State College of Washington, Stanford, and Harvard. If he knew animals as well as he knew people it was because he had known both in their natural habitats. During the mid-1920's, when he became the Zoo director, he prevailed upon Walter P. Chrysler to finance an expedition to Tanganyika to collect giraffes, white-bearded gnus, a long-eared fox, a male kuda, impala, reed buck, hyenas, and wart hogs. After four months, the "City of Calcutta" reached the United States, and photographers' flashbulbs brightened the eyes of the sea-jolted menagerie. He became nationally known as "Mr. Noah," but when the servicemen spoke to him it was never as "Doctor" but invariably as "Sir." Had they felt a familiarity they would really have hounded him for information and stories they couldn't find easily in book.

For example, Dr. and Mrs. Mann (who knowledgeably shared her husband's enthusiasms) occupied a museum-like apartment

on Adams Mill Road, a few blocks from the Zoo. They kept
there for brief stop-overs a baby wart hog, lizards, snakes,
monkeys, two Abyssinian wildcats (which an African fur trader
had given President Roosevelt), a Sumatra tigress, and a baby
lion—all briefly house-handled because of maternal neglect. Dr.
Mann thus relearned an old lesson. Once he handed Mrs. Mann a
lion cub named Susan, nicely wrapped in a candy box. Scarcely
more than a ball of fur at the time, she drank milk every three
hours, grew, and would romp and pull at bedspreads. Here at
last, they felt, was that rarity—a housebroken lion. But when
she was seven weeks old the cub began stalking people. The
belly would move just above the carpet as though the carpet
were jungle undergrowth. Then the testing began. A bone was
tossed and the cub leaped upon it, snarling, and dragged it to a
corner of the room. Susan had crossed the line between
domesticity and savagery. She was placed in a Zoo cage, and
only the Zoo's personnel knew the real Susan.

As in the hotel lobbies, interesting faces appeared, passed,
and were forgotten at the Zoo. Lieutenant Domenico Mortel-
lito, of the Air Force, often wandered the grounds. A native of
Brooklyn, he apprenticed in church murals at the age of nine.
His murals later would be seen in airport lobbies and trains,
Rockefeller Plaza, and one, depicting Noah, in the Zoo
restaurant. Removed by war from his studio in the East Fifties
of New York to the Graphic Presentation Section of the
Statistical Control Division of Air Force headquarters, Mortel-
lito (unlike so many in Washington) described what he did as
drawing up "booklets explaining procedures." He was more
articulate when explaining his love for circuses and animals.

The war created problems for the zookeepers, which were
compounded by the language barrier. It was easy for Roosevelt
and the rationers to explain to the angered victims of Japanese
infamy why coupons were needed for shoes, sugar, coffee, and
gasoline. But it was difficult to inform a giraffe why it could
have no more mimosa leaves and should become content with
hay, apples, and vegetables. The beef shortage was minor,
because for two years horsemeat had been served to many

animals. Most troublesome were those accustomed to tropical fruits and vegetables. Monkeys ate carrots and mixed honey and sweet potatoes instead of bananas—which dropped to fifteen percent of normal supply. The larger apes became the most disagreeable.

Controlled breeding and the use of ersatz foods helped to maintain the National Zoo on its traditional level of excellence, in spite of Dr. Mann's toughest problem—the loss of personnel. And Dr. Mann, unlike the original Noah, had to endure his hardships for longer than forty days and forty nights. But he remained calm. Mann reported to Congress for fiscal year 1943:

> The primary function of the Zoo is to exhibit a wide variety of animal life in the best possible conditions, and in order to accomplish this aim under wartime conditions it was necessary to curtail all phases of maintenance work about the Zoo that could be slighted without harm to the animals. In this way it has been possible to keep the Zoo going in a satisfactory manner in spite of the shortage of manpower, food, and materials incident to wartime.

The report showed that the servicemen had kept their word:

> . . . Conditions have prevented travel by the Zoo personnel for collecting specimens, and the customary array of animals offered for sale by animal dealers has been greatly reduced both in kinds and numbers; therefore, the importance of gifts and deposits is relatively greater than before. The return of members of the armed forces from foreign lands has resulted in a gratifying number of gifts of small animals that have been picked up by these persons as pets or specifically for the Zoo.

The list of donors during the year filled three single-spaced pages of the report, and among them were Señor Dr. Don Francisco Castillo Nàjera, the Mexican Ambassador, who presented a capuchin; the United States Coast Guard, two red foxes, and Senator Claude Pepper of Florida, an alligator. Two polar bear cubs came from the Greenland Administration through Henrik de Kauffman, Envoy Extraordinary and Minister Plenipotentiary for Denmark in Washington. Inevitable philanderings enlivened the Zoo: to the list of hybrids came a baby monkey, the mother a white-faced capuchin, the father probably a brown. And there were neglectful mothers: "Notable among the births was a hybrid gibbon . . . ," Dr. Mann reported to Congress. "The mother discarded the baby after nursing it for a time, and from then on it was raised by hand. At the present time, it is over eleven months old and one of the most popular attractions."

The wartime visitors to the Zoo saw a lot and missed more. There was the head keeper, William Blackburne, a tall man with a leonine face and gentle nature, who kept mostly to himself but would talk when someone asked him questions. His retirement at age eighty-seven before the war ended stunned the park, though he promised to be around in an advisory position.

Blackburne had been with the Zoo for 54 years, and previously had spent a decade with Barnum and Bailey. He remembered making a cage full of big cats do all manner of engaging and dangerous stunts before Queen Victoria when the show toured England. As a member of the Zoo staff, he purchased in 1891 the first lion ever owned by the federal govenment.

The *Washington Daily News* drew from Blackburne his notion of the secret of training animals. An understanding of their personalities was the key, he claimed. "They are just like your friends. Some people you know you wouldn't think of borrowing ten bucks from, while others you wouldn't think twice before putting the bite on them. It is the same with animals."

He liked lions best of all, and was never even scratched by one. Apes are the most intelligent, Blackburne believed, and the deer family the most vicious.

Zoologists are not the great collectors; the years are. Dr. Mann knew this while his young men went to war and his older men retired. The newspapers in his apartment told of war, but all about were his souvenirs of far places and peoples. There was always the low mahogany coffee table with a carved elephant for its base, and the African devil mask on a shelf. And every night, whether the moon was up or down, came the animal voices from the Zoo, drifting through the trees, and from memories in faraway places.

More than occasionally, the sounds were broken momentarily by the cry of "Extra" from the street.

CHAPTER SEVENTEEN

A TAPESTRY OF THE TIMES

THE STARTLING AND HUNGRY cries of "Extra" generally came in the early evening when the tired and often frustrated war worker hoped that he might find a little rest or relaxation in whatever environment he called home. He fumbled for a nickel and went out to get the paper; and whatever the news, the real war stabbed him as the central part of his life and the cause of his own tribulations, which at least for a moment were small when compared to what other men were enduring. But it was impossible even for the skilled propagandists to create a persisting sense of real war. For days on end, many forgot the war. The unaccustomed privations and demands upon their physical and emotional strength dimmed the distant events, all too complex in any case to understand, and, for many, too horrible to think about. They wondered how the soldiers and sailors and airmen could stand it, and the thought hurt because nearly everyone had a brother or son or a close friend out there. They wondered, too, if some form of madness had not invaded the capital. There were curious incidents:

The London Zoo became fearful that a prized seal might be killed in the bombings. So the creature was sent to the Washington Zoo for safety. Someone threw a rock across the fence and into the pool where the seals dived and splashed. The British-owned seal swallowed the rock and died. It was widely said how much better it would have been for the seal to have died at home, a victim of madness from the air instead of from such senselessness as existed in Washington.

At times an uncontrollable devil danced in the capital. Someone stole an army jeep and the Army cried havoc and unleashed its investigators. The vehicle, the newspapers reported, was found by City Detective Sergeant Joseph Sincavity at 18th and E Streets. But where it had been stolen from was classified as a military secret, apparently known only to the Army, the thief, and his cronies.

Ordinarily, little happened around the streetcar barns except the clattering of the cars arriving and departing and the talk of the motormen about the scarcity of rolling stock to accommodate the increasing loads. But as the somber Christmas season neared, a motorman chalked off for the day, entered the barns at East Capitol and 14th Streets around 3 P.M. and boarded a "streamliner" that stood idle on a track. The first indication of surprise came when he started the motor and yelled through the open door, "Hop on folks, the ride's on me." The car moved away; and at every stop its door opened and the same hospitable invitation was extended to waiting passengers. The car picked up speed, zooming through the short tunnel just west of the Senate Office Building. The car's routine destination would have been the turn-about tracks on Mount Pleasant Street, several miles from the barns.

It is impossible to know why anyone would have accepted the ride; but apparently only one person, a woman, finally became suspicious. When the car stopped at 12th Street and Pennsylvania Avenue, famed thoroughfare of inaugural and other parades, and the welcoming cry sounded again, she leaped off and telephoned the police to complain that the motorman was drunk. The transit company, meanwhile, was in full cry, and an inspector stopped the car at 15th Street and New York Avenue, not far from the White House. Some fifteen passengers were told to get out. The motorman was taken to the company's physician, and then brought to the 9th Police Precinct to be booked on a charge of intoxication.

The capital was too much for some inhabitants. A woman

wrote to columnist-counselor Mary Haworth of the *Post* that unless she could get home to the West for a few days she would suffer a nervous breakdown. The Office of Defense Transportation had issued an order to federal agencies to deny Christmas travel leave to employees who lived so distantly that train, plane, or bus must be used. Actually, the order was intended to keep foot-loose pleasure seekers off the carriers so that servicemen on furlough could get home. By the time the distressed woman wrote—early December, 1942—obtaining Pullman accommodations was nearly hopeless. The Baltimore and Ohio Railroad was booked deep into January, and getting plane seats was a dream. Miss Haworth believed the woman could get home because the order was not as stringent as it sounded, and she sternly admonished, "You are getting yourself all worked up for hardly any reason."

Elsewhere in the *Post* it was related that Lieutenant Huntington Thom, USNR, twenty-nine, of 3244 Nebraska Avenue, N.W., son of civic leader Corcoran Thom, president of the American Security and Trust Company, was missing in action in the Solomons. A 1935 graduate of Harvard, he was practicing law when the war began. Here was just another of the too-many-brave-men killed, wounded, or missing. But close to the little news story, a store advertised a "robe n' case for all you football fans." The contraption could be used to protect the body from the cold while the case had a softening effect for the posterior. And the weather, of course, was of acute concern because the lows were dipping into the 30's.

The total impression from the newspapers was that life, and, indeed, the world, operated in two entirely dissimilar ways. There was a war—and yet life was what it always had been. From the front page, a headline told that "U.S. Fliers Sink Jap Warship, Hit Three Others Off Guadalcanal; R.A.F. Leaves Turin in Flames." Meanwhile, inside, theaters pulled hard for attention: *You Were Never Lovelier*, featuring Fred Astaire and Rita Hayworth, at the Earle; *White Cargo*, with Hedy Lamarr and Walter Pidgeon, at Loew's Capitol; Ginger Rogers in *The Major and the Minor* at another downtown house.

The government rationers informed the turkey-hungry capital that pigs' knuckles and sauerkraut, carried over from the 1941 pack, would be plentiful. Readers then turned to the advertisements to learn that a quart of Kentucky bourbon (not the best) could be had for $3.29.

Old-fashioned politics were making a noise. Who would be the nominee in 1944? Mentioned on the Democratic side were Roosevelt, Wallace, Paul McNutt, Jimmy Byrnes, and Douglas, and on the Republican side, Willkie, Dewey, Stassen, Bricker, and Taft. The polls showed Roosevelt and Dewey out in front. And Congress was restive. On December 16, 1942, it adjourned, having been in continuous session longer than any in history. This was front-page news. But turning the pages, Washingtonians learned that Albert de Paris, international hair-stylist, was en route to Washington with Louey Venn of London to glorify the women's hair on the second floor at 1224 Connecticut Avenue. "Monsieur Albert," it was related, "is one of the foremost hair designers on two continents," who as far back as 1936 had created the upswept hairdo.

But the martial spirit, withal, was strong, and the mail carriers felt it. Ambrose O'Connell, First Assistant Postmaster General, while away on a trip composed a poem titled "Carry the Mail," intended to become the postmen's marching song. To get a suitable tune, he recruited the talents of George E. Heisley, Supervisor of the Mechanical Shops in the Post Office Department and director of the Postal Service Orchestra. To Heisley's melody were set O'Connell's lyrics:

> I carry the mail for Uncle Sam,
> I take it through with speed and wham,
> Through rain and snow and gloom of night
> I carry on with all my might.

The entire lyrics when reprinted required nearly a column of newspaper type. When the grand introduction of the March was to be publicly given, the lyricist took off on another trip.

It would be a strange Christmas—more so than the one after Pearl Harbor. That Christmas had been engulfed beyond its

meaning by shock. Now life had settled down, though daily life
could not be disengaged from the war. A somberness rather
than an accelerating joy spread across the capital. Store
windows glittered, but the glitter appeared forced and artificial,
for the sake of making life hold on a little longer for those who
would die and for the others entrapped in the long wait and,
worse, the wondering. And there were Christmas trees, brought
in by nurserymen and farmers from nearby Maryland and
Virginia, but like the store windows they brought little cheer.

The Washington churches and synagogues, without any of the
unctuous moral rectitude that afflicted most divines during the
Civil War and, to an extent during World War I, were concerned
for the war workers and the servicemen, whose welfare was of
greater moment to them than that of their established congregations. With Christmas approaching, churches and synagogues
believed that Washington families should open their homes with
a Christmas dinner for the lonely servicemen.

Robert Tate Allan, church editor of the *Post*, wrote, "Have
you ever stood in a cafeteria line on Christmas Day; or spent a
Christmas Day in a drab boardinghouse room? Thousands of
war workers will be so situated because of travel restrictions."
The Washington Federation of Churches opened its "Share
Your Home At Christmas" program, and uncounted Washington
families made friends, some to remain so long after the war.

The spirit of Christmas infected Frank J. Hogan, whose name
was known to Washingtonians because of his good services to
the capital. A former president of the American Bar Association, he was better known locally as an untiring collector of fine
books. Now, mulling upon a gift for the nation, he decided to
give the Library of Congress his prized original manuscript of
Longfellow's "The Village Blacksmith." Longfellow, Hogan had
learned, was paid $15 for the poem by the *Knickerbocker
Magazine,* in which the poem first appeared during November
1840.

It was impossible for any resident of Washington long to
overlook the poet's knitted brow, the fixedness in the eyes that
was neither complete joy nor sorrow. His image in bronze

reposed in a small square at Connecticut Avenue and M Street, and "Hiawatha" and "Evangeline" seemed in full life beside the statue. One of the poet's arms hung across the chair arm and the hand held a bronze book; the other hand cupped the chin of his lowered face. The statue appeared cold in the wind of the nearing Christmas. He had written once of hearing the bells on Christmas Day, and of peace on earth. But then:

> *And in despair I bowed my head,*
> *"There is no peace on earth," I said;*
> *For hate is strong and mocks the song,*
> *Of peace on earth, good will toward men.*

The Christmas shopping crowds hurried past the statue. There was wide complaint in homes that new toys were hard to find. Far around the world, the British had begun an offensive from India into Burma, with a target of Akyab. The RAF bombed Duisburg, Germany, and in mass flight 26 B-24s roared 4,300 miles to strike Wake Island.

In Dupont Circle, a short walk from the statue, a middle-aged woman tossed crumbs from a bag to a hungry gathering of pigeons.

CHAPTER EIGHTEEN

THE WAR MONTHS PASS

IF THERE HAD BEEN confidence in everyone's mind that the war would end in victory, one of the strongest believers was President Roosevelt. As the year 1943 began, he was already projecting the future America, a prospect which had raised turbulence practically since the Administration's beginning. The industrialists recruited into the war effort had wondered, often out loud, if government—meaning the New Deal—would make what they considered ever-deepening intrusions into the nation's life and its free enterprise tradition when the war was finished. The President lightly touched the subject in the State of the Union Message to the 78th Congress on January 7, foreseeing a world untormented by fear—the demon that he had wrestled in his inaugural speech introducing a New Deal. Apparently, there was nothing alarming in what he said, though it may have been slightly suggestive. The President told the upturned faces:

"Victory in this war is the first and greatest goal before us. Victory in the peace is the next. That means striving toward the enlargement of the security of man here and throughout the world—and, finally, striving for the Fourth Freedom—Freedom from Fear."

It is difficult to understand how he managed to say anything; the address was timed out at 47 minutes and he was interrupted forty times by applause, certainly a delightful sound to a man so appreciative of praise. He spoke of the horrors a future war would bring, because he knew that an atom bomb was in the making. He had now touched the edges of the greatest fear mankind would ever experience. But his fear was kept secret.

The Congressmen returned to their offices, and the President returned to the White House to prepare for a trip to Casablanca, mainly to see what could be done about picking up the remnants of the broken French Empire, while Harry Hopkins gathered up the pieces of his fragmented strength. The two left the night of January 9 aboard a train for Miami with such secrecy that even trusted members of the train crew were replaced by hired help from Roosevelt's hideaway in Maryland. The Washington wartime game of where-is-the-President was again being played. As it progressed, a Pan American Clipper climbed up in the Florida sky, pointed at North Africa. The Conference opened on the 14th, attended by Churchill, General Henri Giraud, and General Charles de Gaulle, a towering figure whose face revealed nothing and whose body suggested a tube of frozen acid. The Frenchmen agreed to do all they could for the Allied Cause; but deep in the mind of De Gaulle was a hope to eventually command the armies—a hope that would be a disturbing factor throughout the entire war. And while they talked, Britain's Royal Air Force spilled a thunder of bombs upon the U-boat base at Lorient, from which the saboteurs had earlier sneaked off for the United States.

March, despite its moods, was always a gentle gift of nature to the people living around Connecticut Avenue and Woodley Road, N.W. The scene evoked uplifting premonitions of approaching spring, a resurrection from the death of winter which expressed itself so noticeably in the grayness of the oaks on the Wardman Park Hotel lawns, and even appeared in the sometimes snow-flecked faces of the crouched lions ornamentally guarding the bridge across Rock Creek Park where the trees down below stood in leafless billows on the hillsides and bottoms. March would pass and the increasing sunlight would filter between the boughs and brighten the wildflowers and the stream that probed the park.

Here was an expensive and genteel neighborhood, a "right address." There was always the flurry of the huge hotel, of course, a blending of excitement and charm; and along the avenue there were pleasant cafes. There was even word that a medical center named The Hopkins Institute functioned in one of the larger apartment buildings, and this of itself lent prestige to the neighborhood.

The Institute, it was understood, was a massage center with therapy administered by skilled practitioners. A few neighborhood people learned that its ownership was in New York City, a further injection of prestige. But on March 8 the residents were shocked upon reading in the newspapers that the Institute was a whorehouse. It had just been raided by the police vice squad under knowledgeable Sergeant Roy Blick and the FBI, which termed the establishment "the most notorious call house in the East."

Eleven women were yanked from the premises, consisting of two five-room apartments of superior elegance, and charged with conspiracy to violate the white slave traffic act. One of the therapists had the entrancing first name of Wonder.

In spite of the dismay in the neighborhood, the raid might have been forgotten within hours. But a horror greeted the news that was to continue for more than a year. The FBI had seized a "rating book" naming the distinguished clientele—Washington's upper class—and detailing their prowess and preferences in therapy. On Capitol Hill and in the highest places of business perspiration beaded dozens of important faces.

The FBI (which apparently had no interest whatever in the patients) delivered the black book to the district attorney. The case was sewed up. The manager, Mildred Powell Carter, age thirty-three, began cooperating with the government, as represented by Assistant U.S. Attorney Jack Fihelly. At first, Fihelly didn't know what he had in the black book, which actually were three dark-colored record books. But soon men came to him, asking, "Ah, uh, have you, uh, did you see this name in the book?" The invariable answer was, "Not yet." When asked if the patrons' names would be revealed, Fihelly would reply "Could be, but I don't know." He always grinned when he said it.

The Institute's financial ratings were intricate. Small letters of the alphabet were placed after each customer's name, indicating the amount paid for service. The key to the code was the name "Fitzgerald," with each letter standing for a number from one to ten, with the exception of the last letter which stood for zero. Why this complicated system was necessary is unknown, because the operation was simple. One room contained a "colonic irrigator," which patients, indulging in self-diagnosis, generally did not believe was indicated. Most frequently called for was the routine therapy—a body massage by a pretty masseuse, with the privilege of spending the night recovering from its effects at a minimum of $20.

The admittance requirements were severe; patients were accepted upon the recommendation of other patients, all highly-placed. One such gentleman developed such an attachment to his therapist that the day after the raid he stormed unabashed into the detective bureau with his lawyer to demand release of the girl.

A year of investigation was spent before the pounce was made. It was discovered that girls were brought to the Institute from as far away as California. It wasn't the girls they were after so much; it was the man in New York, who turned out to be a George F. Whitehead, age forty-three. And the madam might have had a hard time had she not cooperated. White slavery was the reason for the intensity of the pursuit. Of course, there was also a local law forbidding members of opposite sexes from rubbing each other professionally, but with a big war going on and creating tensions such a minor infraction could have been overlooked.

Judge Arthur F. Lederle of Detroit, a visiting justice, presided over the trial. One correspondent was astounded at the sight of the much-publicized "beauties." They were overdressed and over made-up, and their faces were hard and indifferent. They sat in a semicircle of chairs before the bench. A woman reporter noted that each wore "a tailored suit. Several had white, frothy jabots accenting their costumes." Mrs. Carter's testimony consumed most of the second day, when she unsparingly identified each of her former charges. She sat on the stand with hands folded upon a snakeskin purse on her lap, relating how she had arranged parties for the girls.

It soon developed that the Institute was a form of "bank" in the capital's prostitution activities. When acceptable entrepreneurs were short on women, the Institute would fill the breach.

The madam related how she had taken two of the defendants to the Washington Hotel on three successive nights to accommodate a gentleman from Cleveland, Ohio, an extremely nervous man who wanted personal introductions from Mrs. Carter. Unfortunately each of the three checks he had drawn for $75, $80, and $100 on the Cleveland City National Bank had bounced.

The dialogue went like this:

Q. "What took place in the room between the girl and Mr. Mackland?"

A. "They had a party."

Q. "What do you mean by that?"

A. "They undressed and went to bed together."

Asked if she was ever in a room when an unlawful action occurred, the reply was, "Yes. Once when a man was taking too long."

Some relief came when Judge Lederle ordered the "black book" (as it continued to be publicly called) returned to the FBI. It would be kept until it was decided that there was no future need for it and then it would be destroyed. Whitehead, pleading guilty, received a one-to-four-year term in the model Lorton Reformatory situated in the Virginia woodlands, and Mrs. Carter escaped with three-to-nine months. A scattering of two-months-to-one year was tossed among eight of the ladies. Judge Lederle left behind no public record about his sojourn into the manifestations of law. The people around Connecticut Avenue and Woodley Road discovered that life has a way of going on. And the former patients were cured of their ailment, at least for a little while.

Around noon of April 13, 1943, a black automobile brought President Roosevelt to the south side of the Tidal Basin, famed for its rim of Japanese cherry trees, its sunlight and shadows for photographers to study and record for posterity, and young lovers to walk among. The President looked from the window at the domed and columned neoclassic lines of the memorial to Thomas Jefferson—seven years in the planning, four in the building—which he would dedicate that day. Mrs. Roosevelt was with him, and so was Mrs. Woodrow Wilson. They were the most important of the ten thousand important Washingtonians and Virginians who packed the approaches to the Memorial and crowded upon the steps leading to the rotunda 96 feet below the dome. The President knew the Memorial as he knew the philosophy of Jefferson; and he was familiar with the carved words around the wall above the nineteen-foot statue of Jefferson:

I HAVE SWORN UPON THE ALTAR OF GOD ETERNAL HOSTILITY AGAINST EVERY FORM OF TYRANNY OVER THE MIND OF MAN.

Two hundred years had passed since Jefferson's birth, and he was not very old when he shaped the American dream.

Overhead, where Roosevelt sat, rain clouds covered the sky, and the Tidal Basin raised films of spray that laced the walls of the basin.

The war was a long way off; the thoughts were of Jefferson and of his awesome achievements. He could look at a piece of land in Charlottesville and see the form of a great university and then create its architecture; he could draw an inflexible statute of religious freedom for Virginia; he could declare independence for a new nation with a brave and fierce beauty; he could play the violin; he invented many useful household gadgets; he could feel the bite of poverty and keep his gentility, and he found the time to be the third President of the United States.

Now he stood in plaster because the War Production Board needed bronze to help make war. The statue had been fashioned by Sculptor Rudulph Evans in a studio in Westport,

Connecticut, and been transported piece by piece to Washington. Evans had re-created the man. The born frontiersman stood erect and restless. His eyes, from the position of the statue, blazed toward the White House. He was frozen in an imprisonment against his will. His position was the southern wing of a plan: the White House was the northern wing; and the Capitol, the Washington Monument, and the Lincoln Memorial formed an east-west line extending distantly along the Mall.

The crowd near the top of the steps could peer inside and some could see the carvings:

> WE HOLD THESE TRUTHS TO BE SELF-EVIDENT,
> THAT ALL MEN ARE CREATED EQUAL, THAT THEY
> ARE ENDOWED BY THEIR CREATOR WITH CERTAIN
> UNALIENABLE RIGHTS, THAT AMONG THESE ARE
> LIFE, LIBERTY AND THE PURSUIT OF HAPPINESS.

Jefferson had once said something else, if anyone thought of it that day: *"The earth belongs always to the living generation."*

This was an assertion wide open to interpretation. And now a part of the living generation certainly had made a tragedy of the earth which the United States was fighting on islands and on two oceans to undo. Within Jefferson's breadth of vision, this probably would have been a calamitous but transient interlude. When he was old, he had seen his nation like this:

"I have observed this march of civilization advancing from the seacoast, passing over us like a cloud of light, increasing our knowledge and improving our condition . . . And where this progress will stop, no one can say."

Roosevelt had no intention of its stopping in 1943, or within the foreseeable future. Facing the audience, he drew the inevitable comparison between the challenges confronting Jefferson and those imperiling free men now, adding that Jefferson proved that "the seeming eclipse of liberty can well become the dawn of more liberty." The "bold lesson" would be learned by those fighting for freedom now, he said. He termed the gangly red-haired sage of Monticello a man who loved peace and liberty, but who on more than one occasion was compelled to choose between them. "We, too, have been compelled to make that choice."

The nation remembered the anniversary. *The Patriots*, Sidney Kingsley's biographical play about Jefferson, was in its third month on Broadway. Three new books had been published. Some of the 6,500 volumes the Library of Congress had bought from Jefferson in 1815 were placed on public display. And some of his architectural drawings were exhibited in the National Gallery.

The dedication ended, and through the pale April afternoon the statue's plaster eyes stared toward the White House, and there was no dream in the eyes. Roosevelt had told the important people: "Jefferson was no dreamer."

Although much of the great art had gone from Washington, as time went on the servicemen and the war workers discovered a new attraction at the gallery.

The man responsible was Richard Bales. He had grown up in Alexandria and was graduated from the exclusive Episcopal High School. An aunt had once taken him to a concert at Constitution Hall, and he came out wanting to be a conductor. In time, he entered the Eastman School of Music in Rochester, New York. The Depression came, and Bales found himself directing an orchestra in Richmond funded by the Federal Music Project, a New Deal innovation. His next move was to Juilliard, and during the summer of 1940 he obtained private instruction in conducting from the late Serge Koussevitzky of Boston Symphony fame. And about this time he won the friendship of Leonard Bernstein.

The Army examined his eyes and turned him down, so Bales worked in Washington with the British Army Staff. He roamed the National Gallery, brushing his civilian clothes against the uniforms of soldiers, sailors, and marines who didn't imagine that before the war ended the man would be remembered by name, face, and genius by thousands in the Pacific and Europe. During May 1943, he gained the attention of gallery officials and was asked to write a film score—a full fourteen minutes long. Suffering from a case of measles, he finished the job in seventeen days and nights of composing. He became the Gallery's music director and the orchestra grew in reputation with its hall a focal point. Tall, dark-eyed and slender, Bales exuded something more than a rising young talent. He was enthusiasm personified, at its most unrestrained. When his concerts ended he had visibly undergone a personal experience, a triumph within himself. He came out of it all quickly, and answered every possible question the service people and others asked. They were transferred to far places of the world knowing him.

One of his wartime concerts was by the invited Gordon String Quartet, and included several modern works. Upon leaving the hall, Dr. Glenn Dillard Gunn, music critic of the *Times-Herald,* asked a guard in the East Garden Court what he thought of the new music. The guard clamped a hand on his revolver. "If I had my way," he replied, "I would let them have this." Gunn answered, "You are the only music critic I ever met properly dressed for the job."

Many people left the Gallery and the music and drifted into the stores, and upon asking for something would be told, "Don't you know there's a war going on?" At the Gallery they had forgotten.

CHAPTER NINETEEN

WHILE A YEAR DIED

THE FAR-FLUNG SERVICEMEN received a jolt in the thin-paper overseas edition of *Newsweek* of October 11, 1943, which unequivocally stated, "Complacency was still the No. 1 foe on the American home front last week." But the magazine proclaimed that high army officers, materiel production officials, and "globe-trotting senators" had renewed warnings that "the enemy was dying hard—to America's peril." Hard statistics were provided:

Army and Navy casualties had reached 115,201; deaths totaled 21,940. The forthcoming year, which probably would bring the long-screamed-for second front, would pile more dead upon dead, more wounded, and more missing. Only after nearly two years of war had fathers been drafted. (This had brought complaints. A Texan blasted at Washington: "Before I break up my home and let somebody else bring up our four kids, those single and childless guys on draft-dodging nonessential and government jobs ought to be given GI haircuts. If they can't fight, put 'em to work hauling supplies and I'll be glad to do the fighting." Mrs. Roosevelt, back in Washington from the Pacific, commented: "Every other person out there is married. The first thing a soldier does when you talk to him is to pull out a picture of his wife and child. They just think the talk about drafting fathers is funny." The magazine in a footnote said: "Many in the service overseas are Regulars or ex-National

Guardsmen who married either before the draft or the war".)

Considerable fighting lay ahead, the "globe-trotting" Senators made known, and they had traveled 40,000 miles to include such localities as Britain, Casablanca, Marrakech, Cairo, Basra, and Calcutta. They looked upon Guadalcanal, Australia, New Caledonia, and the Fiji Islands. Each of the five—James M. Mead of New York, Richard B. Russell of Georgia, Ralph O. Brewster of Maine, "Happy" Chandler of Kentucky, and Henry Cabot Lodge of Massachusetts—had something worthwhile to report. In essence, it was that the war's conclusion was distant. "Our soldiers know how tough this war is," Brewster told a press conference. "We ought to know how tough it is too." But the complacency was at least partly excusable. At this time the cry again went up that the people were not being adequately informed about the war. As competent an observer as Ernest K. Lindley wrote in *Newsweek:* "Last week three weighty complaints were registered as to the adequacy of the war news supplied to the American people. The first came from eleven leading editors and publishers comprising the Newspaper Advisory Committee of the Office of War Information. The second came from twelve of the principal Washington correspondents in a symposium in the trade magazine *Editor and Publisher,* and the third from the five United States senators who had just completed a tour of the war fronts.

"The substance of these complaints was that (1) too much information is coming from London that should come from Washington, and (2) the American people are not receiving a realistic enough picture of the war."

The columnist informed the news-hungry nation that a recent report to the House of Commons by Churchill contained some ten revelations "of front page importance," and "all of them, of course, were known previously to various high American officials." This, it was added, was not the first time London had scooped Washington; Churchill had done it in nearly every speech. Such news publicly given reached the United States. "The complaint is that it comes from there instead of from Washington."

This column by Lindley and others in like vein had some effect upon the release of war news. Roosevelt had a deeply competitive side. When he realized that Churchill—who was a journalist and experienced in war—was taking the news spotlight, he began loosening up at his news conferences. But the Pentagon never really relaxed insofar as its formal news outlets were concerned. Standing gray and forbidding across the river, it reflected the silence of a prison in the daytime, and at night the lighted windows were clusters of remote stars. Above all, the men who ran it were true to tradition: war is for military people, and outsiders are never to be trusted. What they don't know won't hurt them, and it's none of their business, besides.

As a consequence, there was no wringing of hands over the possibility of Germans or Japanese moving along Pennsylvania Avenue. During the most desperate times, only a few knew the seriousness of the situation at the time of the occurrence. The others went on about their business, and there lay the so-called apathy. And, throughout, the people had an almost blind faith in the military leadership. Ours had never lost a war. It is doubtful, if the military knew of this high estimate placed on them, or cared in the slightest. But the military did know that the people of the United States were determined, and that was satisfactory and entirely sufficient. They simply wanted the people to produce, ask no questions, and keep out of their way. That attitude was all right with most of the people. Objections, as usual, came mainly from the press.

One story did appear in the press which shook the complacency of the American people. At the start of the war, a reporter in Tulsa, Oklahoma, named Jim G. Lucas, a good man on the courthouse and city politics scene, had seen the Associated Press news story calling for combat correspondents for the Marine Corps. He mulled the matter over for a while, and soon found himself embroiled in a strange flat place called Parris Island, where hard men called drill instructors appeared have been born hollering instead of crying. He stood it all as most do without ever understanding how, and was missent after boot training to the Brooklyn Navy Yard. This error was quickly corrected, and soon he was aboard a train for Washington, another strange place, and given quarters at the Navy Yard.

Lucas was a regular church-goer; he had taught a Sunday school class in Tulsa, and hoped he could find one in Washington. He took over a young people's class at long-established Mount Vernon Place Methodist Church, one of the capital's best-known churches situated near the Central Library. (He says now: "I'm not sure how it came about. Most likely, I volunteered. I was never bashful. Dr. John Rustin, then the pastor at Mount Vernon, was a particularly good friend of mine. Now I occasionally hear from some of the young people I taught".)

Lucas left Washington after a while and went off to war. And the next anyone heard from him shook and shocked the capital and the nation. A news story dated Tarawa (Delayed) November 23, 1943 (AP), was signed by Master Technical Sergeant Jim G. Lucas, First Marine Corps combat correspondent to land on Tarawa. The story told of horror in quiet phrases, and the nation finally knew what war was like.

> Five minutes ago we wrested this strategic Gilbert Island outpost and its all-important air strip from the Japanese who seized it from a few missionaries and natives weeks after they attacked Pearl Harbor.

> It has been the bitterest, costliest, most sustained fighting on any front. It has cost us the lives of hundreds of United States Marines (official reports listed 1026 Americans killed.) But we have wiped out a force of 4000 Imperial Japanese Marines—we expected to find only 2000, mostly dead.

As the story progressed, the awful details unfolded:

> The last 75 yards of the pier was white coral grit. There was a brilliant moon—at home I would have called it beautiful. We swore at it viciously. We were perfect targets.

Crouched, we sprinted down the pier, silhouetted against the coral. Snipers opened up, and six men fell, screaming in agony. We lay like logs.

We can't stay here, someone said up the line, they'll shell hell out of us and we'll all be gone.

Advance slowly, five feet between each man. They won't get us all that way.

We started. Three more Marines fell, and we hit the ground. Inch by inch we moved up. Each 10 yards cost us the lives of more Marines. Each time I expected to get mine. Finally, we were within 15 yards of the beach. Ahead were shadows.

The detailed account went on (the sequence of Lucas's story is broken here):

Several hundred Japs were holed up for two days in a bomb-proof shelter at the end of the airstrip, holding up our advance.

Pfc. Robert Harper, 22, Houston, Tex., and Sgt. John Rybin, 25, Laurel, Mont., dashed forward with their flame throwers while automatic riflemen covered them. At the entrance of the bomb shelter, Harper threw his flame on a Jap machine gun nest, charring three enemy Marines beyond recognition. He poured on more fire. There were screams inside the shelter, and the Marines rushed forward to capture their objective.

Harper returned to our post.

"They were all huddled in there scared to death," he said. "I turned on the heat and that was all."

The story was lengthy, and it was a long time before its effects wore off.

The shortage of cigarettes which some on the home front had the foresight to know would come, now struck hard in Washington and across the United States. Most knew that the gigantic name-brand plants in Richmond, Durham, Winston-Salem, and Louisville were producing cigarettes by the millions. But the store clerks only said perfunctorily, "Don't you know there's a war going on?" Government officials seemed mystified, and probably were. Dwindling reserves were cited by the Department of Agriculture. Increased smoking and hoarding were pointed at by the War Food Administration. OPA accused black marketeers, and promised an attack. Only the Anti-Cigarette Alliance rejoiced, and urged the deprived to chew gentian root as a substitute.

It was worse than Prohibition; in those days at least, a bootlegger could always be found.

Stores received limited quantities and many too humanly played favorites. The manager of a German restaurant on 15th Street was fond of a group of news correspondents who ritualistically appeared after 10 A.M. daily for drinks. He would furtively hand around packs, developing a now-you-see-it-now-you-don't sleight-of-hand.

Frustrations were endless. A *Time* correspondent heard during a busy afternoon that a cigarette queue had formed outside a drugstore at 15th and H streets. Hurrying there, he arrived in slow steps at the counter only to be handed a chocolate bar. When he went home that night he found his wife smoking a pipe. A few women tried the substitute, but none, so far as could be ascertained, ever liked it.

A store in the vicinity of 14th and H Streets placed an attractively-wrapped package in a window, labeled "Surprise," and bearing a $1 price tag. The package contained one pack of a name-brand cigarette. There were men in Washington who would give a friend a right arm before giving him a cigarette. There arose a defensive habit of never taking a pack from a pocket in the presence of anyone; rather, fingers slid in and returned with one cigarette.

In Washington at the time were a few heroines. One was a girl from Oregon who came to Washington with a sincere wish to help her country. Her legs were long and beautifully constructed, and she had a rural face that showed an uncommon trust in everything worthwhile. She worked by day in the Pentagon and at night served frequently as a typist in a large news bureau. One night she handed a correspondent a pack of fine cigarettes—as casually as if she were handing him a pencil. The man sprang to embrace her. But being well-bred she shrank back. (It is recalled she muttered something like, "Oh. Did you want those?") Afterward, she brought a pack whenever she arrived. She was never asked where she got the cigarettes; but her gift made him happy.

There must have been thousands like her, the dedicated and brave and hard-working, the honest and wonderful ones, or else the place would have fallen apart.

The final months of 1943 brought both weighty and worthless information to the war-worn people of Washington and the nation. It became known on December 1 in a five-column headline in the New York *Herald Tribune* that "Roosevelt, Churchill, Chiang Met in Cairo, Now Reported on Way to See Stalin in Iran." One of the sessions, it was related, "Took Place in Tent in Egypt in Shadow of Pyramids." Writing from Washington, correspondent Bert Andrews said, "A momentous conference, presumably dealing with the war against Japan, had been completed in Cairo by President Roosevelt, Prime Minister Churchill and Generalissimo Chiang Kai-shek. . . The three men are now reported en route to an unknown destination for a session with Premier Stalin to plan new onslaughts against Germany." (Russia then was not at war with Japan.) Andrews took pains to note early in his story that all of the news available in Washington about the historic meeting and the session that lay ahead had emanated from British sources outside the United States, "for not a single word about them was provided by the information services of the United States government." The story had come from Reuters, the British news agency, out of London. Getting in on the act, the Germans broadcast that the next mystery-shrouded meeting would be held in Teheran, which was, indeed, the case.

Meanwhile, airplane production in the United States reached the phenomenal level in November, 1943, of 9,000 units—averaging one complete warplane every four minutes and forty-eight seconds, a rate of 108,000 a year. "Authoritative sources" said that this reflected a "substantial" increase in production of heavy bombers. These included the new B-29 Super-Flying Fortress with a capability of carrying ten tons of bombs farther than any plane currently in operation. The "flying forts" were expected to be a thundering force in flattening German and Japanese targets during the acceleration of war projected for 1944.

And during the late fall, word had spread freely from the government that Christmas would lose much of its greenery because Christmas trees would be more difficult to obtain because of the shortages of manpower and freight cars. Moreover, in the fashion world of young men, the zoot suit was doomed because of its wastage of cloth. This appalling monstrosity had, since 1941, horrified even the most forbearing of men, hardened to accept almost anything in a world gone mad. Generally of a dark cloth, the jacket shoulders flopped away like a haystack about to tumble from the top; the sleeves were fashioned at least two times too large for the arms, the jacket with two buttons swooped down in square styling to hang almost (if not entirely) to the knees. If this weren't enough, the trousers were some three times too large for the young man's legs, but suddenly tightened to grab the ankles in a squeeze. Despised by servicemen, they were otherwise merely curiosities among so many curious things of the era, including a lady's handbag which revealed its inner contents when the owner held it to the light and peeped through a translucent button.

If all of this created a life of deepening abnormality, coupled with the war reports which affected in some way nearly every family, the people of the United States dramatically took a turn to favoring life over death. In late 1943, statisticians of the

Metropolitan Life Insurance Company had concluded that the year was darkened by only 13,000 suicides as compared to the average of 19,000 before 1941. Fatter bankrolls were given as one reason, the absence of idleness as another. And there were the excitements. For example, people in Washington might transfer themselves into the characters of *Government Girl*, a movie reflecting wartime Washington. It became a big hit everywhere, probably because the capital itself had become little less than a big show in the national mind. And the capital was moving into Christmas.

Christmas Eve came, the third since Pearl Harbor, and once again the store windows tried to brighten the overcast of war. From the crowds on the sidewalks, an elderly man went into a clothing store and asked a lady clerk for a green sweater to send his son, who was serving with the Marines. He was shown a few, but didn't believe that the colors harmonized with the forest green of the Corps. He waited with a show of patience for a marine to come in so he might see exactly how the color would match. A marine chanced along, and the elderly man asked him if a brown sweater would be all right for his son in the Corps. The marine said no, and began unbuttoning his coat. He was wearing a green sweater. "What size does your son wear?" he asked. The man didn't know, but said, "He's about your size." The marine pulled off his sweater and handed it to the man. There was a momentary offer of payment, but the marine refused, saying, "It's a Christmas gift from one marine to another."

It was impossible to know in a city of such size what Christmas would bring to each family. For Mr. and Mrs. Leo C. May, there must have come a joy—not complete, but a joy nevertheless. At least their son, Captain Donald L. May, twenty-five, a graduate of high-toned Friends School in Washington and the Virginia Military Institute, was not dead. The War Department had reported him as missing in action during the Battle for Salerno in September. Now a letter from him said he was a prisoner in a German hospital. There was joy, too, at the Washington Gas Light Company where May had worked as an engineer until entering the service just after Pearl Harbor.

The name of Eisenhower flared in a banner headline of the *Star* on Friday, December 24. He had been given "Supreme Command of Europe Second-Front Invasion." The story under a Hyde Park, N.Y., dateline made known that Roosevelt had announced the appointment in a worldwide broadcast. The President was spending his first Christmas at home since occupying the White House in 1933, and with him were Mrs. Roosevelt and his grandchildren. So the familiar face and the Voice would be absent from the south portico of the White House when the national Christmas tree—to be dark for the second year under wartime restrictions—was honored.

But the people, through habit or reverence, left their homes in the late afternoon and moved through other people more intent on last-minute shopping toward the South Lawn. And, in the absence of the President and other high officials, the occasion was more relaxed, although the ban on cameras prevailed. One presiding official was heard to murmur that it all was "in a way more homey than in other years." The Marine Band played the traditional hymns of Christmas, and the tree stood draped with decorations contributed by schoolchildren. When the music ended and the people had taken their last look at the tree, they went away into the ghost-light of the streets to jostle once again, against late shoppers carrying brightly-wrapped packages toward homes of gaiety, anxiety, or sorrow. Christmas Day was quiet on the streets.

During the next day, the war came closer home: The *Star* told that the Russians had cut Nazi supply roads, and, most importantly, that the United States would supply 73 percent of the men to undertake the invasion of Europe—this according to Senator Edwin C. Johnson of Colorado. No superior prescience was needed to know that this (if it were true) would loose a veritable torrent of American blood.

The weather itself spread gloom. On early Christmas night, in the wake of light rain and snow, a coating of ice began forming on Washington streets and the nearby roads in Maryland and Virginia. Nearly everywhere traffic crawled or came to a

standstill. Emergency rooms of hospitals became filled with
some two hundred persons injured in falls or traffic accidents.
Hundreds of servicemen who had come to Washington from
nearby posts were stranded while the interurban transportation
stood still. For some of these servicemen, their holiday
experience began and ended in the USO lounge at Union
Station; the entertainment included a magic show and music
from an accordian performer. They were served cider, fruit,
candy, and cakes. There were the usual Christmas parties at the
army and navy medical centers. Sightseeing parties banded
together. Others sat down in seeming loneliness in servicemen's
clubs and wrote letters. Out at Walter Reed Hospital, "gift"
long-distance telephone calls were donated by several patriotic
organizations, and some of the patients who were able to get
about gave a Christmas pageant at the hospital. On Christmas
morning a Santa Claus plodded through giving each patient a
stocking full of candies and small gifts. Surprise packages
contained gifts ranging from games to watches. At the Salvation
Army, a free snack bar attracted several hundred guests. A
Christmas supper and party for servicemen was held at the
Central Union Mission near the Capitol.

From all over the country during the Christmas season had
poured the largest mail in the city's history; Postmaster Vincent
C. Burke reported that 200,000 additional sacks were handled
over 1942.

As the season passed, the religious-minded perhaps remembered most the traditional Christmas Day service sponsored by
the Washington Federation of Churches, and held for the first
time at the National Cathedral. Attending were Vice President
and Mrs. Wallace, and Secretary of the Navy and Mrs. Knox.
For the first time in ten years the President was absent. Dr.
Edward Hughes Pruden, pastor of First Baptist Church, left a
sickbed to deliver the sermon. He cautioned the congregation
not to make the mistake of believing that world peace relies
entirely upon world statesmen:

> While we are profoundly grateful for all progress that
> may have been made toward peace at the recent confer-

ences in Cairo and Teheran, we must recognize very frankly that conferences, treaties and military victories can only result in re-arranging men as they are; and that men can be disarranged just as easily as they can be rearranged.

Jesus lived in a world remarkably like our own. He was born into a conquered, occupied country. . . . He demonstrated a wisdom we have not yet learned. He did not speak of a new order or a new world, but of new men.

CHAPTER TWENTY

THE APPROACH TO JUNE AND STORM

FOR THOUSANDS WHO picked up the *Post* on the morning of January 1, 1944, feeling wretched from their revelries of the night before, a dark anguish must have been reflected from the boxed salute in the upper right-hand corner of the paper: "HAPPY NEW YEAR." The day before had been fair, with a high temperature of 40 and a not-unbearable low of 25. Certainly, and despite the war and the shortages and the increasing pressure of work, life was proceeding normally in little corners, and the newspapermen had not forgotten their traditional ways. It was clearly important that the press report the identity of the first baby born in the new year. This being a war year, there was an excited competition at Columbia Hospital between devotees of the Army and the Navy. Mrs. Esther Miller, twenty-three, the wife of an army enlisted man, was pitted against Mrs. Eleanor Butler, nineteen, the wife of a sailor. Mrs. Miller's baby was born at one second after midnight, and one second later Mrs. Butler's baby was clocked into the angry world, scoring a victory for the Army. But everyone was happy. Each infant weighed seven pounds, seven ounces—a remarkable coincidence to talk about for a while before returning to the hospital routine.

Life continued sparkling for those who wanted it that way, and they were many. They searched out the gay spots, to settle among others on Treasure Island, "Washington's Different Cocktail Lounge" offering two orchestras and featuring Chago Rodriguez, "the Goodwill Ambassador of Song." But, simultaneously, James F. Byrnes, Director of War Mobilization, began doubling as an ambassador of restraint. In a New Year message, the spry, dapper official reminded everyone that "thus far, the sacrifices on the home front have been small indeed in comparison with the hardships on the battlefront." He denounced inflation as the big problem.

From this distance in time, while bearing in mind that the poor will always be among us, the prices of food appear to have been reasonable when compared with the general run of pay. For example, in early 1944, York apples sold for 10¢ a pound; grapefruit, five pounds for 25¢; California navel oranges, five pounds for 54¢; Lucerne Grade-A milk, two quarts for 23¢; large grade-A eggs sold for 52¢ a dozen; lean, meaty fresh ham was 31¢ a pound, and a pound loaf of bread cost 8¢. The wild spending came largely on evenings out with women, when prices often rose with the number of drinks the customers swilled. Such free-wheeling spending came largely from men in Washington on contract or other "war" business. The townspeople, on the whole, were restrained, and, knowing the city, had learned every shortcut on spending. Most hard-put, of course, were the men and women government employees within the lower pay grades. They certainly did nothing to encourage inflation.

Meanwhile, in early January, 1944, penny-watching Representative Albert J. Engel, Republican of Michigan, revealed the results of a personal investigation he had conducted into the cost of the Pentagon—a piece of inflation, indeed. He had discovered that the cost figure exceeded a "staggering" $83 million, or $51 million more than the original estimates and the amount authorized by Congress. (Back in 1942, he had pessimistically predicted that the building would wind up costing $70 million.) But growls, however sensible, were so frequent in Washington that the very winds of winter seemed to whirl them away.

There was no way for the creeping days of January to hide the portents implicit in the New Year's Day statements by Roosevelt and Stimson. The President, a chronic sufferer from sinus disorder, had come down with a cold which developed into grippe. He was in and out of a sickbed. But he made known the intentions of the allied nations to launch a great offensive in 1944. "Our armed forces are gathering for new and greater assaults which will bring about the downfall of the Axis aggressors," he said—and by any interpretation this meant, for one phase, an attack upon Europe from across the English Channel. Stimson raised the general anxiety temperature by speaking of "standing upon the threshold of a titanic and decisive struggle. . . . " Strength "in tremendous force" would be loosed both in Europe and the Far Pacific, he said. The President looked beyond the victory of which he seemed assured to the postwar time, declaring that the Allies were giving attention "now" to postwar alleviation of unemployment and other forms of "economic and social distress"—a flashback to his great effort and dedication before the interruption of the big war.

In mid-January, General Eisenhower, beaming with confidence and good humor during his first press conference after his arrival in England as supreme commander, said he had found the pre-invasion machinery "rumbling briskly," and disclosed that Lieutenant General Omar N. Bradley, a square-jawed soldiers' soldier admired by everybody, was the senior American general heading the mounting numbers of men and growing piles of materiel in the United Kingdom. The supreme allied commander in the West stopped short of precisely defining Bradley's future role. Correspondents at the London conference quickly assumed, however, that Bradley would lead the Americans whenever the time came to cross the Channel, while General Sir Bernard L. Montgomery would lead the British invaders. Bradley had been in England for a number of weeks, and behind him lay a brilliant record as commander of the Second Corps in Tunisia and Sicily. The *Washington Post* reacted to Eisenhower's optimism editorially: "General

Eisenhower's statement that we shall win the war in the European theater in 1944 is no idle boast, nor is Admiral King's announcement of a tremendous offensive against Japan this year." The people reacted in the only realistic way: Great offensives and victories meant blood, and there was no possible way for everyone in Washington somehow not to be affected and grieved.

Tucked away in the *Post* of January 13, 1944, was the news that air-raid sirens screaming of blackouts and practice alerts would sound along the eastern seaboard, of which Washington was considered a part, though only on Sundays, and then not more than once every three months. Just at this time, the Russians had captured Sarny, within the Polish border; and, two days before, 1400 United States warplanes had attacked Junkers, Focke-Wulf, and Messerschmitt factories in Germany, with a loss of sixty bombers. The advance saturation bombing preparatory to the overwhelming invasion—to be called D-day—had begun and would mount in fierceness. But as in every month except perhaps the one or two immediately following Pearl Harbor, the people clung to the duality of life—war and peace—and manifested their love of life by packing the National Theater the night of February 14 to enjoy a fine performance of *Life With Father*. And just afterward while a headline told that a "Big Jap Caroline Base" had been bombed, the embattled District of Columbia tax office (troubled by so many residents who claimed they were paying taxes "back home" and wouldn't pay in two places) bombarded 150,000 persons with tax-due notices. None of this touched the immediate lives of the Marines in the distant Pacific: they had just taken a strategic airfield on Eniwetok Atoll in the Marshalls.

Then on February 22, 1944, a front-page eight-column banner unrelated to the war brought a revealing shock that life did go on, and could bring a lingering shudder. "Lawyer Slays Noted Doctor in Triangle," the people learned. Their eyes fell upon the headline's bank, which related, "Dr. J. E. Lind Shot in Auto at Corner of 11th and G," in the heart of the big department store area. Said the *Post* story, "One of the nation's foremost psychiatrists was shot to death by a well-known lawyer in a love triangle at a busy downtown street intersection here as hundreds looked on yesterday afternoon." The doctor, who was fifty-six years old, had analyzed Washington's criminally insane for thirty years at St. Elizabeth's Hospital, and the attorney, who was sixty-seven, specialized in municipal court cases of a run-of-the-mill nature, and could turn tears on and off in his pleadings in the old-fashioned manner of legal eagles. A human interest story on the killing carried a headline, "Told Him to Stay Away From 'That Woman,' Says Grieving Daughter of Slain Psychiatrist. But He Wouldn't Heed Her Advice. . . ." The attorney was arrested on the spot, and a short while later was charged with murder. Not only at the courthouse, where Lawyer Miller was a character and a great favorite, but all about the city the war's distant thunderings were muted by the crack of one pistol.

There was something routine to look at. President Roosevelt was pictured receiving the first lapel tab signifying the first contributor to the Red Cross drive for a $200 million war fund. He wore more heavily the burden of the oncoming invasion, and it was plain by now that a tremendous force would be loosed at Fortress Europe. "Thousands More Yanks Reach Britain," a February headline revealed, noting that the contingent was among the greatest ever sent. Censorship would not allow the correspondents to give the number, but they could say that all were "highly trained" and "ready for combat." The troops were dispersed among U.S. bases "scattered from one end of these islands to the other." Newspapers of Sunday, March 5, disclosed that the Flying Fortresses had struck Berlin, and on the 7th a headline told, "Berlin Pounded, 68 U.S. Bombers Lost." During the foray, "At Least 123 Nazi Planes Shot Down in Fierce Battle."

Then, on March 7, another battle took shape. Representative Engel disclosed that the $83 million Pentagon building was costing taxpayers $7,239,255.95 a year to operate. According to his calculations, the same office space could be rented for

$1.25 a square foot for an annual sum of $4,088,801, Engel told the House. He demanded an explanation from the Pentagon, and so did the reporters, but the War Department's Bureau of Public Relations said it was "withholding comment."

In early March, when the winds were tossing treetops and the women's knee-length skirts, Kann's Department Store took stock of the seasonal view. A huge and illustrated advertisement announced that "Fancy Garters are the Fashion Again. $1.95 and $2.50 a Pair. Enhance Your Leg Appeal With These Provocatively Pert Garters. They're Really Meant to Help You Keep Your Rayon Stockings Smooth and Taut. Ombres, Lace-Trims, Bows, Flowers, or Tailored Rayon Velvets."

Representative Walter H. Judd, Republican, of Minnesota, a lean-faced and serious-eyed former medical missionary to China, appeared before guests from 36 states and eight foreign countries on March 10, 1944, at First Baptist Church to ask a question with the keen edge of an over-hanging sword. He wanted clarification of America's war and peace aims.

"We know what we are against, but what are we for?" he inquired. The nation now had nothing comparable to Woodrow Wilson's Fourteen Points for peace in the first World War, he told his audience, adding that "we may gain a military victory and still not get a decent world." He believed that victory might become a "breathing spell between wars"—and that is precisely what happened.

There, indeed, was a question which the government had never answered in anything like depth. And it was a concern to every human being; but there were other concerns and among them was one not too trivial. Ten ministers, all pastors of churches affiliated with the Southeast Ministerial Council, took time out to take a hard look at the races of mankind, and in the deepest understatement of perhaps the entire century declared that Senator Theodore G. Bilbo, Democrat, of Mississippi, "lacks an understanding of racial relations in Washington," and should be ousted from the chairmanship of the Senate District Committee. Bilbo, built like a fireplug and with a round, furrowed frowning face, would have disputed the conclusion with his practiced growl. He knew exactly what the relations should be according to the notions of his constituency, which unquestionably believed the right man was in the right place to keep matters in hand in that meddlesome city called Washington. It was one of those statements not worth answering—but it surely would elevate his chances for reelection.

Within the silence the capital sang, as though hooked on the tune, the jaunty song "Heigh Ho, Heigh Ho, Off to Work We Go" borrowed from Walt Disney's *Snow White and the Seven Dwarfs*, which on March 31 entered its second week at RKO Keith's Theatre. At this time, several service trades screamed for workers and tossed the problem to their patrons. On April 3 came the announcement that the manpower shortage was acute in restaurants, laundries, and dry cleaning establishments. Services, consequently, would be curtailed through an agreement with the War Manpower Commission. Menus would be drastically reduced. Hotels would limit guests to one face- and one bath-towel a day, and bed linen would be changed once a week. In lower-priced restaurants, paper napkins would be substituted for linen; and there would be no more take-out orders. Laundries would discontinue touching-up wearing apparel by hand; grades of shirt-starching would end, leaving the customer a choice of all starch or no starch. In dry cleaning establishments, preference would go to uniforms and business suits. Last in priority were household articles.

On April 12, the people became sure that besides a veritable outpouring of blood, a flood of money would be required to finance the invasion. Under Secretary of the Navy James V. Forrestal had earlier told Congressional hearings that by July 1, 1944, American forces would have embarked on a military venture of such major importance that any reduction of Navy appropriations should not be considered until "the critical period" was passed. He did not mention the coming invasion during the hearings. It was not until April 12 that it became known that he had asked for $32,647,134,336 for naval activities beginning on the next July—the largest request in the Navy's history.

The awareness of dreadful times to come sharpened on April 18, 1944, when it was learned through radio and newspapers that Britain had clamped curbs on the movements of envoys—the first time that such inflexible restrictions had been imposed in World War II or any other war. Reports from London disclosed that Britain "flatly forbade" neutral and Allied diplomats to leave the country; it subjected all of their communications to censorship, excepting only the missions of Russia, the United States and the British Commonwealth. The veils of secrecy were being woven across the coming invasion more tightly than ever.

A deserved merriment continued at the Stage Door Canteen in the old Belasco Theater on the east side of Lafayette Park; and in April the women in uniform looked wild-eyed at a benefit fashion show and auction. Mrs. Anna Roosevelt Boettiger, daughter of the President, won the raffle ticket for a $185 Hattie Carnegie dress. In the audience were some three hundred socialites. Appearing as models were Mrs. Ira Eaker, wife of the Mediterranean Theater's air chief, in a block print with a Chinese hat; Mrs. Patrick Jay Hurley, wife of a former Secretary of War, in a dramatic long-sleeved black dinner gown, and Mrs. Hugo L. Black, whose husband sat on the Supreme Court, in a blue and gray print both voluminous and soft.

April passed fair with a high of 80 and a low of 45. But the outlook darkened with the headlines telling that "Preinvasion Raids Drive into 19th Day," and "Allies Hurl Might of Air on Nazis In Rising Tempo." U.S. bombers were striking with wide devastation on the coastal defenses in France. But hope for perhaps an early end came with the news that food rationing for the United States was practically over. Meat, it was learned, was made point-free with the exception of steak, beef, and roasts. The only shortages, it was claimed by the officials, were butter, sugar, and canned fruit. There was no mention of cigarettes—a touchy subject because no one as yet had reached a conclusion about the causes of the shortage.

In any case, by this time Washingtonians had come to learn that the good earth of the capital, which nurtured so many flowers to delight the eye, could also be the mother of vegetables to satisfy the stomach. Victory Gardens poked up tomatoes and tiny rows of cucumbers, corn, beets, and beans—and these were a gratification to the small town and rural segments of the population who had brought their green thumbs to the big town. The embattled Germans by 1944 scarcely would have taken time out to learn that they had paid for a sizable tract of Washington land under use as a Victory Garden. This tract, officially known as Lots 5 and 6, lay in the fashionable 2200 block of S Street, N.W., bounded on the north by Bancroft Place and on the east by Phelps Place. The land had been bought by the German government in 1923 as the site for a new Embassy. Architects' plans were ready during the early 1930's, but the uproar caused by Hitler left the Washington project dangling. When the United States and Germany went to war, the lots were seized by the Alien Property Custodian, and, in the official terminology, "a block was put on the property." But persons living nearby began planting vegetables on the abandoned field, and among them was Miss Julia Foraker, a girl who had gone to the best schools—the sort that didn't teach random gardening. She was amazed to find her shovel striking oyster shells in the ground (a circumstance which was never explained) and, eventually, to learn in even more amazement that the carrots did not grow in bunches, like the packages in grocery stores. Another young woman read on a package that cucumbers should be planted in hills and consequently raised a pile of earth the size of a desk.

But over everything hung the thoughts of the invasion, and the guessing game began. More like a gentle whisper upon the boisterous nation came an appeal for God's mercy—like a dim echo from Churchill's Christmas Eve talk seemingly so long ago—from Bishop Henry St. George Tucker, president of the Federal Council of Churches of Christ in America. From New York came word that he had issued an invasion prayer for use on D-Day, a short prayer of only five paragraphs. Simultaneously, the Association of Army and Navy Wives requested that all places of public worship remain open when the invasion was made known. And on May 5, the Office of Defense Transportation asked that travel be cut to a minimum when the attack was launched to enable the wounded to have space for transportation to hospitals in the United States.

Nature appeared to outdo itself with the flaming flowers of spring. Older residents of Washington said that they had never before seen such a profusion of color—azaleas in red, scarlet, and apricot, yellow tulips, and some of rose and purple. Just beyond the city, some fields were carpets of gold buttercups. A walker along a byway on May 7 reported "the flash of a red cardinal and the fluttering of a yellow and sable butterfly." Nearly everyone wanted to be outdoors, and some went to the Chesapeake and Ohio Canal on weekends to watch the mule-drawn barges pass up and down the waterway which traces its origin to George Washington's aspiration for a water route to the West. Aboard the barge one afternoon was a Royal Air Force flier traveling at two miles an hour when he had been accustomed to four hundred.

Sunday, May 21, brought word that the headquarters of General Eisenhower had broadcast its first direct order to Europe's underground fighters. They were told to make a careful note of every activity of the Germans. And then it became known that on May 24, "7,000 Flights Rock Europe in Day; Americans Raid Berlin 11th Time."

News came from the courthouse on Thursday, June 1. An eight-column front-page banner in the *Post* pushed the war aside to say that "Jury Quickly Frees Miller in Lind Slaying." The jury had deliberated an hour and twenty minutes, and the verdict was brought in at 6:41 P.M. in the nearing twilight—but it undoubtedly must have seemed like the most glorious of sunrises to the barrister, who had been on trial for two weeks. A ripple of approval came from the crowded courtroom, and Miller was visibly stirred.

The case fell from the public mind. The invasion again took precedence. The 5th and 6th of June were chilly, and some people took off their spring clothing and put on tweeds. The flowers flamed in the beauty of defiance.

CHAPTER TWENTY-ONE

D-DAY AT LAST

THROUGH THE WINDOWS came the smells of damp grass and the awakening flowers, and the bronze moon that had shone so brightly in the night's temperature of 58 lay low and pale as the day came on with promise of clear weather. The pigeons were stirring along the walkways of the downtown parks, and occasionally a man or woman passed with an unusually worried expression. By this time in June 1944, the strain of the war was showing and there was no way of knowing by looking at a face whether it had been touched by one of those notifications from the Pentagon or simply the strain of a way of life that no one could live with for too long.

But the early morning of June 6 brought tingling magic to the iron-riveted world. It came curiously. In newspaper and radio offices, bells rang on the tickers at 12:37 A.M. The flash related "German Trans-ocean Agency claims Allied invasion has begun." There had already been one false alarm about the Channel crossing—coded OVERLORD. Could this from the Germans be another? Berlin Radio continued steadily to hammer out the message for three hours. Paratroopers had landed near the Seine estuary. The harbor of Le Havre was shelled. But most of the United States didn't hear it. The people slept.

Finally it was announced that Colonel R. Ernest Dupuy, press aide to General Eisenhower, was to speak from London. The four major networks were told to stand by.

"This is Supreme Headquarters, Allied Expeditionary Force." The communiqué would be released in ten seconds, and the Colonel slowly counted to ten. Then he spoke, in the cool businesslike voice known to newsmen because he had been Chief of the News Division at the War Department in Washington from 1941 to 1943. The invasion, he said, had begun on the northern coast of France.

And still most people slept. The President's bedroom was darkened by drawn blackout curtains. He had read private dispatches until the invasion was announced.

Newsmen were quickly in their offices or on the streets. One had been shaken awake by his wife around 2 A.M., to be told excitedly, "They want you on the phone. They say it's urgent." Then the voice came through, "This is it, get in here." He dressed quickly, and on the sidewalk waited interminably for a taxi. The entire neighborhood was as silent as the dreaming moon. The night was haunted and frightening and it seemed as though it would never end, as though time had been suspended.

The President had already written a prayer, composed between telephone calls from the Pentagon and his other work. He would be the first President in American history to lead the entire nation in prayer—made possible because of radio. He had read and reread the words that he would say:

> Almighty God: our sons, pride of our nation, this day have set upon a mighty endeavor, a struggle to preserve our republic, our religion and our civilization and to set free a suffering humanity. Lead them straight and true; give strength to their arms, stoutness to their hearts. . . . The enemy may hurl back our forces. But we shall return again and again; and we know that by Thy grace . . . our sons will triumph.
>
> Some will never return. Embrace these, Father, and receive them, Thy heroic servants, into Thy kingdom. . . .

The headlines of June 6 were set in the biggest type in the shops. "Allied Land in France, Eisenhower Announces," the *Washington Post* trumpeted. The bank headline told, "Nazis

Admit First Blow Success as Vast Forces Hit Normandy Coast."

Another column related: "President Roosevelt last night hailed the liberation of Rome [2 days earlier], but warned that the final victory over Germany 'still lies some distance ahead.' " It was all too much to receive too quickly—a frightful uncertainty on the one hand, a victory on the other, an assurance of even more dreadful things to come, and the certainty of death rising inexorably in the month of spring and bloom. And within it all the hum of voices remote and unheard: "War-conscious Washington has never been more so than now," society editor Hope Ridings Miller wrote in the *Post.* "The fall of Rome was THE topic at all get-togethers here Sunday."

During the day, someone asked General Marshall if he had spent the night at his desk. "I had done my work before," he replied. He had gone to the Soviet Embassy to receive the Order of Suvorov, then to bed at his Fort Myer quarters.

The people on buses and streetcars reacted to the news, and stranger talked to stranger as they had on the night of Pearl Harbor in front of the White House. But they quieted down quickly; and many upon reaching their offices asked time off to go to church and pray. The capital's usual affairs went on. One reporter summed it up: "No gaiety, no parades, no work stoppages." There were mere interruptions: Blood donor centers became crowded with people wanting to empty their veins into the men crossing the Channel. At 11 A.M. forty girls came in from one insurance office.

The 86,000 public schoolchildren went into assemblies to pay tribute to invasion forces. At McKinley High School, Principal Frank C. Daniel read from the Bible: "O give thanks unto the Lord, for He is good. . . . He brought them out of darkness and the shadow of death. . . . " (This would be unlawful now under a Supreme Court ruling.) Children gathered with government employees and Congressmen at St. Peter's Catholic Church at 2nd and C Streets, and a photographer snapped the young sad faces and the hands clasped in prayer.

In United States District Court, 110 candidates for United States citizenship stood solemnly while Milton W. King, president of the District of Columbia Bar Association asked, "What have I done today that a boy should die for me tonight?"

As June wore on, there came brief reflections from soldiers revealing—more deeply than all the headlines could do—what war could mean to lands, how the human spirit would be wrenched by monstrous sights, but above all how good from a distance the United States appeared. A letter came from Corporal Tracy Dunn, thirty-three, who had graduated from Tuskegee Institute in 1933 and done postgraduate work at Bluefield (West Virginia) State Teachers' College. Before entering the service he had worked in the reference department of the Library of Congress. From the war he wrote in June:

> If you want to fall in love with the dear old U.S.A., just see Europe and Africa. Each day I live in the shade of death. Everywhere I have been the people are starving and in this part of the world starvation is more than lack of food. Life is gone, and when I see these living-dead I know what I am fighting for. If I can keep my homeland from such a famine, my life is not too much to give.

At 4 P.M. on July 6, 1944, Washingtonians moved as slowly as their business allowed through a heat of 94, a suffering sufficient to obscure the memories of past bad days and dragging years. Few might have chosen to look toward the sky where the heat seemed to originate; but the sky was important that day and at that hour because out of it had just come an important man—Brigadier General Charles André Joseph Marie de Gaulle, who, on June 18, 1940, had fled his homeland of France to settle unquietly in England as the leader of French Resistance. When the C-54 touched ground and taxied to a halt a platoon of French air cadets and three squadrons of United States airmen came to attention.

Soon, the first roar of a seventeen-gun salute broke the silence, and the General emerged from the plane. He seemed very cold in the heat, and he was tall against the hugeness of the plane, taller in appearance than his reputed six-feet-four. He looked about upon a land he had never visited before with the look of a man who did not want to show an interest. But he indulged the delicate traces of a smile. The face tightened again while the Air Force Band played "The Marseillaise" and "The Star Spangled Banner." The General saluted, and when the band finished he shook hands with State Department protocol chief George T. Summerlin, after an introduction by Henri Hoppenot, the General's representative in the United States. He moved along to General Marshal with a handshake and a "very glad." He shook the hands of Admiral King, General Arnold, Lieutenant General Vandergrift of the Marines, and a scattering of White House aides. There was no dallying about with a man whose reserve paradoxically demanded action. He was hurried off to the White House.

Roosevelt, in his Oval Office, had his feet firmly on the earth. He confronted the iceberg with a wind of warmth: "My, I'm glad to see you," he said, and after a flutter of small talk proposed that they go upstairs for some tea.

Early that evening, Secretary of State Hull gave a gold-plate dinner for De Gaulle at the Carlton Hotel—an important and fancy affair which Hull wanted to keep a quiet one, perhaps for diplomatic reasons, perhaps because he knew De Gaulle was tired. Hull himself was tired, and was meditating on retirement from public life. The face of the Frenchman, especially the eyes, showed fatigue and he appeared thinner than the photographs had shown. But he drank and ate a great deal, sipping Manhattans, French sauterne, Portuguese champagne, and American burgundy; and consuming with a curious daintiness his squab and asparagus tips. He offered few words, simply saying that the United States and France stood in agreement on the essential things.

The Carlton had been and was a gathering place of important people, so much so that important and unimportant loungers in the lobby seldom looked up from their newspapers or conversations to watch the passersby. But at 10:42 P.M., when the tall Frenchman, whose clamped features were quickly identifiable, passed through the lobby to leave the hotel the loungers rose and applauded—a gesture unprecedented in the Carlton. In response to their enthusiasm came the merest trace of a hand-wave from the General.

A busy next day lay ahead, At Henri Hoppenot's sumptuous residence on Massachusetts Avenue, De Gaulle's committee in the United States wove its plans to press the liberation, and bring about a France in full flower. The General spoke there, projecting his words into fixed and lasting history: "France will emerge once again," he said. The import of his words was clear: The past would fade; every German must be killed or chased out of France, and Frenchmen must rely upon themselves to form their future.

Out at Walter Reed Hospital, the heat seared the grass, and on the grass or on the benches in the shade sat wounded soldiers wearing red jumpers. They had been indifferently idling away the hot afternoon; but suddenly a commotion occurred along the driveway to the large main building. A slow procession of cars was moving in, and out of one stepped De Gaulle like a stiff wax figure. From the other cars stepped State Department officials with the measured movements of diplomats, and out of other cars jumped reporters with their eyes fixed ahead to where the General was about to mount the steps into the building. The reporters knew where the General was going. It was a courtesy and a friendly visit to ailing 83-year-old General John J. Pershing. In the World War I General's quarters, the two conversed through an interpreter. To De Gaulle's question about the "situation," Pershing replied that it favored the Allies (which De Gaulle certainly knew, but this was a courtesy visit). To another question, Pershing answered that it would take some time to find out about the general world situation. De Gaulle reflected that Mahomet had once said that without war the world would come into stagnation. To this, General Pershing sharply remarked that we had never had peace long enough to know.

During a brief interlude in his four-day stay, De Gaulle visited Mount Vernon, and took a long look at the heavy black key to the Bastille, a present to George Washington from Lafayette. Curiously, he wondered if deer were kept on the estate, and was told there were none. During a later press conference, he appeared more relaxed. He did not fear that the United States had designs on French territory, and he wanted a French army of occupation kept in the Rhineland perhaps for many years.

The United States government had played a cautious hand with the Frenchman; every possible courtesy was directed toward his vanity, and toward furthering harmony between the two nations. But none of this meant that the United States recognized De Gaulle's Committee of National Liberation as the government of France. The President merely accepted the committee as a working tool. The General himself kept a level aim: In the making of the peace, France must have standing equal to that of the United States, Britain, and Russia. And above all, France must rise in glory.

For the average Washington resident, it meant merely that somebody else of great importance had been in town, and now was gone. And to sum it up, the-hell-with-it. The heat was murderous.

Now that a landing had been accomplished, it became easy for many to believe that the war in Europe would end fairly quickly. The belief was widespread that it would not continue through another summer, though sensible people knew that, considering Nazi fanaticism, the way would be hard and costly in lives. But there was a lift of spirits in July and August, swept along by such invigorating songs as "I'll Be Seeing You," and "Swinging on a Star." And yet there was no positive escape from the realities. The wounded soldiers were becoming more and more in evidence on the streets, and some didn't want to leave. One would tell *The New York Times*: "We meet three kinds of people. Some are intelligent enough not to stare and ask questions. Some are well-meaning and want to do something, but they always say the wrong thing. And then there are long-nosed gossips who ask us foolish questions and try to pry." Their main hope was that people wouldn't stare and wouldn't ask questions.

There was certainly conflict in the air. Despite the "promise" of the European situation, the government continued to pile war workers upon crowded Washington, and too many had no decent place to stay. Prior to June, 1944, an appeal for rooms by the Metropolitan Area War Housing Center had brought "good" results. A second appeal was issued for rooms in June—directed at Washington, Arlington, and Alexandria homeowners—for the hundreds of workers, especially girls, who would have arrived by August. The War Department, indeed, said that 2,600 girls would be employed between June 1 and August 1 for service in the Pentagon and in other War Department offices. The greatest shortage of rooms was in Arlington, mostly an apartment community, where five hundred listings a month were needed to meet demands. Some theorist in the government —without the slightest knowledge that half a loaf is a hundred percent better than none—announced that rooms with single beds were preferred.

CHAPTER TWENTY-TWO

OF MIDSTREAM AND THE HORSE

THE CIVILIAN POPULATION of Washington and the nation
scarcely realized that President Roosevelt since Pearl Harbor
had continuously exercised the prerogatives of commander-in-
chief more determinedly than any war President since Abraham
Lincoln. And with his involvement in military strategy and his
personal intervention in the problems of armament production
he had departed far from the old image—idolized or disliked—of
himself. Now in July 1944, the time had come for the
Democratic National Convention, and the Democratic politicians were preparing a resounding howl for the 19th of July in
Chicago. The convention's choice, to all but the most unrealis-
tic, had already been settled upon. Having broken the
two-term tradition in 1940, Roosevelt was now finishing his
third, and on July 11 made known to no general surprise that
he would run again if nominated—perhaps the most superfluous
"if" of the year. Crime-buster Thomas E. Dewey had been
nominated by the Republicans on June 28, and was conducting
a cautious campaign, though indicating his future points of
attack. The country needed a change, he asserted, and its affairs
were under the management of tired men.
    The President gave no outward indication of weariness, but
he was fatally ill. He had lost considerable weight; his neck had
shrunk within his collar, and his cheeks had turned cavernous
and pale. His afflicted legs were troubling him unmercifully.

With his physical decline (which shook Robert Sherwood upon first sight of him after a protracted absence) came the burdens of the raging Second Front and a growing political problem: Who would run with him as Vice President? Roosevelt wanted Henry Wallace, or, at any rate, was intensely loyal to his compatriot of the exciting New Deal days. Wallace had the support of uncounted liberals but was so stamped as an extremist—even as a strange personality who dabbled in occult sciences—that the party's leaders knew he would jeopardize the ticket. Most acutely conscious of the Wallace risk were Bob Hannegan, the party chairman; Edwin Pauley, the party treasurer and California oil magnate; Edward Flynn, New York political boss, and Sidney Hillman, head of the Political Action Committee of the heavy-muscled Congress of Industrial Organizations. Actually Hillman would desert Wallace only if the Vice President's chances appeared hopeless. Boss Flynn had given the President a strong notification of Wallace's likelihood of damaging the party's chances. At Roosevelt's request, Flynn had made a personal tour of the important political areas and on his return had branded Wallace as perhaps the most objectionable of all probable candidates. The President's loyalty to his friend visibly cracked. But he would not say whom he preferred as his running mate. His facility for fencing, which long had frustrated correspondents at his press conferences, reached an unprecedented height. Possible candidates were mentioned—William O. Douglas of the Supreme Court; James Byrnes of South Carolina, former Supreme Court Justice and a powerhouse in the war effort, and Senator Harry S Truman of Missouri.

The President's equivocation became unbearable to the political professionals as the convention neared. So in quiet desperation they sat down with the President the night of July 11, not to pressure him, because they knew him too well, but to make use of their ears. Roosevelt radiated charm, entirely unappreciated by his guests—Hannegan, Flynn, Mayor (Boss) Edward J. Kelly of Chicago, Pauley, Postmaster General Frank Walker, George Allen, a fun-loving friend of capital officials and military leaders, and John Boettiger, Roosevelt's son-in-law. The conversation was casual and the names of men in public life were mentioned. But not once did the President utter a name and say, in effect, He is the man.

Around this time it was rumored that "someone" had read a list of possible Vice Presidential candidates to Roosevelt and he had given, by inflection of voice, a mild assent to each name. When Truman's name was mentioned, the assent had sounded enthusiastic. Flynn would write long afterward that he had detected something in the President's tone when the Missourian's name was injected into the otherwise disappointing conference. It is now fairly well established that when Roosevelt despaired finally of Wallace he settled on Truman for several reasons: He had admired his work on the notably honest and competent "Truman Committee" on war expenditures; Truman was liked on The Hill; was admired by Labor to a substantial extent, and was not disliked by any major power group in the nation.

Truman, indeed, was a peculiarity in official Washington. He was satisfied with where he was and with what he was doing. He had reached the United States Senate—a long way from a corn row and a defunct haberdashery—on January 3, 1935, in his fifty-first year, and had walked self-consciously to take the oath knowing he was typed as "the Senator from Pendergast"—of having had connections with the political machine of Boss Pendergast in Kansas City. He had determined to remove the label. Before coming to Washington, he had read the biographies of his colleagues-to-be, and they had helped to shape his later relations. He tried to be convivial but his attempts became buried under the piles of work on the floor and in his suite in the Senate Office Building. His days began at 7 A.M., and at 7 P.M. he tried to get home, though always with work under his arm. Home at first was a furnished apartment at 3016 Tilden Street; later an apartment building called the Warwick on Cathedral Avenue and, later yet, 4701 Connecticut Avenue, where he thought he might stay a long time. His neighbors at each address saw a slight, erect man with a strangeness in the eyes. The eyes were both piercing and friendly, and the man was unfailingly courteous in a small-town way. But he didn't socialize much. He seemed intent on his home life with his wife, Bess, and daughter, Margaret, and on the work bundled under his arm. If he appeared restless and talked in a straight-to-the-point manner it was under no whip of ambition. He certainly knew that Hannegan and others were pressing him toward the Vice Presidency, but he himself, now admired by his senatorial colleagues and practically the master of Missouri politics, wanted to be let alone.

To make himself perfectly clear, he had, in response to a telephone call from Byrnes, promised to place the South Carolinian's name in nomination at the convention. And having committed himself he hung up the phone at his home in Independence, Missouri, and with his wife and daughter started off in the family Chrysler for Chicago.

Behind the scenes, Byrnes' stock was rising and Hannegan and Pauley frantically prevailed upon Roosevelt to stop his West Coast-bound train in Chicago to get an endorsement for Truman lest a floor fight come between Byrnes and Wallace, with Wallace the winner and the party the loser. Hannegan had a personal letter in which the President had said he would be pleased to have either Douglas or Truman run with him. Now, Hannegan asked, would the President at least change the order of the names? Roosevelt complied, and the train sped off for San Diego. The President was bound for Pearl Harbor to discuss strategy with Admiral Nimitz and General MacArthur. The commander-in-chief was at work, leaving the politicians to squabble over the President's running mate.

Truman's fate was determined by a now famous telephone call. He had been asked to come to Hannegan's hotel suite in Chicago for a talk. Entering the room, he beheld bosses Flynn, Kelly, and New Jersey's Hague, along with Hannegan, Pauley, and the postmaster general. As they were telling him he *must* run for party and country, they were interrupted by the telephone. Hannegan and Truman were seated on the edge of a bed, and the party's chairman caught up the receiver.

Roosevelt's voice was so loud Truman could hear it.

"Bob, have you got that fellow lined up yet?"

"No, Mr. President. He is the contrariest Missouri mule I've ever dealt with."

Roosevelt replied, "Well, you tell him that if he wants to break up the Democratic Party in the middle of a war that's his responsibility." The phone became silent, and Hannegan looked at his fellow Missourian.

"My God," Truman said.

At the convention, the reading clerk had droned on. . . . For Truman, 1,100; for Wallace, 66; for Douglas, 4; absent, 6, making a total of 1,176 votes."

If he wanted the honor and the office it did not show on his face the evening the convention sent him on the first step toward the Presidency. Many who knew the President's state of health realized that *two* candidates for the highest office had been nominated.

Perhaps no national convention nominee ever moved through acclaim to acknowledge the honor with more visible reluctance than Truman displayed. He appeared slightly uncertain, unprepared. When the noise subsided, he spoke: "You don't know how much I appreciate this very great honor which has come to the great State of Missouri." He was interrupted by yells and handclaps. He picked his words like a man searching for a lost thread: "There is also connected with it a very great responsibility, which I am perfectly willing to assume." And he would help President Roosevelt to "shorten the war and win the peace."

That is about all there was to it. With Mrs. Truman he left the convention, passing through noisy well-wishers and, managing a smile behind which there was no elation. Surrounded by police and Secret Service men, the couple walked like two lonely people, dependent only on each other, toward a waiting automobile.

Mrs. Truman asked her husband, "Are we going to have to go through this all the rest of our lives?" Harry Truman didn't reply, but he knew the answer; and if he had ever experienced fear in his life he must have been scratched by it then. He had read history assiduously and knew there were certain men whom the fates would not let alone. He had come all the way to this from a small farm, and he had come sometimes involuntarily, able to control himself but never the pressures that moved him.

The two drove through the hot Chicago night and the street noises to the Stevens Hotel where he was the man of the hour. In the suites held by news correspondents scores of typewriters told all about him. And back at the convention hall blue and yellow and red and orange balloons lay trapped against the ceiling, unable to rise higher in his honor, and in Roosevelt's honor, and in the expectation of another victory.

But as the automobiles jammed with sweaty and jubilant delegates moved from Chicago and the trains and planes carried others away to beat the bushes and pound the sidewalks for a hoped-for landslide on November 7, a few close to the President knew his state of mind, and worried. The worry was accentuated, now that the voice had come by radio to the conventioneers, accepting their nomination and faith in him. How much did he *really* care? And again, and more urgently now, would he be his old self in the political mudpile after so long in the studied and apparently enjoyed role of commander-in-chief? There was a psychological factor, to boot. Franklin D. Roosevelt, old pro and unshakable egotist, had an abiding contempt for Thomas E. Dewey. (He was to say later that Dewey was performing like a movie gang-buster with him as the villain of the piece.) Would the haughtiness in the aristocrat's nature cause him only to swat idly at the self-assured intruder, like a man irritated by a fly? And there was an even deeper concern: How fully was he aware of the so vivid decline in his health, and could he stand the rigors ahead?

On Tuesday, August 1, Dewey spoke to the nation from Pittsburgh on a six-day swing from New York toward St. Louis and the Republican Governors' Conference. Facing fifty newspapermen on the 17th floor of the Hotel William Penn, Dewey struck hard at the commander-in-chief role, declaring with a prosecutor's alternately trumpeting and softly lancing voice that the next President would have to be a peacetime magistrate as well. There would lie problems in all the residues of the New Deal, and toward these the Administration was making "no progress." He continued: " . . . We will elect a President most of whose term will be in peacetime. And, as I see it, the United States simply cannot face another period like the Roosevelt depression, which lasted for eight years, continuously from 1933 to 1940, inclusive. It may not be long before the most vital thing that faces every American is his opportunity to work, either for himself or for someone else. I am entirely satisfied that with competent government the opportunities in this country are still unlimited. We do not need to surrender our liberties to a totalitarian New Deal, and we cannot afford to."

A reporter spoke up, asking about the Democrats' talk of "changing horses in the middle of the stream." Dewey unquestionably was prepared for that one. "I should say that that argument was demolished at Chicago," he quipped. "They changed half of the horse" (the reference being to the break-off from Wallace). Everybody laughed, and Dewey showed that he could.

It was the sort of first-class quip that Roosevelt himself would have liked to have made to an opponent, and that must have intensified the sting. There was nothing to do but feed the horse named Dewey enough rope to hang himself on. But Dewey trotted along. In Des Moines, Iowa, on September 11, he said that the Roosevelt Administration had done "absolutely nothing" during the 1930's to prepare the nation for war, and lacked the competence to solve postwar problems. This was sticking to the issues, as Dewey saw them, but he somehow couldn't let Roosevelt as a person alone. A reporter asked if he would recognize Roosevelt's long federal government experience by placing him in an ex-officio Cabinet post. Dewey managed a laugh.

"I'm not indulging in Cabinet making at this time," he disclosed.

There had been some talk about Roosevelt's dog; and,

moreover, the Republicans had seized upon a photograph of the President taken when he made his acceptance speech. His failing health was clearly shown. The newspapers gave the picture wide dissemination, and the Republican publicity services included it in the campaign literature.

Roosevelt contrived a counterattack. He chose a friendly audience—the International Brotherhood of Teamsters, who were holding a pow-wow loaded with good food, fellowship and spirits at the Statler Hotel in Washington. As the President, who was guest speaker, delivered his remarks, they were broadcast to the nation:

> The Republican leaders have not been content to make personal attacks upon me—or my wife—or my sons—they include my little dog, Fala. Unlike the members of my family, Fala resents this. When he learned that the Republican fiction writers had concocted a story that I had left him behind on an Aleutian island and had sent a destroyer back to find him—at a cost to the taxpayers of two or three or twenty million dollars—his Scotch soul was furious. He has not been the same dog since. I am accustomed to hearing malicious falsehoods about myself but I think I have a right to object to libelous statements about my dog.

The voice came through the radio, soft, lulling, hurt, angry, and good-humored, the emotions incredibly blending. The nation laughed, and the laughter sliced into Dewey. Roosevelt aimed a second barb:

> Well, here we are together again—after four years—and what years they have been! I am actually four years older—which seems to annoy some people. In fact, millions of us are more than eleven years older than when we started in to clear up the mess that was dumped in our laps in 1933.

He had struck at the "tired old men" theme of his opposition, and had placed the blame for the depression upon Dewey's party. The speech had a powerfully stimulating effect on his own faithful by accelerating voter registration, which had alarmingly sagged because thousands had assumed that Roosevelt would win. Cheer spread through the party: he was back in there fighting. And across the country his supporters wanted in.

Washington, under controversial interpretation of the Constitution, was a voteless city. Thousands, of course, who had come from other parts of the country could exercise the right of absentee ballot, but none employed by the government below policy-making (very high level) positions could under the Hatch Act engage in partisan politics. But it is safe to surmise that if the result of the election had depended on the capital Dewey would have been overwhelmed. This is postulated on the fact that since the early 1930's, Roosevelt had created a mammoth bureaucracy of which every building block was a job. During his incumbency, more than a passing nod had been given Civil Service—meaning the *career* service and the safeguarding of jobs on the Register.

But during election years the air was blackened by those awful words. "To the victor belongs the spoils." Election years are incubators for butterflies with a penchant for fluttering in the stomachs of government employees, and the year 1944 was no exception. Actually, it was a bad year. After eleven years on the bench, the Republicans were eager to play. The question hung: How meaningful was Civil Service? Could it interpose between the employee and a rapacious rider of the G.O.P. elephant who came to town, saw "the Big Fix," and got the job someone had held since Roosevelt came in? It was a matter to wonder and worry about. Very probably, only a few really believed that Dewey would win. But the champ was stretching his luck. And more than luck, his hold upon the people. The third stretch had been frightening. Even Jim Farley, the finest politician except Roosevelt himself, had walked out.

And Dewey was by no means out of the running. Persons close to the President remembered a poignant occurrence. When Roosevelt reached Seattle after the midsummer Pacific trip, he broadcast to the nation from the Bremerton Navy Yard. For the first time in a long while he wore his leg braces and stood at the lectern in obvious pain. It broke through his courage and showed in his voice. The people wondered because they had heard, little by convincing little, of his physical decline. His standing went down in the next polls, and Dewey's ascended. A *maybe* tortured the job holders in Washington. But there was no uncertainty about the nature of Dewey. If elected, he would make as clean a sweep as any law allowed, or any change of administration had ever witnessed.

Participants in a distant war of horror and a battle of words between politicians at home, Washingtonians allowed some events to slide by which in peacetime would have aroused wide interest.

The Constitution of the United States and the Declaration of Independence were coming home. It appears that around August 1944, the military authorities concluded that there was no longer a danger of enemy attack on the Library of Congress and the documents might be safely returned. Joyfully and solemnly, Verner W. Clapp on September 19 handed the Chief Clerk of the Fort Knox Bullion Depository a receipt for the documents.

Early on the morning of Sunday, October 1, 1944, Captain William F. Santelmann, inheritor of the baton of Sousa in the U.S. Marine Band, assembled his musicians for ceremonies at the Library. Here was another great event for the world-renowned organization which had sounded throughout American history. It had made its official debut January 1, 1801, at the White House in a concert for President John Adams, enlivening the first New Year's reception. Counting its birthdays from July 11, 1798, the band had played for every President except George Washington.

The doors of the Library opened at 11:30 A.M. A distinguished throng of guests gathered around the nation's bedrock documents, beside which stood a Marine Guard of Honor, to be relieved successively in coming weeks by guards from the Army and Navy. Archibald MacLeish spoke briefly to the world and the Honor Guard:

Our nation differs from all others in this—that it was not
created by geographic or by racial accident but by the free
choice of the human spirit. . . . It is appropriate that these
fragile objects which bear so great a weight of meaning to
our people, and, indeed, to all the peoples of the world,
should be entrusted to the guard of men who have
themselves seen active service in a war against the enemies
of everything this Constitution and this Declaration stand
for. We leave them to your care with confidence.

Santelmann raised his baton and "The Star Spangled Banner"
rang through the vaulted hall.

Whatever anyone may have thought of Franklin D.
Roosevelt, everyone except the loser likes a winner. And
especially a charming winner who radiates something which
makes everyone feel that he also has been a winner. Even a
rainy November day can't drench the feeling. So a host of
people began dressing earlier than usual that morning and
headed for Union Station Plaza or to the sidewalks of
Pennsylvania Avenue leading to the White House. The man with
the thumping victory over Dewey was coming home and a
tumult of handclaps and triumphant yells was in order.
Morevover, any fear about the jobs was washed away as by the
rain.

When the special train wheezed and stopped at 8:28 A.M., a
police-estimated crowd of thirty thousand was waiting in the
Plaza with rain dripping from their hats or umbrellas of many
colorings, and misting the Capitol dome, aloof above the wet
treetops a few blocks away. To the west of the Plaza crowd
other thousands stood. Reporters pressed the police for the size
of the entire crowd and the police, as always, looked skyward
for information and after a while said it was somewhere around
200,000—below the number that had greeted the King and
Queen of England in 1939, but sizable by any considerations
for a city of this size.

Down by the tracks where security was tight, the Cabinet
awaited the time to board the train and shake the champ's
hand. Secretary Stimson was the first to board, spry for his 77

years. Nearby was a black automobile with bulletproof windows. On the front seat beside the chauffeur, Johnny Boettiger, the 62-year-old President's 5-year-old grandson, looked about with a child's delight at the trains. At 9 A.M. he saw his grandfather appear on the train's rear platform. Nearby, the stiffening Metropolitan Police Band raised its instruments and blared "Hail to the Chief," silencing the voices beside the train.

Soon the President was in the automobile. He wore a gray raincoat buttoned snugly at the collar, and the side-pinched gray campaign hat was high upon his broad forehead. He smiled, but the face was wan. Next to him and pressing closely was Harry Truman in a black raincoat. He did not smile. His face and eyes appeared hard, and perhaps a little sad. Next to Truman was Henry Wallace, his head slightly lowered and a mystical half-smile on his face. The car moved away.

The President began talking, casually as though he were surprised by the attention, into microphones which radiomen placed in the car.

"This is a very wonderful welcome home," he said. Then, "I hope that some of the scribes in the papers won't intimate that I expect to make Washington my permanent residence." He laughed at this little reply to the accusations that he would run for President until he died.

Washington's selected motorcycle officers, trained to form a perfect V in leading important parades, sliced through the rain along Delaware Avenue and down Pennsylvania, the engines inaudible under the blare of bands and the roar of cheers and handclapping. The President drew a laprobe almost to his neck. Where he had passed, the crowds broke apart and began walking toward their offices. Shortly after 9:30, Roosevelt was at his desk, facing another press conference. He said he had no news, and some of the campaign-weary men and women would remember that a few audibly said, "Thank God."

But he did fumble in his desk to produce his pre-election guess sealed in an envelope. He had ventured 335 to 196 electoral votes. He had, in fact, ridden an electoral landslide—432 to 99.

He had been voter No. 251 at Hyde Park Village. Having slept late, he had arrived after noon in sunshine and accepted a piece of candy from Election Inspector Mildred M. Todd. He munched while giving his occupation as "tree grower." After a few moments, an agitated clanking of metal came from the voting machine behind the green curtain, and from Roosevelt, "The goddamned thing won't work." Someone got the machine quickly adjusted. That evening he ate scrambled eggs and sat down with friends to tabulate the returns. Reporters with a precise sense of history say he went to bed at 3:50 A.M.

CHAPTER TWENTY-THREE

THE UNITED NATIONS SPROUTS AMONG THE OAKS

FROM THE WHITE HOUSE to the late Georgian estate named Dumbarton Oaks at 3101 R Street in Georgetown is a mere brisk walk for an able man, but the distance extends between two worlds. The mansion, or its smaller beginnings, had stood behind the trees since around 1800 on land that was a part of Ninian Beall's Rock of Dumbarton grant from majesty across the seas. In time, the holdings passed into ownership of various persons of affluence and prestige, and the never dusty records show that John C. Calhoun of South Carolina, the "flower of States' Rights," lived there while serving as a Senator and congealing his philosophies which would have their part in turning the nation into a charnel house. Long before 1944 the mansion was enough by itself to warrant hours of viewing, but the most discriminating of visitors often said that one must travel widely in Europe to find the equal of the Dumbarton gardens, reaching downward from the house to Rock Creek. Within the expanse of flowers and large and small hideaways of grassy knolls, all view of the city was lost, obliterating the present and, best of all, the future.

Until 1940, the estate had been owned by Mr. and Mrs. Robert Woods Bliss. Ambassador Bliss had served the nation well in Argentina, and enjoyed enormous wealth indirectly from the manufacture of Castoria, for which, according to its promoters in generations past, children clamored. The couple

225

had amassed a fabulous collection of Byzantine and early Christian art to the point where, apparently, they believed a great university should take over. Harvard was selected, and in 1940 Dumbarton Oaks became, through the university, a world center of study in the erudite field which so entranced Ambassador and Mrs. Bliss. The Blisses moved out; Harvard moved in; and within the mansion and under the oaks even while the war was thundering scholars from many lands became lost in thought.

In October 1944, throngs of strange men appeared, and behind them moved a rippling kite-tail of correspondents of the diplomatic beat so long accustomed to the State Department's jargon that they spoke of "assurances" instead of "promises," or said "I can live with that," when they meant that the proposition was satisfactory. The correspondents arrived in taxicabs. The solemn men, representatives of the United States, Great Britain, Russia, and China, alighted from black automobiles after the expressionless chauffeurs leaped out and opened the rear doors without a look into the faces of the diplomats.

Their hope was to make the lives lost on Omaha Beach and in the Pacific islands worthwhile—however distressing the losses. They wanted *this* war to end with a meaning. Alfred Lord Tennyson had envisioned a parliament of man and a federation of the world, and Woodrow Wilson had sliced off his life on the sharp edges of the ideal.

The diplomats talked for seven weeks, mostly at a long table in a room of distracting beauty, where long windows indulged a view of lawns where the little birds that remain into November hopped from bush to tree limb and back upon the grass again. The conference ended with a resolve that a security organization to be known as the United Nations be established. It could take "such action by air, naval or land forces as may be necessary to maintain or restore international peace." A tentative charter was drawn to be deliberated upon at a later time by all but the present enemy powers. The meeting would begin on April 12, 1945, in San Francisco.

The Dumbarton Oaks Conference was ended; the hopeful among the peoples of the world took heart; the doubters, who knew the appeal of drum and trumpet poisoning the veins of men since almost the first man, said, in effect, here-we-go-again; and the great house with its trees was returned to the purposes of scholarship. From nearby Montrose Park the shrill voices of children drifted through the oaks and through the sounds of the birds and the sighs of November winds that had no destination.

CHAPTER TWENTY-FOUR

GRAY CHRISTMAS

THE WEEKS PASSED into December, which had never meant much more than Christmas, and it was hard to believe that the capital was nearing its fourth Christmas overcast by war. And yet there might be something to celebrate besides the birth of Christ: vague rumors, never from responsible authority, had spread during the fall that the war in Europe might be ended by Christmas. With the arrival of fall, the Allied armies were pressing against the Rhine; Luxembourg and Belgium were liberated, and the Germans fought mostly in retreat—though with a stubborness that nonetheless would surely be broken. The victory, never doubted, appeared to be startlingly near. And then what would happen? The Allies would combine against Japan, and the little paper-lantern people who had been more deadly than was ever supposed would be overrun. That shouldn't take very long, although it would certainly be costly.

Christmas and its approach bring soul-searchings that touch the past more than the present. The question now was, what had all of this meant? Or what had it proven? There was a meaning: evil sores which had erupted upon two sides of the earth were healing after terribly drastic surgery. And maybe, but just maybe, it wouldn't happen again. The proper men who had talked for so long behind the Georgetown oaks might, after all, have at least set in motion a formula for peace. And what was proven? There was the certainty that the individualistic

American could be disciplined and to a large extent regimented with a minimum of grumbling when the cause was justified. But as the introspections deepened and became unsparingly honest, it was admitted that the American at home had not undergone too much suffering—aside from the deaths in the Pacific and in Europe.

What hardships there had been would soon be over. Women would stop their interminable talk about nylons. These would return in the little long boxes to the store counters. And it would be nothing to say to an alert clerk, "a pack of Camels, a carton of Chesterfields, two cartons of Luckies." And the coupons for shoes, gasoline, sugar, and all the other necessities might disappear in a headline one morning. People—other people, of course—would be flushed from the town, opening space for comfortable living, space for walking on the sidewalks, accommodations in restaurants, and opportunities for permanent jobs in a magnificent city that would be wonderful to live in once this infernal crowd got out.

In the meantime, however, the small discomforts and privations continued. Newspapers of December 2 related that there would be no more chicken—or at any rate very little—and these tidings came at a time when better days seemed just around the corner. The War Food Administration explained that all chickens produced in Virginia, West Virginia, and Delaware would be bought by the Army Quartermaster Corps, and all persons between Richmond and New York would "find fewer chickens." And, then, "Consumers who are not able to purchase chickens as often as they would like are asked to remember that chicken is for fighters first"—a direct steal from the replies of store clerks about everything. Eastern seaboard people would, however, continue to eat turkeys, guineas, ducks, squabs, and geese. Why the chickens had not been seized to begin with was not made clear. Rather the old whipping boy, the black marketeer, was blamed. These gentry, it was pointed out, had caused the Quartermaster Corps to lag in chicken purchases by 110 million pounds.

Meanwhile, on the smoking front, the cigarette shortage

became more acute. Mindful of the abrasive effect upon public morale, the editorial board of the *Washington Post* joined in analysis of the problem, devoting its lead editorial of December 2 to the cigarette shortage. It concluded that "the major cause of the cigarette shortage is simply that there are fewer cigarettes than are needed to satisfy the demands of smokers." Following this profound observation, the editorialist gave the deprived some statistics to inhale. The 1944 output was streaming at record levels. There should be 241 billion cigarettes after the number shipped overseas was subtracted, or 23 billion more than the entire output of 1941. The people, it was urged, might decide to smoke less and make cigarettes last longer. The newspaper rejected rationing, believing it "would present almost insuperable enforcement difficulties."

To help drown thoughts of all this, there was some booze around, with rum in the greatest quantity. Old Crow was advertised (though it was not announced where it could be found) and an advertisement invited all to "Say It With Three Feathers, Now on Hand at Its Pre-War Cost . . . $3.75 for 4/5 Quart." Groceries, to judge by the ads, were abundant, but seemed less in evidence when one entered the stores. An 11-ounce can of soup sold for 10¢; two quarts of milk for 23¢; eggs went for 45¢ a dozen; grapes for 23¢ a pound. A full-page ad from the huge Hecht Department Store reminded readers without noticeable relevance that "Catherine the Great Was a Great Hand for Handbags."

In mid-December, gasoline rationing reached a crisis. Cars ran dry in the streets in the capital's worst gas famine. The few physicians had in many instances to be carried on their rounds by police and fire department vehicles. Had motorists not nursed their cars to curbs there might have been a Mack Sennett comedy mixup of automobiles in a heterogeneous obstruction of thoroughfares. On December 17, more than five thousand phoned the American Automobile Association to find out where gas station pumps had fuel. They had to go to work. Many stations had closed and would remain so for two days until the new ten-day gas allotment period would begin. The buses which had an approved arrangement with wholesalers kept running, and the keen of ambulances still sounded.

The government explained the causes of the shortage. Tank cars had been removed from the East to other areas for reasons of necessity; a large number of tank ships had been converted from civilian use; and the government had resolved to amass adequate reserves of gasoline for the use of farmers during the spring planting. A headline on December 21 read, "Gas Stations Still Turn Away Hard-Pressed D.C. Motorists."

All that thousands could do while remaining at home was to hum their troubles away. They chose old favorites like Irving Berlin's "Always" and "I'll Get By," as well as newer ones such as "Don't Fence Me In." Berlin's popular "White Christmas" rode melodiously on the vague hope of peace by the year's end.

The women had been told soon after Pearl Harbor that sober dress reflected patriotism, something hard to abide by but nevertheless accepted. Now as the war neared its end they perked up and junked the tiny hats that had been in vogue for years, and put on tall and nearly brimless headwear. These fashions had originated in Paris during the jubilation after the Germans were chased out. The irrepressible something new would affect fashion generally until the war ended.

There was a pre-Christmas lull touched by the unquenchable excitement of window shopping and the arrangements for small parties. Christmas would come fast enough for everyone except the children.

Vice President-elect Harry Truman viewed the future and said he would principally be a liaison man between the White House and the Senate. He would avoid Henry Wallace's mistake—the helter-skelter pursuit of chores which he had so apparently thrived on. Truman had begun to socialize a little more, but he continued to work doggedly in the fixed belief that he had never got anything except by work. Life and war kept a fairly even balance.

But with benumbing suddenness the war again overshadowed everything. An eight-column banner headline in the *Washington Post* of December 18 carried the jolting news: "Nazis Open Big Offensive, Enter Belgium." And below: "Foe Strikes With Tanks, Planes on 60-Mile Front."

People grabbed for the papers, reading, "The German army reinvaded Belgium and Luxembourg in an all-out offensive yesterday, denting U.S. First Army lines with thousands of troops and scores of tanks attacking on a 60-mile front. This first major counter-offensive since Normandy was gaining in intensity." The story was signed by Associated Press Correspondent Edward Kennedy, well known in Washington. The news fell on a partly cloudy day, whipped by winds in temperatures around the mid-30's.

Christmas cheer was whirled away as by the winds. And the cheer would remain in abeyance. It scarcely returned when on the 20th a headline related: "First Army Fights Back to Balk Major Breakthrough; North Flank Assault Slowed in Bloody Battles."

This was the Battle of the Bulge, Von Rundstedt's surprise breakthrough hatched up by his desperate leader, who still believed that some magic in his fantastic dream would now save his frightened and actually cringing life and the life of his almost flattened fatherland. Washingtonians reading the New York *Herald Tribune* of December 19 might have gained some fortitude. Leo Cullinane wrote:

> Authoritative War Department sources calmly discounted today the over-all effect of the new German counter-offensive against the American 1st Army in Western Europe, saying, "It is nothing to get excited about," and cited two reasons why it was made at this time.
>
> 1. Sheer military necessity. The Germans, having been hedged in by overwhelming American forces, called upon the major portion of their reserve strength to break through and reduce the extent of Allied operations.
> 2. Propaganda purposes. The Allies have been pounding the Germans hard and sending them reeling back constantly for weeks on end, and the new move is calculated to give the German people at home a "psychological lift" particularly during the holiday season.

From the front a news blackout curtain began falling. In

Washington there remained a few more days before Christmas. The people knew that the soldiers were fighting in cold and snow and wondered how many more such Christmases would yet pile up. The soldiers and the airmen had experienced setbacks before but had always won in the end and there was glory somewhere far away, but now there was again nothing but uncertainty and doubt, and from these no release.

On Christmas Eve morning of 1944, police radios blared that "A bear is prowling about in the rear of 3905 Reservoir Road, Northwest!" It would develop that Edmund Leonard, of Haymarket, Virginia, who had been a hunter since childhood days, looked from a window of his brother's home at the Reservoir Road address and shouted, "Whoops. A bear." His brother Robert along with his wife and their three red-haired daughters, Peggy, two, Marian, six, and Ruby, nine, sprang from decorating the Christmas tree and rushed to a window.

"It sure is," Robert agreed. Having no guns in the house, they called the police. The report sounded through the police radio in the newsroom of the *Post* and a reporter telephoned the Zoo. An attendant was sent to the bear cages and returned to say that every bear was accounted for. Soon, six Metropolitan and Park Service police reached the Leonard home. They were told that the bear had gone to a nearby brook to drink. The police followed the tracks and came upon a lost and frightened Chow dog, which answered obediently to a whistled summons. The owner, Howard Jones, had a happier Christmas in getting his dog back.

On this fourth Christmas Eve of the war years, an estimated 300,000 people turned out to worship—and many to wonder, no doubt, how many more such Christmas Eves lay ahead. Inside Union Station, people stood beside a Christmas tree at the Traveler's Aid desk and sang carols from 6 P.M. to midnight. A soldier shared his carol sheet with a hatless man in a fur coat whose vocalizing flowed from a mouth topped by a huge mustache. Among the crowd were ordinary travelers, policemen, waitresses, and kitchen help from the station's

restaurant. The sound became unearthly in the vaulted
immensity:

> *Silent night, holy night,*
> *All is calm, all is bright. . . .*

The War Hospitality Committee made sure that uniformed
men and women had seats during the midnight services in
formal places of worship. The crowds overflowed. At the
candlelight service held at National City Christian Church near
Thomas Circle, Army Staff Sergeant Virgil Fox played the organ
(he was later to become nationally renowned for his artistry);
Pfc. Erno Valasek of the Air Force was the violinist; Army
Sergeant Richard Weagley was tenor soloist; and the narration
was given by Corporal Mark Austad of the Marine Corps. A
brass ensemble from the U.S. Navy Band contributed to the
music.

Servicemen and civilians helped 350 needy families have a
better Christmas at the Central Union Mission.

At the *Post,* compositors were adjusting the six-column
headline, "Yanks Dent Nazis' Southern Flank at Four Points
Along 25-Mile Front; 7000 Allied Planes Hammer 'Bulge.' "
This would greet early risers on Christmas morning.

The weather was depressing—indeed, everything had been
depressing except the hope-filled hymns of the night before. In
the parks, the pigeons huddled under the drippings of light and
intermittent rain falling through the bare trees. The temperature
was noticeably lowering, and the few people on the streets
hunched deeply into their outer wraps. Strangers in the city had
a hard time finding food. Most restaurants had closed because
of the holiday. Hotel dining rooms and a few less pretentious
places remained open but were packed beyond capacity
throughout midday and the afternoon. The wait to be seated
generally lasted longer than an hour. The price of a plate of
turkey, the fixings, and the inevitable polished green peas was
$3.50. A loneliness invested the streets everywhere downtown.
There was little traffic, and along the streets men and women in

uniforms walked, in a quietness that was a part of the day, of the gray sky, of the slight but soaking rain. Beneath the high rafters of the Church of the Epiphany on G Street near 13th, a few people sat. They had just wandered in; there was no formal service. In one of the pews a WAVE sat with her head bowed, and once she took a handkerchief and wiped her eyes. Near her was a woman in expensive furs. She sat for a long time with her head bowed. When she left, she dropped several bills into a box at the door and wandered off down the street.

A short time after Christmas, on January 7, 1945, Washingtonians discovered through a by-line in the *Post* that Edward T. Folliard—so long known to them and respected—was serving as a war correspondent for his paper and was at the Bulge. His story was datelined January 4 and "With the U.S. Third Army—Luxembourg." Here was a report strengthened by the human-interest details which the people really wanted. Folliard described the prisoners of war taken by the 26th "Yankee" Division in the Ardennes, and he saw many of them as the very antithesis of a theoretical Nazi Superman. "Some of the Germans would be rated as worse than 4-F at home," he wrote.

> This is the Ardennes and it is not blitzkrieg country—certainly not at this time of the year. Snow blankets the land and it is so cold that trigger fingers get numb if taken out of gloves to light a cigarette.
>
> It is a country of towering hills and deep gorges, a great country for forests and corkscrew hills that make the Washington-Annapolis Highway look like a slide rule. . . . Washingtonians would have to say it is not quite so precipitous as the sprawling God's country down in Virginia, but more so than the rolling country up around Frederick and Braddock Heights in Maryland.
>
> . . . The German salient looks much different up here from what it does on a newspaper map. On the map, the tactical problem looks very simple. You have a bulge in the Allied line extending something like 50 miles from the German frontier.

A German outfit dug in around a village (here) can play hell with a fellow that wants to escape the place. They set up their guns and spray the roads for miles around. You would wonder how anybody or anything could ever drive them out.

The exquisite understatement was as though Folliard was talking to the people in the city where he had been born. He went along:

Well, the Yankee Division did drive them out, and so helped mightily to open the way to Bastogne which rises to the northeast. Maj. Gen. Willard S. Paul, Division Commander, is a lickety-split fellow who is described by the outfit's star officer as "the movingest man who I ever saw."

Folliard then described how he "came down from Paris by way of Rheims and the American Ninth Air Force" on through Belgium to join the Yankee Division:

Passing its [Yankee Division] battle route, virtually every house in the villages had been battered and gutted. . . . Nevertheless, the natives were coming back to start all over again.

The roads were strewn with signs of battle-wrecked German tanks and field pieces, battered German helmets, fresh graves surmounted by hastily-fashioned crosses, and here and there a human corpse lying alone in a ditch.

Every village, it seemed, had its wayside shrine, a little hut inside which reposed a statue of Jesus or Mother Mary. These were being used as shelters by American sentries.

General Paul shows us the map and points out the high points where the Germans are dug in. The going is slow, maddeningly slow for this "movingest man."

It's like spending a night out in Rock Creek Park without a fire, only worse. For one thing, it's colder, and for another, there are men out there who want to kill us. They may be 4-F's, but they've got guns, and being Germans they know how to use them.

CHAPTER TWENTY-FIVE

INAUGURAL IN THE SNOW

IT WAS IMPOSSIBLE to know that by February 1945, the German attack would be broken. The gap was closing under drives by General Patton from the south and the British in the north. Brussels and Antwerp were free of the Nazi reach and the Allied armor rolled forward again and the infantrymen sloughed off mile by mile. There was criticism of the Allied command, but actually the German assault had damaged the Nazi chances—slight though the chances were at this point of the war. The last of their failing strength had been hurled upon favorable ground and become exhausted. The war in Europe became once more what it had been, but not enough of the details in terms of suffering and bravery were known in the United States. All they knew was that the men had done it again.

But something curious had happened in the meantime: the joy of victory had lost its edge. There was something monotonous in the sight of men and women crowding into the nightclubs and a hollowness in the sound of the bands. The war, seemingly endless, had taken precedence over life. Few had appeared to give a damn back in November when the President had announced casually that his fourth-term Inaugural would be held on the south portico of the White House rather than on the east front of the Capitol, the traditional place of swearings-in. Moreover, there would be no parades, hurrahs, thumpings, and

237

barkings of such dogs as Poundmaster Frank Marks had failed to catch. The unprecedented fourth-term ceremony, scheduled for Saturday, January 20, 1945, would be scaled down to save materials ordinarily used for seating stands along the Avenue, and floats and other trivialities attendant upon a Chief Magistrate's oath to "preserve, protect and defend the Constitution."

There was but scant public reaction upon learning that a selected audience would gain admittance to the White House South Lawn, while others might witness the ceremony through the iron fence palings or from the Ellipse across the street. It wasn't so much that the Roosevelt Inaugural was like a fourth-told tale, but that people were saturated with sights and sounds, all of them seeming the same. As a conversation piece, it was much more interesting that men had gone to buy safety razors and were shown selections made of unusable plastic. Or had tried to replace broken parts of alarm clocks and been frowned out of the stores. Life had degenerated into pettinesses, burdensome in the accumulation. Roosevelt would probably go on forever and that could be endured—according to the majority point of view—but when would this war end? All the talk of a conclusion heard during the past summer had faded in the fogs of the Ardennes.

Just before the Inaugural, it became known that the President had retreated before an issue raised inside the White House. He had ordered chicken a la king for the two thousand luncheon guests. But back came the word: there would be no such dish. Mrs. Henrietta Nesbit, the housekeeper, bespectacled and strong-jawed, told the President that "We are not going to have that because it's hot. And you can't keep it hot for all those people." Gwen Morgan, of the United Press, discovered that the dictum had come from Mrs. Nesbit's swivel chair, where she was "enthroned" at a desk "covered with cook books, both foreign and domestic, that would make a collector's eyes gleam. . . . " And paradoxically, the very simplicity of the Inaugural was making the arrangements the worst of any. Mrs. Nesbit explained: "No ceremony at the

Capitol, no parade, but just a few minutes of talk out on the porch, and then—bang!—the hordes are upon us. Why, it's all going to be right underfoot."

Mrs. Roosevelt got in a word. The luncheon would be "very slim, indeed." There would be chicken salad (in which Mrs. Roosevelt later said there was more celery than chicken), rolls, coffee, and unfrosted cake. There would be no butter for the rolls, inasmuch as it was customarily served only at breakfast.

The two thousand guests were twice the number invited to the third Inaugural luncheon. Thus, there would have to be 90 gallons of chicken salad, accounting for 200 chickens (apparently no one mentioned the Quartermaster Corps dilemma), 190 dozen rolls, 165 cakes, and 100 gallons of coffee. There would be three buffet tables and one hundred waiters to serve those crowded from the spread-out repast. The East Room, the State Dining Room, and another downstairs would be the centers of the feeding.

This, even so, was all too much, and brought from Mrs. Nesbit the hard observation that "Why, just an affair for eight hundred persons absolutely fills the White House." Compounding this, a clean-up must get under way between 2 and 4 P.M., for a tea scheduled for 4:30 P.M. would bring 1,800 new faces into the East Room and Dining Room. This crowd would devour 200 dozen small cookies and 100 marble cakes, minus icing.

There was but one thing to do: "The best we can." That was the way Mrs. Nesbit accepted the situation, while the Commander-in-Chief, engrossed in the surprising turn in Europe, withdrew from the fray.

The peculiar shape of the Inaugural was most observable to six cameramen, one reporter, four federal officials and an army sergeant who looked down from the 555-foot Washington Monument a half-mile away. The White House gleamed like a sculptured ice block on a flooring of snow. The red and blue of an American flag placed flat against the portico was a lone dab of color. The flag on the staff near the microphones was limp in the cold quiet day. Facing the portico the selected guests formed a huddled block of black; behind the huddle lay a wide expanse of snow-covered lawn entrapped by the curving black fence; and pressed against the fence was a raggedly-formed crowd peering toward the portico. Hundreds of people stood across the street and many stomped their feet to relieve the cold. Some looked upward at a sky that was low and leaden.

Statistics, of which Washington was so enamored, would come later: 7,806 people were admitted to the lawn, while 5,000 had gathered around the fence and upon the Ellipse. Six-figure crowds had stood before the Capitol and along the Avenue during inaugurations past. Now the Avenue displayed only the flags, and its accustomed daily activity.

Notables on the lawn and balcony looked about for other notables and spotted Mrs. Woodrow Wilson. They reflected that she had not been seen much in public lately, and was looking quite well. Bernard Baruch was quietly present; then down the steps came spry Jimmy Byrnes, now the War Mobilization Director, to chat with acquaintances on the lawn; on the balcony Samuel Rosenman took pictures. Representative Everett M. Dirksen, the Illinois Republican who had wanted the nomination until Dewey shoved him aside, had been among the earliest to appear for a place in the snow on the lawn. Republicans were very noticeable, among them Senators Leverett Saltonstall of Massachusetts, Warren R. Austin of Vermont, Arthur Capper of Kansas, and Harlan J. Bushfield of South Dakota. And there was Representative Earl Wilson of Indiana, who had sometime back agitated for a curfew for government girls, which made him quite popular back home but something else in Washington.

Eleven of the President's 13 grandchildren stood on the west steps. With them and their nurses were Diana Hopkins and the three children of Crown Prince Olaf and Crown Princess Martha of Norway. Upon the porch were Anna Eleanor Dall, seventeen, oldest of the grandchildren, and her brother, Curtis Dall, Jr. They were the well-known "Sistie" and "Buzzie" to family and public alike, remembered from the first term.

In favored positions on the lawn stood wounded soldiers from Walter Reed and Maryland's Forest Glen hospitals—fifty quiet men. They had come mostly from Europe, but some had been wounded in the Pacific theater. One volunteered that Mrs. Roosevelt had sent the invitations. The overcoat one of them wore could not cover the place where his right leg had been.

Harry Hopkins wore a felt hat with the brim turned up, and in elegant contrast Mrs. Anna Roosevelt Boettiger wore a silver fox jacket and fondled a large bouquet of white violets. If the sun had shone, Lord Halifax, puffing meditatively on a pipe, would have cast a long shadow on the lawn. Mrs. Elliott Roosevelt (Faye Emerson) wore mink and carried a bouquet of blue violets.

The black splotches of crowd on the snow jerked suddenly when the Marine Band opened with "El Capitan." It was 11:25 A.M. Stiffening to the music were the military conductors of the great martial symphony abroad—General Marshall and Admiral King among them. There was only one other glimpse of stiff formality: a silk hat was worn by Governor Charles M. Dale of New Hampshire.

The President took the oath from Chief Justice Stone. Roosevelt had stood without a hat or topcoat in the cold on the arm of his eldest son, James—now a Marine Corps colonel wearing the green service uniform and an overseas cap. The President's hand gripped a yellowed 259-year-old family Bible, opened to I *Corinthians,* the "Faith, hope and charity" passage.

He spoke to the world that morning: "In the days and years that are to come we shall work for a just and durable peace as today we work and fight for total victory in war."

Harry Truman, now Vice President after being sworn in by Henry Wallace, had told a reporter: "I have worked hard all my life. That's the only recipe for success I know. I'm going to be the hardest working vice president you ever saw."

The benediction and the National Anthem closed the Inauguration.

The remainder of the day was left to Mrs. Nesbit.

CHAPTER TWENTY-SIX

"THERE IS NO ARMOR AGAINST FATE. . . . "

THURSDAY, APRIL 12, 1945, was just another day in Washington, as a December 7 so long ago had been, and in its center was the same man, Franklin Delano Roosevelt. Just as on that December day it was believed that a war that seemed inevitable would be somehow averted by a man who could perform miracles, those who thought fleetingly of the President's failing health on that quiet afternoon of April 12 were probably convinced that his genius for life would conquer it. Death might beckon to him, but if death was a gentleman it would not persist; it would withdraw before the engaging smile and the flip of the fingers holding the long cigarette holder.

But, incredibly, Franklin Roosevelt was dead. The word came to many people in the usual ways—by telephone to friends who probably had already heard of it, across backyard fences, and by the familiar "Have you heard?" spoken to strangers, just as strangers had spoken to strangers the night of Pearl Harbor. Steve Early telephoned the Washington wire services at 5:40 P.M., saying, "Here is a flash. The President died suddenly this afternoon. . . . " The voice was low and steady but shocked.

The capital was still by nightfall, and there was a widespread feeling that the report wasn't true. The notion had come earlier to a correspondent for *Time* while driving with a photographer to Charlottesville, Virginia, to cover a fairly routine assignment.

When the announcement came through the car's radio, the correspondent said it couldn't be true. Like others, he felt that Roosevelt was indestructible, a power beyond such an everyday occurrence as death. But the photographer, who had been close to Roosevelt during the past months, turned the car around in the road and found a filling station and telephoned Washington. Then he said without the slightest inflection, "We're going back in."

Earlier that day, Mrs. Roosevelt had been the guest of honor at a tea for the benefit of children's clinics. The event was held in the exclusive Sulgrave Club at Dupont Circle. It would be remembered that she displayed her usual gaiety. Just that morning she had heard from Warm Springs that the President had eaten a substantial breakfast and was feeling fine. She was chatting pleasantly with Mrs. Woodrow Wilson when someone broke in to say there was a telephone call. A short while later Mrs. Roosevelt returned to say, regretfully, that she must leave.

When she reached the second-floor Sitting Room in the White House Steve Early told her, "The President has slept away." She sat silently for a few moments and then said, "I am more sorry for the people of the country and the world than I am for us."

On Capitol Hill, Vice President Truman went for one of his frequent afternoon visits to the office of his old friend Speaker Rayburn. He was poured a drink of bourbon and tap water. The telephone rang; the Vice President was wanted. Steve Early told him the Georgian news. It was remembered that Truman's face changed strangely, then paled. He walked from the office without saying a word, but Rayburn sensed what Truman had been told. He spoke quickly, "We'll all stand by you, Harry." It was also remembered that only the day before, Truman, while talking casually to reporters, had said that all he had ever wanted to be in Washington was a Senator.

At the White House, Mrs. Roosevelt told Truman, "The President has passed away." His reply came through a choked throat, "What can I do?" Mrs. Roosevelt asked if they could help him.

She wrote to her sons: "He did his job to the end as he would want you to do. Bless you and all our love—Mother." She dressed in black and in the early night took a plane for Georgia.

Truman was sworn in by Chief Justice Stone in the Cabinet Room of the White House Executive Offices. His left hand grasped a small black Bible with red-edged leaves. His right hand was raised in oath to the height of his shoulder. A white handkerchief peeped in three sharp points from his coat lapel pocket, and he wore a prim bow tie. His eyes were sad and staring. Mrs. Truman stood on his left, and there was nothing in her eyes but grief. The face of their daughter was expressionless. When it was finished there came a round of handshaking but no one smiled.

When Washingtonians finally became convinced that the President was dead, crowds that varied in size kept vigil in Lafayette Park through the night and into the next day. Throughout the city and the Maryland and Virginia countrysides people arranged to be on the streets between Union Station and the White House when the cortege would pass during the morning of Saturday, April 14. (Had the time element permitted and travel been unrestricted, the capital certainly would have become overwhelmed by crowds from every part of the nation.) That was about all the respect they could show. They could not, of course, attend the simple funeral services to be held that afternoon in the White House.

The great men of the world paused in all the madness to say that they were grieved, and American flags blew in foreign winds at half-staff. Churchill said that the President's death was "the loss of the British nation and of the cause of freedom in every land." And "profound regret" settled upon King George VI. Stalin believed that "the American people and the United Nations have lost in Franklin Roosevelt a great politician of world significance and a pioneer in the organization of peace and security after the war."

There was nothing normal about Washington on the morning of April 14 except the first gropings of the flowers and the pale featherings of the trees in a bright but humid day. Stores, showplaces, and government offices were closed. Twenty-six hotels announced through their Association that dancing and other diversions would be discontinued until Monday. Church and synagogue doors were open and people came in to pray and meditate. The National Theater canceled two performances of the Maurice Schwartz play *Three Generations*. A reminder hung upon the day: On another April 14, President Lincoln—the first of three great war Presidents—had been fatally struck down. The capital suddenly now was without song or love or laughter.

The people stood five deep on the sidewalks between Union Station and the White House. There was a brief flurry when a woman fainted in the crush or under the worst part of it all—the nerve-wracking silence. The special train arrived at Union Station at 9:50 A.M. As the mile-long procession moved westward from the station the crowds turned, staring. But the soldiers lining the avenue with bayoneted rifles didn't flinch. A faint breeze came from nowhere and rippled the flags at half-staff on the buildings. The world seemed in motion again, whirled along in the furious roar from the skies of Flying Fortresses and Liberator bombers. The Marine Band played, and to a *Washington Star* reporter, the music "was almost unbearable in its solemn tones." The roar of the planes faded into the distance, but the sounds of sobbing could be heard, near and sometimes loud. There was an almost uniform gesture along the line as the people passed: people put their hands to their faces, pressed their faces for a moment, and then released their hands.

The band played Teckham's "Our Fallen Heroes," the "Marche Pathetique," and "Our Illustrious Dead." Behind it marched in dress uniform 680 midshipmen of the 3rd Battalion of the United States Naval Academy. The beating of drums was heard, and the pounding of feet. Reconnaissance cars moved four abreast, each bearing eight helmeted soldiers. Armored cars passed, and machine guns poked upward.

The flag-draped coffin on the black caisson moved slowly behind the six white horses, flanked by an honor guard. The crowd tried to move with it. The procession went on. The Navy

Band led four companies of marines, four companies of sailors, and companies of WAACs, WAVES, and the women of the other services. The automobiles bearing the family and President Truman and Cabinet and diplomatic officials passed by. Far along, the Washington Monument reached high into the April blue, but nobody looked at it.

The procession turned toward 15th Street within sight of the White House, and there the crowd was dense and quiet. For a full half hour two British army officers had stood beside the Treasury Building without saying a word to each other. When the caisson rolled by they stiffened in salute. Their eyes followed the caisson for a while and their hands snapped down. Without a word they moved along with the crowd.

The crowd of mourners—estimated at 400,000—was densest in the vicinity of Lafayette Park. They were men and women and servicemen and servicewomen and infants held on people's shoulders. Some looked for a while at an old Negro woman sitting on the sidewalk and crying, "Oh. He's gone. He's gone forever. I loved him so. He's never coming back."

The caisson made a crackling sound when it rolled into the White House drive. The coffin was carried in. The white horses and the caisson stood before the door, and the crowd peered from the park. The day was so quiet now that the smallest birds could be heard. The sun had become hot, but its heat was overlooked in the hour of drums and death.

In the East Room, the casket was centered upon a small Oriental rug. A wall of flowers brightened the gun-metal gray bronze coffin. The scent of the flowers was heavy in the room and the lighting from the three chandeliers was dim. But the lighting illuminated the gold of two hundred straight-back gold-colored chairs. In front of these and in the center were a dozen chairs upholstered in green brocade. These were for the family.

Mrs. Roosevelt entered the room and everyone stood; President Truman entered and everyone kept his seat. (Observers of this action did not believe that any discourtesy was intended; the mourners were preoccupied.) Harry Hopkins, who had arrived from the Mayo Clinic in Minnesota, was as pale as death himself. The service, conducted by Bishop Angus Dun of the Episcopal Diocese of Washington, was simple and lasted 23 minutes. At the start the mourners stood and sang "The Eternal Father," the Navy hymn. At the close they sang "Faith of Our Fathers." The diplomats and the others left to go about their business affairs, to be conducted now under an untried man. But the Washington people kept their vigil across the Avenue.

The people meant to honor Roosevelt to the last. That night when the body was conveyed back to Union Station, a crowd of some 200,000 packed 15th Street and Constitution Avenue, and the Station Plaza. While the Army Air Force Band played "The Star Spangled Banner," the casket was placed at 9:47 P.M. aboard the last car of the seventeen-car train. A short while later, a light, warm rain began falling. Charles Harrison, forty-nine, the porter on the car that bore the body to Hyde Park, said, after a moment of thought: "This is the greatest honor of my life, although it's a very sad thing."

Estate) and during her tenure after the government took control it was her duty to greet the guests and see to their comfort. This was an important position in Washington because, with the exception of the cannon salutes and the bands at the airport, the first and most important impressions came from the Blair House custodian.

Mrs. Geaney knew the unpretentiousness of the Truman family and must have felt few qualms. During April 1944, she had escorted President and Mrs. Roosevelt through the premises, showing the sterling collections, furniture, and other rarities that had been in the Blair family for four generations. She remembered it as "a wonderful few hours."

But it wasn't always that easy. The visit in 1943 of Amir Faisal and Amir Khalid, two princes from Saudi Arabia, had required special preparations.

"I wanted to make them comfortable, yet I didn't know very much about the customs of their country and what kind of food they would eat," Mrs. Geaney recalled. So she read books about Arabia and asked questions. At dinnertime, the princes were delighted by a meal of lamb and rice marvelously like the food enjoyed back home.

Her life was packed with excitement but with very little awe.

"They are all just human people with important problems on their minds when they come here," she once explained. "It's my job to make them feel right at home, and give them the best in real American hospitality." Unlike the majority of Washington householders, Mrs. Geaney had no "help" problem. "I have a faithful, efficient staff that stays with me. You know, I think they like the excitement as much as I do."

Many things besides the war and a world waiting for peace played on the President's mind. For one thing, there must be changes sooner or later in the men around him, and one of these would be a new press secretary. The importance of finding the right man could not be overestimated. The press secretary literally guides the President in his relations with the news media and can produce favorable reactions through right timing and sound judgment, or can cause incalculable damage by advising or personally uttering one inappropriate phrase. It certainly lay on Truman's mind when he held his first press conference on April 17 in the Oval Office. The space was jammed by 348 reporters—an unprecedented number who did an unprecedented thing in applauding when the session ended. Then the President went on the radio to tell the nation's fighting men around the world that all was well in Washington.

His first week went by: He talked with British Foreign Secretary Anthony Eden; he received a delegation of Republican leaders led by Senator Robert A. Taft of Ohio, who expressed complete bipartisan support; he signed a bill—his first—prolonging the Lend-Lease Act, and he found moments to help the Veterans of Foreign Wars open their annual fund-raising drive by buying a poppy from Margaret Ann Forde, age five. Then he got around to doing something about a press secretary.

Two choices weighed on his mind. There was brisk and hard-driving Samuel A. O'Neal, former reporter for the St. Louis *Post-Dispatch* and presently publicity director for the Democratic National Committee, which wallowed in an expanse of plush offices on the second floor of the Mayflower Hotel while constantly agonizing the air with cries of financial impoverishment. And there was Missourian Charles G. Ross—a man with a double appeal to such a personality as Harry Truman because the ties stretched back half a century. The two had sat close by at school desks in Independence, and they had remained in touch through adult life, though Ross had chosen a newspaperman's role and Truman that of haberdasher and politician. O'Neal was an extrovert, and Ross the precise opposite. O'Neal had a touch of the dandy and a flair with clothes. Ross could wear a seersucker suit in summer and wind a long leg across the arm of a chair, suggesting a Lincoln posture. But while Lincoln might slowly rise and articulate his thoughts in whispers of beauty, Ross could fling himself upon a typewriter and raise hell with the calling of names. He had done that in 1931 in an article called "The Country's Plight—What Can Be Done About It?", an analysis of Herbert Hoover's administration. A Pulitzer Prize had fallen in his lap, and now, in 1945, while he was importantly engaged with the *Post-Dispatch*, a message from Truman fell on his head. Ross did not want to involve himself in the White House, and, furthermore, the move would mean a cut in salary from $35,000 to $10,000 a year. Joseph Pulitzer, owner of the newspaper, was also reluctant, until the President phoned him; the Presidential desire, traditionally, has been a command. A short time later, the "weatherbird" on the newspaper's front page reported, "Truman Kidnapped Charlie Ross." (Another Charlie Ross had been a famous kidnapping victim.)

After agreeing to take the job, Ross asked for one thing—he wanted to cover the San Francisco conference first. Truman assented. Heading West aboard the correspondents' special train, Ross was enthusiastically congratulated on his appointment. The congratulations bothered him, because he had understood the appointment would be kept secret until the conference adjourned. Obviously, somebody had talked.

The news had leaked out in a curious way. Miss Matilda Brown, who had taught English to Truman and Ross at the Independence high school, had sent congratulations to Truman after his nomination in Chicago. The message was filled with sentimental reminiscences. Truman had shown the letter to Ross, and said he would phone the teacher sometime. They did so the night Ross agreed to become press secretary. When the phone rang, Miss Brown was busy in her kitchen. Truman spoke:

"Miss Tillie, I've just appointed Charlie Ross my personal press secretary. I wanted you to be the first to know about it. We're here together now, talking over old times." Ross picked up the phone, and Miss Brown exclaimed, "Bless your heart! I'm glad you boys are going to work together again. Now you help Harry all you can, Charlie."

When Ross became ensconced in an office with a thick red carpet, black fireplace, and pea-green walls, his desk was only two doors removed from Harry Truman's. But now when they spoke, Ross called him "Mr. President," and Truman addressed him as "Charlie."

CHAPTER TWENTY-EIGHT

FROM THE DARKNESS FLASHED A LIGHT

WASHINGTON HAD A MASS peculiarity: It was seldom noisily demonstrative. The people liked parades and might turn out in suffocating numbers—though some credited this to the Roosevelt era when government employees were shooed into the streets to give paraded dignitaries a fine, if false, impression—but there was never such emotionalism as New York City, say, could display on a New Year's Eve or during a parade for a home-coming hero. The capital, like a self-assured old lady, was more inclined to show visible shock or sorrow—as it had on Pearl Harbor day and at Roosevelt's death—than to exult in triumph.

On May 8, 1945, when it was officially announced that Germany had unconditionally surrendered, Washington continued going about its business, except for a few isolated and unimportant flare-ups. The people had known of the surrender some hours previously through an historic Associated Press scoop, and had heard that New York and other places about the nation had gone wild. But Washingtonians waited for the official word, and during the waiting planned for little more than quiet programs at neighborhood centers and brief minutes of meditation in places of worship.

Germany had capitulated at 2:41 A.M., May 7, in the red brick schoolhouse which Eisenhower had used for months as his headquarters. Edward Kennedy, lean and leathery from years on the battlefronts and now chief of the Associated Press staff in France, broke the news some 24 hours ahead of the officially authorized announcement. The military men in France knew that the lid could not be contained on such an event, and had wanted the announcement time moved up. Civilian authority wanted a combined announcement by the United States, Great Britain, and Russia. Kennedy's news story brought him disaccreditation by the Army as a war correspondent, and a long controversy shook newspaper circles concerning the proprieties. Many editors praised Kennedy as having scored one of the greatest news scoops in journalistic history, while some condemned him for having broken a release date.

Actually, he had been scooped himself. The Germans, not to be outdone in everything, had spread the word. The tattletale was none other than Count Ludwig Schwerin von Krosigk, successor to Joachim von Ribbentrop as foreign minister. But the German's outburst was without confirmation of any kind until Kennedy's brief dispatch was telephoned from Paris to London nearly an hour later, to be flashed on the Associated Press wires in the United States at 9:35 A.M., May 7. (The Associated Press later said it did not know the report was unofficial.)

The morning newspapers of May 8 were not thrown against the doors with unusual exuberance. The householders may have picked up their papers less casually than usual because beyond mistake the war in Europe had ended or, in any event, Germany's fighting-will had been broken. The headlines told it confidently. A one-line eight-column banner in the *Post* proclaimed: "Germany Surrenders Unconditionally," and the bank head promised, "Big Three Will Proclaim VE-Day at 9 This Morning." News Editor John Shirley Hurst wrote:

> After almost six years of the bitterest, most devastating conflict the world has ever known, Germany has surrendered unconditionally to the Allies. President Truman, Prime Minister Churchill and Premier Marshall Stalin are scheduled to proclaim the historic victory to

the world in simultaneous broadcasts at 9 A.M. today.

Elsewhere it was noted by the newspaper that President Truman was sixty-one years old that day, and that a man arrested for some trivial offense had fallen dead while going through the formalities with a desk sergeant in a precinct stationhouse. Life continued.

The people went to work as usual, and most asked time off to hear the President. He was in the Executive Office of the White House at 8:35 A.M., and was to receive the press and then to confront Victory face to face. He encountered, along the way, Senator Kenneth McKellar of Tennessee, president pro tem of the Senate, who exuded a "Happy birthday, Mr. President," for which attention the President thanked him. The broadcast was readied. Standing by were Mrs. Truman, Margaret, and an assortment of army and navy officers of high rank.

The voice came through in a flat tone with a depth of fierceness and earnestness:

> This is a solemn but glorious hour. General Eisenhower informs me that the forces of Germany have surrendered to the United Nations. The flags of freedom fly all over Europe. For this victory we join in offering our thanks to the Providence which has guided and sustained us through the dark days of adversity. . . . We can repay the debt we owe to our God, to our dead, and to our children only by work, by ceaseless devotion to the responsibilities which lie ahead of us. If I could give you a single watchword for the coming months, that word is work—work and more work. We must work to finish the war. Our victory is only half won.

The people went back to work under promise of afternoon showers and cooler weather. The *Post* would term it a "strangely quiet" observance, totally unlike the reaction in New York where 500,000 people swarmed into Times Square. Some knelt in the streets to pray, while others stood five deep in bars.

Confetti and torn paper fluttered from high buildings, bringing from Mayor La Guardia a plea to conserve paper.

The word came to the mangled young men in Walter Reed General Hospital, quiet within green acres near Washington's Maryland suburbs. There, two short programs were held for the staff and the wounded men. A reporter looked at them and wrote, "There were serious young faces, many thin and taut." To them, Brigadier General Lloyd E. Jones, of the hospital staff, said:

"All of you have made some sacrifice. I am certain that whether your service was in North Africa, the Pacific, Alaska, or the Continent of Europe, you have by your service and sacrifice contributed to the glory of Victory Day in Europe."

Pfc. Joseph Marchlewski of New Kensington, Pennsylvania, a paratrooper who had lost a leg in Normandy, told a reporter, "I'm glad it's over because of all the other guys who are being saved from this kind of suffering. I've been in a hospital for eleven months and I know."

The Senate was not in session, but the House unanimously passed a resolution extending congratulations to the armed forces and members of the Allied nations "for their magnificent accomplishment."

The accomplishment had been sealed by German Colonel General Gustav Jodl, chief of staff of the German army, by signature in the cathedral city of Rheims, by a window with open curtains in a schoolhouse. He stood as stiff as a soldier in death, but could mutter, "I can see no alternative; signature or chaos." He had asked to speak formally:

> With this signature, the German people and armed forces are, for better or for worse, delivered into the victors' hands. In this war, which lasted more than five years, both have achieved and suffered more than perhaps any other people in the world. In this hour, I can only express the hope that the victor will treat generously with them.

He said not a word of the ghastly deaths and tortures which

he knew—and which those who heard his appeal also knew—that his government had brought upon millions in gas chambers and concentration camps. Immediately after the signing, he learned from Eisenhower that he and his nation could expect nothing.

When the Germans left, Eisenhower picked up the two pens used in the ceremony and held them in the V-sign. His smile was reflected by those of the men about him, including Russian General Ivan Susloparov, Supreme Headquarters deputy chief of staff; SHAEF Naval Aide Captain Harry C. Butcher; Deputy Supreme Commander Sir Arthur Tedder and Lieutenant General Walter Bedell Smith, Eisenhower's chief of staff, who signed for the Allies.

General "Beedle" Smith was a tart-tongued officer of the old Army who never wasted a word, always said what was on his mind, was feared by some and admired by all. Churchill, among his heartiest admirers, called him a bulldog because of his tenacity, and others reflected that he had the face and the legs of one. He was a master of logistics, and was widely credited with understanding and assembling the tremendous number of details that had made the invasion of Europe possible. More than intelligence was needed; it had required a hardness and an inflexibility, both of which showed in his brown eyes. Now, at fifty, he stood beside Eisenhower in the schoolhouse, gripping a cigarette, and his smile was the slightest of any man there.

A native of Indianapolis, he had not gone to West Point; but after high school had entered the Army to become a reserve officer and serve in France in World War I. He was now loaded with honors. In January 1944, King George VI of England had created him Knight Commander of the Order of the Bath. This had topped all of the honors, as far as Britain was concerned, paid to Americans after the Allied landings in North Africa. Tunisia had taken note, and he had become a Grand Officer of Nishan Iftikar; Morocco had made him a Grand Officer of Alouite, and the French had bestowed a Commander of the *Légion d'honneur*. He wanted no attention paid to himself—but he did want some paid to the American public. He believed emphatically in the people's right to have correct information.

His army life had carried him to distantly scattered posts; but at the time that he signed the European war into the shadows of history, he called his home 4314 36th Street, N.W., Washington, D.C., a residence he had taken in 1939 but had not seen now in twenty months. Reporters went to ask Mrs. Smith what she thought of her husband's leading role, but she spoke only through a relative. She had "never made a statement for the family," but as for the conclusion of the European war she was "very happy, as I know the rest of the world must be."

"Beedle" Smith would come home, and the peacetime man was said to be entirely different. He was gregarious, loved dogs and horses, and the Red Radiance roses he grew in his garden.

Shortly after May 1, Washington and the nation knew that the great dome of the Capitol would soon blaze in light under the night sky. The word had come from the floor of the House of Representatives. On May 1, Representative J. Buell Snyder, Democrat of Pennsylvania, remarked that the lights were on again in London and in Russia. He urged that the Capitol be lighted "the moment President Truman announces that Germany has capitulated or surrendered."

Speaker Sam Rayburn replied, "If the gentleman will yield, the Chair has already ordered that this be done." A long burst of applause rose from the floor. David Lynn, Capitol architect, soon made known that the floodlights on the grounds had been checked and that upon the recommendation of Rayburn, the chief electrician would turn on the lights at once if the President's announcement came at night. And if the news came during the daytime, the illumination would appear at dusk.

When the President's announcement came at 8:30 P.M., Tuesday, May 8, 1945, a loveliness appeared on the night sky. The dome of the Capitol gleamed in a bath of light, and the light flowed upward over the gown of the goddess. It had been a long time since Pearl Harbor when the light had gone out.

The light cast as many meanings as the fanciful and the coldly realistic could find in the glow. For a few, the Capitol was simply a sight again impressed on the Washington night; for more, it symbolized the long-desired defeat of Germany. For service people who looked up the Avenue it meant at least a halfway point through misery and danger. For a tall suntanned Kansan named Eisenhower who would come to the capital on June 18, after a long absence, it would mean a light to guide a search for the most difficult thing on earth to find—a lasting peace which, humanly, his soldier's mind craved more than the glory of arms.

CHAPTER TWENTY-NINE

HURRAHS IN THE HEAT

ON JUNE 18, 1945, Washington sprang a surprise—largely upon itself. It found that it really had a voice that could roar and hands that could tear paper into bits and cascade them from windows. What might penetrate the traditional core of calm imbedded in Washingtonians was always difficult to predict. Historically, they had exulted for Generals Grant, Meade of Gettysburg, Sherman of Georgia fame, and the Western and Eastern armies that had paraded in the May following the end of the Civil War. And for General Pershing, who now lay aged and ill in Walter Reed Hospital with only three more years to live.

And they would do it for General Eisenhower, a man equally special, who was coming to Washington that day. There was a terrible magic in the battles he had planned and the victory he had forged, and more. His modesty was engaging, and his face looked like a part of everybody; the mass face of America was reflected in his features. And if he was not an ordinary man he looked like one who tended an inner hearth for anybody to sit beside. Beyond his military skills, he had (almost like Jeb Stuart) the actor's "quick light charm"—purposeful or not—the stuff, in total, that many high offices and monuments are made of.

The *Washington Star* of Sunday, June 17, alerted the capital with a lead-story headline: "City Prepares Hero's Welcome to

Eisenhower." A parade, it was said, would signalize a full day of greeting.

"A grateful city tomorrow will give a hero's welcome to a modest Kansas farm boy who became supreme commander of our victorious forces in Europe." People talked about it by telephone, and in office, store, and street corner.

London had just thanked him loudly. A tremendous crowd had assembled entirely in his honor, and Eisenhower had spoken of the ties between his country and England which had tightened during the war. He praised England's love of liberty and its cultural enrichment of the world, and he gloried in the armies which had beaten the Germans down. But he left no one with the impression that he should be remembered. He had merely remarked that he was a man from Kansas, and the Londoners knew that he would soon be gone, and by way of parting had given him a token sword and a place for his name on the roll of fame, and made him an honorary freeman of London's city proper.

June 18 brought a hellish heat and humidity. Before 9 A.M., men and women wearing the lightest clothing they could grab walked and rode downtown in such masses that the entire population seemed in flux. Mrs. Eisenhower selected a simple black dress, a black hat with pink flowers, and high-heeled open-toed shoes. The temperature began climbing into the 90's. The crowds waited silently on the sidewalks, fanning themselves with newspapers or with their hands. A man fell in a faint, and undoubtedly others dropped, but it was no day for statistics. More importantly, somewhere there were twenty bands of waiting musicians, and a man who had been only an image to thousands would soon pass by in person.

And somewhere along the coast the General's plane was roaring, and with him were 54 officers and enlisted men, and an escort from the coast of one hundred bombers and fighter planes.

When the General's plane, flaring tiny painted flags of the allied nations, touched down at the Air Transport Command Terminal at 11 A.M., Mrs. Eisenhower, who had walked forward

just behind General Marshall, was the first to greet him. As the
two embraced, 108 cameramen, a record number for the
terminal, focused in, pressing so close that Marshall snapped his
fingers and military police moved the photographers back three
yards. A short way off, a second plane had landed with the
word *Sunflower*—the Kansas state flower—shining in paint.

Generals Marshall and Eisenhower shook hands. The
General's fellow passengers began leaving the plane, of whom
the lowest-ranking GI was Pfc. Vernon H. Jansen of Lorraine,
Kansas, a veteran of thirty months' service in the Medical Corps.
Eisenhower headed for the Pentagon in Command Car No. 1,
for greetings with old friends. When Eisenhower was leaving the
huge building, Pvt. Pat C. Carloggia, twenty-two, who had been
wounded at Bastogne, reached for the General's hand.
Eisenhower remembered him, and a decoration he had given.
"You're the man who drew my picture while you were lying on
a stretcher," he recalled.

While the caravan crossed Memorial Bridge, Eisenhower could
see the massed faces of the people who had waited in the heat
for hours to get a glimpse of him. High above the heat, the
engines of the escort planes roared. From the sidewalks in town
rose the appeals of vendors with flags and buttons showing the
faces of Eisenhower, MacArthur, Truman, and Roosevelt.
Mostly the people bought ice cream.

The crowd became so dense at 14th Street and the Avenue
that people leaned against each other, absorbing each other's
heat. From the favoring windows of the Willard Hotel faces
looked down.

Before noon the procession and the music stopped before the
north entrance of the District Building, where the spruced-up
Commissioners gave Eisenhower a key to the city, with
apologies that it was not large enough to indicate the gratitude
of the people. Eisenhower responded " . . . All my years as
commander-in-chief, all of my life, I have never been so proud
and so thankful as to have been given the key to the capital city
of my country. This is undoubtedly the high spot in my life."

The General, apart from the noises of war, had probably

never heard such a roar before. Above the cheers and the handclapping, the word "Ike" echoed incessantly. Whatever he thought lay hidden behind the smile. He had not been to the United States since the invasion of Europe and the ways of the people of Washington were unknown to him. He did his best to reciprocate; he waved to the crowd while his automobile moved at the head of eighteen army cars bearing the returning veterans. (There are a number of young men and women in Washington now who prize a memory that as children Eisenhower looked directly at them, held the gaze for a while, and smiled and waved.) He moved toward Capitol Hill and the torn bits of paper fluttered upon his trail.

When he strode brisk and suntanned down the center aisle of the House chamber to address the Congress, the acclaim from the floor and the packed galleries grew deafening, like a cue picked up from the crowd outside. It lasted two minutes and would have raged longer, but the General raised a hand and the chamber became quiet. When Speaker Rayburn's introduction ended, Eisenhower meticulously adjusted his glasses and began reading his speech in a determined and earnest voice. He chopped off each sentence like a farmer chopping at a log. Twelve microphones carried his words to the nation.

He believed that the "problems of peace can and must be met," and that was really what the soldiers wanted. There had been one victory, and another lay ahead.

Around 1 P.M. at a luncheon in the Statler Hotel, Eisenhower thanked God that he was home, and before the day ended President Truman added an oak leaf cluster to his Distinguished Service Medal. Truman, once himself a soldier, remarked that he would rather have that distinction than be President.

The following day, Eisenhower flew to New York City where a seventeen-gun salute at LaGuardia Airport greeted him and millions lined the curbs under showers of falling paper. He admired a hand-carved gold medal presented to him, saying to the mayor, "New York simply cannot do this to a Kansas farmer boy and keep its reputation for sophistication."

He was more serious to a crowd that jammed City Hall Park:

If we are going to live the years of peace, we must be strong and we must be ready to cooperate in the spirit of true tolerance and forbearance. It isn't enough that we devise every kind of international machinery to keep the peace. We must also be strong ourselves. Weakness cannot cooperate with anything. Only strength can cooperate.

And that night at the Waldorf-Astoria he begged for peace:

Peace is an absolute necessity to this world. The nations cannot stand another world catastrophe of war. . . . We cannot be isolated from the world.

Eisenhower had been the second army man of World War II to be honored at a joint session of Congress. On May 21, 1945, T/Sgt. Jake W. Lindsey of Lucedale, Mississippi, erect and proud, had appeared to become the one-hundredth recipient of the Congressional Medal of Honor. With him as he faced the Congress were President Truman and General Marshall. In the middle of the formalities, the President observed that the Allies were preparing to unleash overwhelming forces against the Japanese, and the honor to Lindsey and others who had won the medal was "a proud and moving occasion for every American."

Marshall, who had chatted with the 24-year-old soldier before the ceremony began, read the citation. On November 16, 1944, Lindsey had gone ahead of his unit near Hamich, Germany, and while wounded had moved through intense machine-gun and tank fire to clear a way for advance. It was above and beyond the call of duty—but citations can never relate the full extent of bravery.

These were the men that Eisenhower had kept in mind, the ones who had returned the light to the Capitol dome for whatever might come of it.

CHAPTER THIRTY

PEACE COMES LIKE A SCREAMING EAGLE

IF ANYONE HAD asked the average Washingtonian what was happening during July 1945, he probably would have replied that it was hot as all hell, because the summer had been unusually searing, scorching people at times beyond thought of anything else. And it might have been casually remarked that Jimmy Byrnes, the brisk climber from one important post to another, had succeeded Edward Stettinius as Secretary of State. Just how this came about was generally unknown, but Truman had made the proposal to his former senatorial colleague aboard a train en route to Washington after Roosevelt's funeral at Hyde Park. The appointment came on July 1—the new President's first Cabinet selection.

Ever since Pearl Harbor, the shifting about of high officeholders had been incessant, so the more interesting news now was the word on July 15 that the ration value of butter was reduced from 24 points per pound to 15 points. It was known that butter supplies were turning stale in warehouses. Beyond this, great expectations were growing. Half of the war was ended, and it was only a matter of a little more time before nylon stockings, cigarettes, quality clothing, gasoline, and sugar would return, the very things which in combination mean *life*. Life loomed more important than it ever had before. And hopefully the world would be rid for all time of the kind of madness that Hitler and the Japanese war-makers had spread.

But that had been expected from the start and thus involved only a little more waiting near the end of the era of long waiting in Washington. In the meantime, the petunias, zinnias, and roses daintily held their colorings in the heat for the men and women who at lunchtime sat on the park benches or sprawled on the grass, talking of office matters and impending dates and the downtown shows. Very little had changed since the past year, and the year before that, and even since 1942. War regulated the way of life.

It would be learned that President Truman had taken off for Potsdam for a conference regarding war and peace—with considerable attention to be paid to the handling of Japan once she was beaten down. Truman had boarded the Cruiser "Augusta" on Saturday, July 7, at Newport News, Virginia, with 52 persons, including experts from the State Department, Charley Ross, Byrnes, and Admiral Leahy. Ploughing the ocean as an escort was the "Philadelphia." There was no danger; Germany was out of the war and the Japanese navy was but a distant remnant of sunken or near-useless iron. Ross gave daily briefings by radiophone to some twenty correspondents aboard the escort cruiser. Truman exuded life as though the waves had drenched him and washed his troubles clean. He frequently wore sport shirts and moved about the ship like a boy on a playground. He ate often with the junior officers, and at the crew's mess—for he could not be anyone but Harry Truman, though the closest chum of his life would not unbend from calling him "Mr. President." He would disembark at Antwerp, and later would meet the British and Russian delegations. Then he would display the dignity his strange destiny demanded, and in the back of his mind he would conceal his knowledge of the atom bomb—the best-kept secret of all time, which he had heard about in full briefing only some two weeks after being sworn into office.

More mundanely, back in Washington on the day the President departed, the problem of finding housing accommodations for veterans and their families was tossed around at a special meeting of the District of Columbia War Hospitality Committee. No one had a quick solution, but there was much talk of using the Washington Tourist Camp, recently reopened just off the southern end of 14th Street.

But to the people, something more than housing was missing. Truman's flat Midwestern inflections sounded odd against the memory of the two great voices that were gone. Roosevelt's was silenced in death, and Churchill's had in July become smothered in the ascent to power of the Labor Party under colorless Clement Richard Attlee. Only a third remained of the triumvirate of Roosevelt, Churchill, and Stalin—and who at the time knew the full measure of Roosevelt's successor or the potential for murder and world alteration behind the Russian's mask? It was curious what two voices, one lulling, the other bursting in a rocket of oratory, had done to advance success in a war. As early August came, word flew about the capital that the Japanese were considering bowing out of the war. But there had been many rumors before, and the people, scarcely having regained breath from their welcome to Eisenhower, were calm. There was strong cause, however, to believe the rumors.

On August 6, 1945, persons stopping at newsstands saw the headlines about the dropping of a bomb of awesome power on a little-known place called Hiroshima in Japan. On Tuesday, August 7, the New York *Herald Tribune's* eight-column banner line disclosed: "First Atomic Bomb Smashes Japanese City; New Weapon Equals 20,000 Tons of TNT; Truman Tells Foe to Quit." It became known that the "basic force of the universe had been unleashed." Another headline related that Truman had visited ship's messes to tell about the bomb, and had personally informed the entire crew of the "Augusta" at sea. The strength of his conviction about the action was unconcealed. The reaction aboard the ship was, "Send some more of 'em over Japan and we'll all go home."

Out of the past came a reminder of the solemn men who had stepped with frozen faces from the black automobiles under the trees of Dumbarton Oaks in Georgetown during the autumn of

1944. On August 8, President Truman signed the Senate document ratifying the United Nations Charter to which the representatives of fifty nations subscribed solemnly in San Francisco. Truman used three pens to make the United States the first nation to bring the Charter into force. The first signature had been that of Byrnes. Ratification by the Senate had come July 28.

As the war neared its decisive end, the hurryings back and forth across the land by businessmen and war workers, intent upon completing final transactions, disturbed the State Department, moving it to take action on the transportation problem. It instructed all diplomatic posts in the Western Hemisphere to take all measures to induce would-be travelers to stay out of the United States and, if they had to come, to avoid rail and air transportation. Orders were issued within the department to curtail all official travel unless it related directly to the war against Japan. This war was brought vividly to Washington with the opening of *Back to Bataan* at RKO Keith's.

In their expectations of an early peace, the people learned some news of passing interest. Mrs. Truman had arrived in Washington from St. Louis on the 11:20 A.M. train of August 9, to find her husband waiting for her at the station. And contrary to nearly everybody's belief, bulging Washington did not have the largest number of federal employees. California ranked first, with 313,000; New York State was second with 297,800; and the District of Columbia came third with 256,300.

More disturbing news was also learned: On August 10, the *Star* publicized complaints from amputees at Walter Reed Hospital that there were long delays in getting artificial limbs. T/Sgt. John D. Hull, of Baltimore (a radio operator on a B-24 shot down during a raid on the Ploesti oil fields), in a pep talk to employees of J. E. Hanger, Inc., manufacturers of artificial limbs, said that he was ready to learn to walk a month before he received his leg. The hospital spokesmen said a bottleneck had developed mainly because of the unusually high influx of patients, and because the legs were not coming from manufacturers. (As of July 31, 1945, Walter Reed was serving 1,009 amputees.) McCarthy Hanger, vice president of the firm (which was serving a hospital other than Walter Reed), said his employees were turning out six hundred limbs a month and had been asked to increase production. A difficulty was in finding qualified employees to meet the increasing demands. But to Sergeant Hull, "It means a lot to a guy like me to walk down the street smoking a cigarette. How can you do it on crutches?"

The long-expected and inevitable cutbacks in industry began to come. War Mobilization Director John W. Snyder announced that the Navy would eliminate ship construction projects totaling $1.2 billion, and army ground forces would cutback $1 billion.

No one outside the deepest centers of officialdom knew precisely how close the end of the war lay. But the airwaves brought a broad hint at 7:35 A.M., August 10. From Tokyo radio came the message, in English—apparently intended mainly for the United States which was and had been carrying the heaviest load of the Pacific fighting:

> The Japanese Government today addressed the following communications to Swiss and Swedish Governments, respectively, for transmission to the United States, Great Britain, China, and the Soviet Union: In obedience to the gracious command of His Majesty the Emperor, who, ever anxious to enhance the cause of world peace, desires earnestly to bring about an early termination of hostilities with a view to saving mankind from the calamities to be imposed upon them by further continuation of the war, the Japanese Government are ready to accept the terms enumerated in the joint declaration which was issued at Potsdam . . . with the understanding that the said declaration does not comprise any demand which prejudices the prerogatives of His Majesty as a sovereign ruler.

Across the United States, radios broadcast the Japanese overture. Outside the White House at 8:25 A.M. came a slapping sound as painters laid a coating of gleaming white on the mansion, as though sprucing it up for a special occasion. At the same hour, President Truman walked into his office, knowing of the Japanese offer. Shortly after came Byrnes, Leahy, Forrestal, and Stimson. And in the meantime, the coded message passed through the tedious rounds of the neutral intermediaries, the Swedes and the Swiss. Friday afternoon was spent by the Big Four in consultation on the formulation of a reply as promulgated by Truman. The role of the god-emperor was the sensitive area. The reply came down hard on the point:

> From the moment of surrender the authority of the emperor and the Japanese government to rule the state shall be subject to the supreme commander of the Allied powers who will take such steps as he deems proper to effectuate the surrender terms. The emperor will be required to authorize and insure the signature by the government of Japan and the Japanese Imperial General Headquarters of the surrender terms . . . and shall issue his commands . . . to all of the forces to cease active operations and to surrender their arms, and to issue such other orders as the supreme commander may require to give effect to the surrender terms.

The long wait began, and by now the fate of Japan—already a certainty—had been doubly assured by the entry of Russia into the Far Eastern arena on August 9. Japan first flashed the news with an excited account of how the Soviets, under command of Marshal Alexander M. Vasilevsky, had loosed a furiously rolling attack with tanks, infantry, and artillery across the Manchurian border. The Japanese fought for a while, and then reeled backward.

A small crowd of people had stood silently in Lafayette Park, drifting away but always reassembling, ever since Friday, August 10. They looked across Pennsylvania Avenue at the White House, and it looked very quiet behind the heavy foliage of the trees. The painters went on with their work as if nothing mattered except beautifying the mansion. But there were the ominous barriers on the sidewalk by the high iron fence, and there were soldiers—not many, but enough. There was nothing definite as yet; there was only the agony of suspense. And there was a feeling that could not be allayed: the Japanese were tricky, and fanatical. Maybe, after everything, after even this, the Japanese homeland would have to be invaded, with dreadful loss of life. Men were being brought back from Europe for just such an eventuality. The White House during the afternoon dispelled any notion that the big break would come about on Friday. But negotiations were in progress. The Allied reply went out on Saturday under the signature of Byrnes, acting for the Big Four. There was now absolutely nothing to do but wait. Wait, and, in some cases, to wonder if fighting men who had survived the war in Europe must die in a more distant part of the world.

Washington churches were packed on Sunday; but the weather was beautiful and thousands made off to beaches on the nearby eastern seaboard; others watched the flight of golf balls on the courses near the capital but probably more stayed at home waiting for the word to come through the radio. Word came at 9:34 P.M., and NBC, CBS, Mutual, and the American Broadcasting Company grabbed it. The networks credited the United Press—which had produced the false Armistice in November 1918. Now it related, "Washington—Japan Accepts Surrender Terms of the Allies." Only a few minutes were needed for UP to learn that it was not the source of the "news," and it sent out a disclaimer. The networks killed the story, but the havoc had begun. Celebrations flared across the nation, but by Monday the people had quieted down, a little angry that they had been bamboozled.

But the rather small crowd kept vigil in Lafayette Park, and reporters wandered around, asking questions. Alvin Turner, of Maryland Park, a clerk in the Veterans Administration, said, "I'm here to get the news. They never tell us anything at the Bureau [they didn't know anything to tell] and there're no radios, either. If it comes, I'll rush back and run through the halls telling everyone." Barbara Lee Steel, who had graduated

from Bryn Mawr in the spring, said, "I'll blubber like a baby. I
did the other day"—actually the night of the false report. Jean
Cushing, of Bethesda, Maryland, asked what she would do if
peace were announced in five minutes, replied, "Since three of
my friends died on Okinawa, I guess I'll just go back to work."
Some said they didn't know just why they were waiting. A few
had come only to eat lunch in the outdoors; others were "just
tired" and "the grass looked good." It was the fourth day of
waiting for Mrs. Mary A. Brown, a quiet gray-haired
grandmother, who sat on an unshaded bench beside her
nine-year-old granddaughter, Bernice. She was "too nervous and
full of herself" to remain at home. She showed the reporter a
photograph of her son, Lieutenant Aubrey C. Brown, USNR, on
duty in the Pacific for nearly three years. A native
Washingtonian, Brown had been assistant manager of the
Mayflower Hotel. Mrs. Brown said, "And do you know, as soon
as the radio tells us that the peace has been signed I am going
over and call Aubrey long-distance. I don't care if it costs all I
have."

Downtown, Mrs. Mae West and Mary McDonald, employes of
a candy store in the 1000 block of F Street, prepared for the
expected peace by nailing boards across the store's plate-glass
windows to prevent breakage during the inevitable celebration.
Farther downtown, Inspector Oscar J. Letterman personally led
police in a raid on a numbers and horse-racing emporium
thriving in Apartment No. 2 of a building in the 500 block of
Second Street. "It was one of the largest places of its kind I've
ever seen," the astounded inspector told reporters. The daily
receipts were estimated at $5,000. During the pounce, the
telephones rang incessantly, and three policemen answered
"about one hundred times." The operation, which had
flourished for eight untroubled years, ended with the carting
away of the proprietor, two adding machines, three telephones,
two large bags of money, and several thousand numbers slips.
Meanwhile, in the White House Rose Garden, President Truman
presented the Distinguished Service Medal to Byrnes for his
"major contribution to the war effort." And in its enormous

building facing the Mall, the Department of Agriculture ordered the Commercial Credit Corporation to release twelve million pounds of fatback and other salt pork products for sale in Southern areas which had suffered from the pork shortage out of proportion to other areas because salt pork is a staple of the region's diet. "It is a question of letting the pork go or not getting the cotton crop harvested," an official explained to a nation which, at this critical moment in history, could not possibly have cared less.

The Duke of Windsor was granted a pleasant thirty-minute talk with President Truman and recalled his visit to the 35th Division, in which Truman had been a captain of artillery during World War I. There was big excitement at the Zoo with the arrival from Colombia, South America, of two playful baby capybaras—largest representatives of the world's rodent family. One was a male and the other a female; they were six months old and weighed fifteen pounds each. Dr. Mann hunched over them, staring. They would grow to 85 pounds and would be three feet long and two feet tall. In the shipment came two screamers—long-toed birds that are kept among the chickens in South America to scare off marauding hawks. And there came one hummingbird, lone survivor of six that began the trip.

At nightfall on the 13th the people stood quietly waiting in Lafayette Park.

There was nothing unusual during the early evening of Tuesday, August 14, 1945; near the northern suburbs where the lawns are larger, the evening smell of flowers and grass was pleasant for the old ladies and retired gentlemen sitting on the porches; and downtown the crowds were pushing their way onto public vehicles to start for home and a night of rest.

At 7 P.M., President Truman, wearing a dark double-breasted suit and striped tie, stood in his office before a desk that was nearly clear of all paper. On his right sat Jimmy Byrnes, and beside Byrnes Admiral Leahy; on his left sat Cordell Hull with a weariness on his face; and lined precisely behind were some ten notables, with Postmaster General Bob Hanegan, one of fate's principal helpers in placing Truman in the White House, at the far right of the back-standers. Truman began reading from a sheet of paper held tightly in his right hand. Japan had sued for peace. There would be formalities, but the war was ended.

The first reaction struck the Chesapeake & Potomac Telephone Company. The news of the surrender brought "a sudden hush," but it didn't last long. The dead phones came to life in a jam of local and long-distance calls. People rushed from their houses with no thought of what they were wearing to become part of a crowd of half a million that was already downtown or heading that way. A dense mass pushed and squirmed through Lafayette Park, crossed the Avenue in a rush and forced its way through police guards and MPs to the iron palings of the White House fence, probably few remembering the hush of Pearl Harbor night three years, eight months, and seven days past.

The incessant blare of automobile horns numbed the air and echoed off the massive government buildings. Truck drivers stalled in traffic jams made their vehicles backfire, and somewhere submerged within the roar were the shouts of human voices. Three words rode the crest, "We want Harry!" The President and Mrs. Truman appeared on the north porch. The President waved and smiled, and the crowd became silent after a final scream of "Speech, speech!" Truman began talking through a microphone:

> Ladies and gentlemen, this is the great day. This is the day we have been looking for since December 7, 1941.
>
> This is the day when fascism and police government ceases in the world.
>
> This is the day for the democracies.
>
> This is the day when we can start on our real task of implementation of free government in the world.
>
> We are faced with the greatest task we ever have been faced with. The emergency is as great as it was on December 7, 1941.
>
> It is going to take the help of all of us to do it. I know we are going to do it.

Fraser Edwards of the *Washington Daily News* wrote of "a swaying, swirling sea of humanity that howled and shrieked and hugged and kissed and just went daffy with delight." (This was good reporting, but incomplete. The "hugging and kissing" grew into unabashed fornication on the steps of the Treasury Department and in Lafayette Park.) The half million people appeared to be equally divided among the sexes, and the emotions of the women seemed the most extreme. A girl reporter on the *Times-Herald* wrote, "If I were a mother, I'd certainly have my daughter locked up tonight."

Streets and pavements became piled with broken bottles, cast-off clothing, and torn paper. An estimated hundred government girls, WAVES, and sailors marched singing up 14th Street, headed by a majorette manipulating a broomstick. In the midst of the Pennsylvania Avenue crush, a CBS sound truck was stalled and rebroadcast England's announcement of the war's conclusion, closing with a loud "God Save the King." The crowd applauded, and three British sailors stood at stiff salute. A crowd in front of the *Post* cheered as a serviceman and his girl jumped from a car, stripped, exchanged clothing and leaped back into the automobile. An aged Negro won applause as he paraded beside the curb with a faded American flag, trailing a mongrel on a tattered leash. Washington's Chinatown on H Street threw aside plans for a formal celebration and burst loose with wild noise; American and Chinese flags sprung quickly from the fronts of buildings, as firecrackers sounded and thin acrid smoke filled the air. Several marines grabbed kerosene lamps from a construction site and paraded through G Street. At 10:30 P.M., an elderly white-haired woman stationed herself near E Street and Pennsylvania Avenue and kissed servicemen who passed. They smiled, and a few of them called her "Mom."

Every nightclub in downtown Washington was packed, and patrons with seats held them doggedly. A sailor spoke to a waiter, "I know you are probably a veteran, too. No hard feelings. But we would like our drinks when you get time." Around 9:30 P.M., the Lotus and the Trade Winds closed, fearing the rising excitement in the crowds pressing at the doors. An hour later, the Neptune Room bade all good night, and closed with difficulty. The Casino Royale and the Cafe of All Nations clung determinedly on. But the patrons of the Russian Troika looked with no more than their usual enjoyment at the floor show, and those at the Statler and Mayflower were decorous.

From somewhere, a soldier got hold of a white horse and rode it from the Avenue up 11th Street to gather cheers and then rode off. On E Street, two soldiers, each suffering the loss of a leg, waved their crutches and laughed while a crowd of soldiers and WAACs marched by holding hands. A sailor, his sea legs even less steady, made it along F Street continuously yelling, "Hot dog! No more court martials." On Capitol Hill, a soldier jumped into a fountain, and when friends pulled him out he jumped in again. On F Street, an old woman stood sobbing, and when asked, "Did you lose a son?" replied, "No. I'm just happy."

A polite British sailor tipped his cap to a WAVE, asking, "May I kiss you, now that the war is over?" He was told, "You sure can, sailor."

A Negro cab driver shouted, "I'm the happiest man in the world, yes, the happiest man. I've got two brothers over there. They'll be coming home. I'd have had another brother coming back, but he was killed on New Guinea." (It is regretted that the reporter who heard this did not get the man's name.)

The churches and synagogues were never empty during the night. Civilians and servicemen sat in the pews, some of them with bowed heads, all of them oblivious to the uproar outside. In residential sections, noisy parties began spontaneously. Children paraded up and down, beating drums and waving flags. Parents gave up trying to send them to bed.

Despite the hysteria, the crowd was considerate of one another and of property. Emergency Hospital treated only 160 persons, and there were reports of only three windows being shattered. The Red Cross arranged several first-aid stations and prepared for big business, but the first three celebrants who appeared were drunks.

The celebration raged until the sun rose. President Truman did not overlook the faces of Washington he knew so well: federal and District of Columbia employees were granted a two-day holiday, and of them the President said:

> One of the hardest working groups of war workers during the past four years—and perhaps the least appreciated by the public—have been the federal employees in Washington and throughout the country. They have carried on the day-to-day operations of the Government which are essential to the support of our fighting men and to the carrying on of the war. On behalf of the Nation, I formally express thanks to them.

Most of them could say that they had done what they were told to do, and for many exhaustion had not been enough. Their efforts—however obscured in the vastness of war—were theirs and their country's and always would be. There was something substantial about them (from today's perspective) that makes them seem good, and their era golden. What the times had done to them no one can say with sureness. But "in God's mercy," which Churchill had asked for on Christmas Eve of 1941 while the national tree grew a bloom of lights, they had performed and in a large way endured. Many emerged strong where before they had been weak; and many had grown wise, leaving behind their unease and innocence. And life had returned to gather up their wisdom and their strength. But would the life resulting from the marriage of drudgery and victory be worth the pain? The entire world was wondering.

Yet there was certainty for all in one thing: people passing through Franklin Square during the victory celebration saw a man walking a restless dog who was straining at the leash. The dog carried a newspaper in his mouth—a newspaper with the plainly-visible headline: "The War is Over."

BIBLIOGRAPHY

The Associated Press News Annual, New York, Rinehart & Company, 1946.

Catton, Bruce. *The War Lords of Washington*, New York, Harcourt, Brace and Company, 1948.

Churchill, Winston. *The Unrelenting Struggle*, Boston, Little Brown and Company, 1942

Current Biography, New York, H. W. Wilson Company, 1941, 1942.

International News Service. *It Happened In 1945*, New York, Essential Books, Duell, Sloan and Pearce, 1946.

Mearns, David C. *The Story of a Parchment*, The Declaration of Independence, reprinted from the Annual Report of the Librarian of Congress for the Fiscal Year ending June 30, 1949, United States Government Printing Office, 1950.

National Gallery of Art, Washington, D.C. Text by John Walker, Harry N. Abrams, Inc., New York

New York Herald Tribune. *Front Page History of the Second World War*, New York Tribune, Inc., 1946.

Phillips, Cabell (ed.). *Dateline: Washington*, New York, Double-Day and Company, Inc., 1949.

——(ed.). *The Truman Presidency*, New York, The Macmillan Company, 1966.

Rachlis, Eugene. *They Came To Kill*, New York, Random House, 1961.

Roosevelt, Eleanor. *The Autobiography of Eleanor Roosevelt*, New York, Harper & Brothers, 1961.

Savage, Katherine. *The Story of the Second World War*, New York, Scholastic Book Services, a division of Scholastic Magazine, Inc., 1957-58.

Sherwood, Robert E. *Roosevelt and Hopkins: An Intimate History*, New York, Harper and Brothers, 1948.

Truman, Harry S. *Memoirs*, New York, Doubleday and Company, Inc., 1956.

Wilson, Rose Page. *General Marshall Remembered,* Englewood Cliffs, N.J., Prentice-Hall, Inc., 1968.

INDEX

Abwehr 2 (Intelligence 2), 115, 116, 122
Adams, John Quincy, 67, 221
Adams, Phelps H., 157
Africa
    Allied landings in, 104, 156
    German victories in, 108, 109, 110
Agriculture Department, U.S., 187
Air Force, U.S.
    bombings of, *see* Air warfare
    women in, 145
Air-raid sirens, 197
Air Raid Warden Service, 22
Air warfare
    in European Theater, 111, 172, 174,
      189, 197, 198, 201, 203, 204, 245
    in Pacific Theater, 93-94, 172, 189,
      197
Airplane production, 10
    rise in, 187
Akyab, Burma, British attack on, 172
Alcoholic beverages
    availability of, 230
    rationing of, 113
Alexandria, Egypt, 109
Algeria, Allied landings in, 156
Alien Property Custodian, 202
Aliens, enemy, rounding up of, 29
Allan, Robert Tate, 171
    on day of Pearl Harbor attack, 15-16
Allen, George, 213
Amagansett, Long Island, landing of
    saboteurs on, 118, 119-20, 122
America First Committee, 13, 36
American University, 42, 66
Andrews, Bert, 188
Andrews, Edward R., 21
Andrews, Marshall, 76
Annapolis, Md., historic documents in,
    62
Anti-Cigarette Alliance, 187
ARCADIA conference, 57
Ardennes Offensive, 231-33, 235-37
Argentina, German penetration in, 85-86
Arizona, U.S.S., 34
Arlington, Va., housing shortage in, 211
Arms contracts, pursuit of, 40-41
Army, U.S.
    damage in Pearl Harbor to, 34
    recruitment for, 18
    women in, *see* Women's Auxiliary
      Army Corps (WAAC)
    See also Servicemen; War Department,
      U.S.; World War II

Arnold, Gen. Henry Harley "Hap," 208
    personal qualities of, 144
Art galleries, 66
    See also names of specific art galleries
Artificial limbs, shortage of, 268-69
Asheville, N.C., art treasures removed to,
    69
Association of Army and Navy Wives, 202
Astaire, Fred, 169
Atomic bomb
    as best-kept secret, 266
    dropped on Hiroshima, 267
    press treatment of, 104
Attlee, Clement, 267
Austad, Mark, 234
Austerity, *see* Clothing, shortages in;
    Food shortages; Materials' shortage
Austin, Warren R., at fourth-term in-
    auguration, 240
Autry, Gene, 37

B-29 Super-Flying Fortress, 189, 198,
    245
Bales, Richard, 180-81
Ball, Ernie, 15
Baltimore, Md., historic documents at,
    62
Bank deposits, 46
Baruch, Bernard, 3, 153
    at fourth-term inauguration, 240
    personal qualities of, 144
    as source of news, 102-3
Battle of the Bulge, 231-33, 235-37
Baugh, Samuel, 1, 14
Beal, William, 16
Beall, Ninian, 225
Beer, rationing of, 113
Belasco Theater, 201
Belgium
    Allied liberation of, 228
    Ardennes offensive in, 232
Benét, Stephen Vincent, 43
Berlin, Germany, air bombings of, 198,
    203
Berlin, Irving, popular songs of, 231
Bernstein, Leonard, 180
Biddle, Francis, 51
    German saboteurs and, 123, 124, 125
    in Interdepartmental Security Com-
      mittee, 105, 106
Bilbo, Theodore G., 199-200
Biltmore mansion, art treasures removed
    to, 69